A GUIDE TO
DIVORCE
MEDIATION

A GUIDE TO DIVORCE MEDIATION

HOW TO REACH A FAIR, LEGAL SETTLEMENT AT A FRACTION OF THE COST

GARY J. FRIEDMAN, J.D.

PART ONE: AN INTRODUCTION TO MEDIATION
CO-WRITTEN BY JACK HIMMELSTEIN

WORKMAN PUBLISHING • NEW YORK

*"If I am not for myself,
who is for me?
And being for myself alone,
what am I?"*
—HILLEL "THE ELDER"

Library of Congress Cataloging-in-Publication Data
Friedman Gary J.
A guide to divorce mediation: how to reach a fair, legal settlement at a fraction of the cost
p. cm.
Includes index.
ISBN 1-56305-478-7 — ISBN 1-56305-245-8 (pbk.)
1. Divorce—Law and legislation—United States—Popular works.
2. Divorce Mediation—United States. I. Title
KF535.Z9F68 1993
346.7301'66—dc20   92-50933
                                     CIP

Workman books are available at special discounts when purchased in bulk for premiums and sales promotions as well as for fund-raising or educational use. Special editions or book excerpts can also be created to specification. For details, contact the Special Sales Director at the address below.

Workman Publishing Company, Inc.
708 Broadway
New York, NY 10003

Manufactured in the United States of America

First printing May 1993
10 9 8 7 6 5 4 3 2 1

*To my parents, Irwin Friedman and Ruth Wells
Friedman, and to Harry Sloan: Each believed in my
possibilities before I did.*

ACKNOWLEDGMENTS

I spent 1988-89 on sabbatical with my family in Aix-en-Provence, France, reflecting on my work as a mediator and particularly on the cases that I'd found most challenging. With a rented French typewriter, I wrote up these cases in an effort to better understand them. Upon reading my musings, my wife, Trish McCall, suggested they had the makings of a book.

Lauren Friedman, Rosemary Jellison, Susan Keel, Jennie Mayle, Sukie Miller, Marilyn Watkins—all good friends—agreed with her and encouraged me to move forward.

Lacey Fosburgh, Bob Kriegel and Marilyn Harris Kriegel, Howard Lesnick, Carole Levine, Stuart Miller, and Martina Reaves guided me through the transition from reflections to a book with their thoughtful advice and criticism.

Candice Fuhrman, my agent, Suzanne Lipsett, a freelance editor who became my teacher, and Workman editors Suzanne Rafer and Margot Herrera made the book a reality through their talent, clarity, patience, and persistence.

My office administrator and assistant, Amy Battin, generously and enthusiastically once again proved herself indispensable.

The Stanford Center on Conflict and Negotiation provided invaluable assistance at a critical time.

My clients and the participants in my training programs, through their willingness to bring themselves so fully to the process, have confirmed to me the value of this work.

Far too significant to describe in words has been the abundant support of my family: Trish, Sydney, Cassidy, Nicholas, and Will.

AUTHOR'S NOTE

*M*y approach to mediation, as reflected in this book, is the result of fifteen years of close collaboration with my friend and colleague, Jack Himmelstein. Jack, principally a teacher, and I, principally a practitioner, joined together to develop new approaches to teaching and practicing law that would be in tune with our values. These included the commitment to justice and the belief that parties in conflict can play an active role in resolving their differences. I have often described our relationship by saying, "I practice mediation and Jack explains to me what I have done." In that manner and through our ongoing dialogue, we have continuously evolved our approach and trained hundreds of other lawyers in the United States and Europe.

This book flowed out of that collaboration. Throughout the book I use the word "I" in describing what I do, yet at a deeper level "we" would often be more accurate.

Although I mediated the cases that form the body of this book and gave them written form, the ideas set forth are largely an expression of those we developed together. The conceptual overview in Part One was written by both of us and is literally a joint product.

CONTENTS

FROM ADVERSARY LAWYER TO MEDIATOR

The year was 1976, and I was a successful trial lawyer struggling to make my legal practice and my personal values converge. During that critical period for me, my friends Lorna and Jay presented me with a challenge that would change my life. Arriving at my office without telling me why they wanted to talk, they asked me to help them reach an amicable divorce. I was saddened but not altogether surprised by their decision to divorce but was unprepared for how they envisaged my role. They wanted me to act as lawyer for *both* of them. Even though I had started to think of my law practice as "alternative," I was caught off guard. While I was interested in finding new ways of lawyering, what Lorna and Jay were suggesting seemed impossible. I didn't know of any lawyer who had ever done something like this.

I knew that divorces could be complicated, both emotionally and legally, and saw their request as naive, however well intentioned. While explaining my reaction, I heard myself uttering some rather traditional remarks. "Although I support your desire to keep the divorce amicable, to fully protect both of your interests you really are going to need separate lawyers. As a lawyer, I could only represent *one* of you," I told them. "To try to represent you both would result in a conflict of interest. Even representing one of you would be hard to do, since I'm a friend to you both. So maybe it's best for me to recommend lawyers for each of you. I have a couple in mind."

A look of impatience crossed Lorna's face. "What mumbo jumbo," she snapped. "I thought you were different, but you're just like all the rest. We don't *want* you to take sides. We just want you to help us make the decisions necessary to settle everything. If we knew the law, we'd probably be able to do this ourselves."

"But the law is much more complicated than you think," I objected. Still, an internal debate had begun in my mind. *What's wrong with their request?* I asked myself. *To help these two sort through the issues and untangle their interests, why do I have to be on one side against the other?* I found that I was still exclusively viewing myself as my client's *protector* in a dispute. *But I know these people. I know they're both smart enough to look out for themselves. I suppose there's a chance that one or the other might come out unfairly—but that's a possibility in any disagreement, even with lawyers. If it seems to me that one of them is taking advantage of the other, why can't I simply tell them what I see and let them figure out what they want to do? Why can't I simply give them access to the law without having to be a proponent of a position?*

A more familiar voice broke in. *You can't do that. You know what's going to happen. They'll get into a fight and you'll end up stuck in the middle. This can only lead to trouble for them and you.*

But I could feel the weight of my friends' disappointment and, the more I thought about it, my own. It came to me that this was the opportunity I had been searching for—the chance to stop doing battle and to help people I cared about work together to make decisions.

"Look, I think you're right," I said to them. "I want to help you work out an agreement. But I want you to know that I've never done this before, and I'm going to need your help. If there's ever been a case of the blind leading the blind into completely un-charted territory, this is it." I felt an enormous sense of relief coupled with the sense of a great challenge.

The next four months were very difficult. There was a lot of confusion, some heavy fighting, a string of misunderstandings about my role (not the least of which were my own), and some frustrating backtracking. But—more or less—the process worked. And it did indeed prove very different from any of my previous legal experience. *I* didn't make the agreement for Lorna and Jay; they did it themselves. When it was all over, I was excited, even inspired. I had sensed before that there was another way to resolve stalemated disagreements; now I *knew* there was.

Within six months I was working with many divorcing couples and other people in dispute who wanted to avoid litigation and adversary lawyers. Two years later, "sitting in the middle" had become my main role as a lawyer, and it was by far the most satis-fying work I had ever done. By 1978, I had given what I was doing a name: *mediation.* While mediation had a long history, it had not been tried with cases traditionally considered resolvable only by lawyers representing separate sides. The term was popping up around the country in the mid-seventies, but I discovered that often those practicing or teaching what they called mediation had very different ideas from my own. I continued feeling my way, and the more I evolved as a mediator, the more effective and, for both me and my clients, personally satisfying the work became.

BACKTRACK:
THE LITIGATOR'S LIFE

A shortcut to describing the essence of mediation is explaining what it *isn't* and why it evolved as it did. I began my law career as a trial lawyer with my family's firm. Coming as I did from a legal background, I was well groomed for the law. I found it exciting and financially rewarding, and I was good at it. After practicing successfully in this mode for five years in the early seventies, I began to grow increasingly disheartened, particularly when I saw the human costs of the litigation process—relationships seemed only to be worsened by the adversary experience. I often felt estranged from my clients, even after what was clearly a "win." Though the results were usually what I considered good, the clients often felt dissatisfied. Something was missing—for both of us. I wanted to be interrelating with clients on a level of mutual respect, but I began to see that the more wholeheartedly I acted on their behalf the more disempowered they became.

One of the hallmarks of my success had been a particular flair for what is called "client control"—doing what is needed to gain the clients' implicit permission to make decisions for them. I worked hard to gain for them what *I* thought was best, steering them in the process to acquiesce to the wisdom of my thinking. Clients turned control over to me and in the process disenfranchised themselves. The cost of losing control over decision making was a price many clients were willing to pay for the relief of knowing that the case was now in their lawyer's hands. Increasingly, I felt ill at ease with the burden of figuring out what was best for a client and then battling the other lawyer—and often my client—to achieve that result.

Another thing that disturbed me about the litigator's life was the high value placed on negative human qualities. Fear of losing face, of just plain losing, or of being sued by the client often seemed to be at least as powerful a motivator as the search for justice. But even worse, aggression, defensiveness, and blame were the main currency I dealt with as a lawyer, both in the way I approached opposing lawyers and in my interactions with my clients. And truth—which in my personal life I valued above all— was often considered irrelevant.

Once my misgivings surfaced, they quickly became intolerable. My professional success rapidly lost its personal meaning. I quit the firm, certain that my legal career was behind me. I moved to California, and for a year I studied the spiritual and psychological dimensions of human relationships, including my own.

At the end of the year, I realized I had been kidding myself: I couldn't leave the law behind; it was what I knew and loved. What I had to leave was not law itself but law as it was *traditionally* practiced. The question was not what I would do instead, but rather how I could practice law in a way that both met my clients' needs and still conformed to my personal values.

With encouragement and support from two wise and understanding friends, Jack Himmelstein, a law professor, and the late Harry Sloan, a psychotherapist, I took up the practice of law again—tentatively, but intent upon experimenting and challenging traditional assumptions about what lawyers are supposed to be and do. It was then that Lorna and Jay asked me to help with their divorce. Taking their case was like learning to walk after being immobilized for a long time.

My transformation from advocate into mediator was slow and, I now see, profound. Increasingly, I came to believe that it was essential for my clients to make their own decisions in resolving their disputes. The decisions called for were far too central to their lives to permit a settlement imposed from the outside, extending far beyond the professional's expertise into the deepest reaches of the clients' private lives. I began to sense that if people were given the room and support—no small feat, as it turns out, for me or for them—they could do it themselves based on their own personal sense of justice.

But if I no longer achieved settlements in disputes on behalf of my clients, what did I have to offer? Since people hire lawyers because they are unable to reach an agreement on their own, how, if not as a decision maker, could I help them through an impasse? If I weren't going to protect one against the other, how could I know whether they were protecting themselves? Could I really serve my clients without being aggressive, manipulative, forcefully persuasive? How was I to quash the lawyer's desire to play the white knight who saves the day and earns the client's undying gratitude? How could I neutralize my well-sharpened sense of blame in order to play the unbiased middleman? And where was I to gain my satisfaction if I gave up my desire to *win?*

Partly by intuition and partly by hard analysis on my own and with others, I began finding answers to these questions. Where previously I had relied on my analytical mind, I now sought to balance that understanding with the insights of my heart and intuition. Over time, I started to perceive my role as that of bringing people together rather than making one guy a winner and the other a loser.

THE EVOLVING CONCEPT

Simply stated, my goal became helping people make decisions together. But I had my own condition for accepting cases for mediation: The people in conflict had to accept full responsibility for the decision making, had to understand as completely as possible the context and consequences of the decisions to be made, and had to deal directly with each other. The goal was *not* simply for them to reach an agreement in an informal setting. Nor was the process a laissez-faire one, in which I simply turned over decision-making responsibility willy-nilly to them. The mediation had to honor certain principles along the way, even if that made it harder to reach an agreement. This view sometimes caused tension in the room. Indeed, many of those who come to my office with the intention of mediating rather than litigating their dispute are surprised when I refuse to agree to their terms. For example:

- Hilda and Frank arrive at my office with the request that I make the decisions about what would work best for them and put that in writing. I decline.
- Bill and June enter mediation to finalize an agreement they have reached on their own. It quickly becomes clear that Bill has been the sole decision maker, both in their marriage and in their settlement. Since the resulting agreement is not very different from what the law would have provided, many mediators would be willing to comply with their request. I am not.
- Mel and Evelyn, recognizing the intense mutual hostility that has kept them embroiled in legal battle for years, come to my office and ask me to talk to them in separate rooms, running back and forth between them until a settlement can be hacked out. I refuse.

In each of these examples, my response was unconventional. For me to be willing to mediate with them, each of the above couples would have to agree to try to work together to make their own mutually acceptable decisions. Many approaches to mediation focus exclusively on the settlement terms, but for me, *how* the settlement is reached is as important as the settlement itself.

THE EVOLUTION OF THIS BOOK

*O*ver the past fifteen years, I have mediated about a thousand cases. During that time, I have become a teacher of the mediation process in law schools, professional training programs, and public presentations. It's often been said that I refuse to use a "paint-by-numbers" method; instead of teaching mediation as a series of clearly describable techniques, I have relied heavily on role playing and other forms of teaching by example. Many of my students and clients have suggested I describe my method in a book, but for a long time I was unable to find a way to convey the particular blend of legal, psychological, and spiritual perspectives that distinguishes mediation as it has evolved in my practice.

I plead guilty to having been inexplicit, but it has not been because I have wished to keep to myself the secrets of successful mediation. The difficulty in explaining the essence of the process has to do with the nature of human conflict itself. All disputes, from sibling rivalry to wars between nations, are matters of human relationship, and all human relationships, when one looks closely at what they comprise, are almost unbelievably complex.

Nevertheless, although most people who come to me for mediation usually have legal and economic matters uppermost in their minds, they eventually reach an agreement only by digging below the surface issues—such as spousal support and co-parenting—to confront and change their relationship. The significance of mediation as an alternative method of resolving conflict lies in the process of examining, clarifying, and adjusting human relationships in all their intricacy and emotional depth. When you consider that every conflict is as unique as the people involved in it, the complexity appears to be nearly overwhelming. I finally decided that the way to convey the essence and value of mediation was the way I did it in class—by presenting and commenting on a series of mediations from my files. Part Two of the book consists of twelve mediations based loosely on cases I have had over the years. While the dynamics and exchanges presented are true, I have invented all names, characteristics, and specific circumstances to thoroughly preserve my clients' privacy.

This book, then, is written from inside the mediation process —and from inside the mediator. In my practice I mediate all sorts of disputes, but I have limited the cases in this book exclusively to divorce. Separation and divorce are familiar microcosms for all human disputes, and the same basic approach ultimately applies

THE MEDIATION TRIANGLE

When I refer to the mediator's position as "sitting in the middle," I don't mean I position myself between the two disputants. Actually, if you and your spouse came to me to mediate your divorce, we would form an equilateral triangle—literally. That triangle has a symbolic as well as a practical meaning: It represents the essential aspects of our relationship.

First, I am on the same level as you. I do not have the power to decide your case or in any other way act as a judge. I have no fixed result in my mind to urge you toward. In fact there is a broad range of possible decisions you could reach.

Second, I am not on either person's side. I will help each of you express yourself as fully as I can, but I won't become an advocate for either of you.

Third, by sitting in the middle, I am able to help you deal directly with each other.

Fourth, from our different vantage points we all have different perspectives, and we can use them to achieve a mutual understanding.

Not everyone in the throes of dispute feels comfortable about sitting face to face; in fact, few do. But comfort isn't a prerequisite for mediation; what *is* required is your *willingness* to stand on your own and deal directly with each other.

The way I think about my place in the middle and why I make the choices I do are central themes throughout this book, but three conditions are essential to my style of mediation:

1. Client Responsibility You assume the major responsibility for making the decisions that will settle your dispute.

2. Mediator in the Middle My job is to stay neutral, actively working to understand each person's views as fully as possible and, ultimately, to help you understand yourselves and each other without becoming a decision maker or advocate for either person. At the same time, I need to work actively not to collude in a process that allows either of you to take advantage of the other.

3. Integrating the Law The law is but one of several possible bases that may guide the decisions you will make. Your own personal sense of fairness, for example, is usually at least as important as the law, and finding bases of decision making that honor *each* person is essential to the process.

to them as to warring corporations or to businesses being torn apart by jealousy and disrespect. At the same time, staying with disputes that are superficially similar has the advantage of showing in bold relief the uniqueness at the base of each and every case.

And because I wrote this book for myself as well as for those seeking to understand mediation—perhaps because they wish to resolve their own disputes through mediation—I have also chosen to write about those divorce cases that have been the most problematic for me and that I have not been able to forget. These cases offer insights not only into the mediation process and the mediator's role, but also the nature of humans as social beings.

The potential for growth and change exists at the beginning of every case—though, as you will see, not every mediation succeeds. But just as every relationship differs because of the unique personalities of the people involved, so does every case unfold in its own way and reach a unique conclusion. It is possible to describe some parts of the process in a general way, and I do so in Part One. But it is through the case studies that I show how mediation works and dramatize the fresh, productive insights it can yield into our common experience.

This might make mediation sound like a mere "softening" of the adversary approach to conflict, but in fact it is a careful, sensitive *paring away* of layer after layer of experience. It cuts through stances of posturing, threatening, cajoling, and blaming to the underlying issues of disappointment, pain, hope, aspiration, and fairness. Ideally, the result for both participants is a deeper understanding of themselves and the other, and of the fundamental human relationship between them.

THE DISPUTANTS' REWARDS

*F*rom the point of view of the disputants, this is not only a decision-making process about who gets the house or how much support will be paid (although it certainly includes that) but also a fundamental reorientation. Our normal tendency is to want to forget about the past, sever ties, and move on. Yet people who are willing to face what has happened between them and to speak honestly to each other about it, while also addressing what they want for the future, have the chance to reach a settlement that has integrity. That is the challenge and opportunity that this process presents.

PART ONE:
AN
INTRODUCTION
TO MEDIATION

CHOOSING

MEDIATION

When I think about explaining the process of mediation, I find it natural to think of describing it as I would if you were in my office. Most aspects of the explanation I am about to give have been present in one mediation or another as part of the give-and-take with any new parties. The description is more detailed than what I would give in any one mediation, and I would likely not give specific examples from other mediations as I do here. But otherwise, this is what I think people need to know. So I ask you to allow me to talk with you as if you might be entering this process.

In considering the decision to mediate, you need to understand how mediation compares with its alternatives. Briefly, the options for reaching a settlement following the decision to divorce or separate are these:

- You and your spouse sit down together without any outside help to make all decisions as to parenting and property and write an agreement.

- Each of you hires a lawyer to represent you separately in the negotiations.

- With or without lawyers, you both agree to turn over the necessary decisions to a judge or an arbitrator.

■ You and your spouse meet together with a neutral third party, a mediator, who helps you make the decisions together and writes the agreement.

Each option has its own advantages and disadvantages. Let's look at them one at a time.

1. Deciding Together. This option works best when you are able to deal effectively with each other and to understand the various implications of your decisions. The main advantage of proceeding without outside help is that you retain complete control over the decision making. Even the most argumentative couple usually can make *some* decisions, even if they are limited to how the kitchenware is to be divided. But in relationships where one member is used to making all the decisions, or when there are complex legal, economic, psychological, or personal concerns, deciding together unaided can be dangerous, and the outcome will probably not be legally binding unless you take further steps to formalize your agreement. Still, if you can communicate well together, if each of you understands all the consequences, and if each of you can assert yourself fully, this can be an ideal way to separate.

2. Hiring Lawyers. Many people equate hiring lawyers with going to court, but in reality only a small percentage of cases are ever decided by a judge. Most cases are resolved by the lawyers negotiating directly with each other. Indeed, a principal reason to get legal representation is to prevent you from having to deal directly with each other. Furthermore, your lawyers are there to protect your legal rights, so the results of the negotiation are likely to approximate what the lawyers believe a judge would probably decide. In this sense, while most cases never actually go to court, the negotiations take place in the shadow of the court.

The chief disadvantage of hiring lawyers is that you basically turn your decision making over to them. Some lawyers do represent their clients' desires, but many attribute to clients what *they*, the lawyers, think the clients ought to want. This "protective" stance can frustrate clients and—when the two lawyers square off against each other with their respective defensive stances—prolong the conflict and exacerbate bad feelings between the couple. But perhaps most disturbing in the long run, the decisions reached in litigation are likely not to be personally suited to the family.

3. Accepting an Outsider's Decision. Submitting the dispute to a judge or arbitrator is the last resort in all divorces, and although frequently threatened by lawyers and/or their clients, it rarely happens. In cases where negotiations become deadlocked, this alternative offers a sure way to reach a decision. There are, however, a couple of caveats. The timing of the decision can sometimes be outside the clients' and their lawyers' control. Also, no matter how full the presentation, judges or arbitrators usually lack the knowledge and time to consider different ways of customizing a settlement to meet the particular clients' needs. And significantly, though most people expect a judge's decision to be final, with certain issues—such as support or custody—the door is left open for the parties to come back to ask for changes.

4. Mediation's advantages lie in the clients' control of the process, their flexibility in making fully informed, customized decisions, and their ability to deal with each other in a manner that has personal integrity for them. But as with the other options, it has its disadvantages as well. Many spouses just can't overcome the tension between them to work together. And for those who do, the danger still exists that one person will overpower the other.

WHEN TO MEDIATE

*T*iming can be crucial to the success of mediation. People going through a separation are often on an emotional roller coaster, and changes can occur suddenly, with little warning. Most often, when couples do eventually enter mediation, one party—usually the one who initiated the separation—has achieved willingness before the other. This means that the spouse who is "ahead" of the other must be willing to slow down enough to allow the other to "catch up" emotionally.

Nevertheless, you need not have actually decided to divorce to begin mediation. The process can be useful if both of you are ready to separate and are facing only those decisions necessary to do so. Sometimes one spouse doesn't believe the seriousness of the other's desire to separate until they arrive together in mediation. And every so often the initiating party has second thoughts about separating once the mediation process is under way. I've seen one party arrive with reluctance, the other with clear readiness, and then the two reverse roles during the course of mediation. Ultimately, both parties need to accept separation before they are ready to work on the separation decisions, although that clarity sometimes comes after the two parties enter the process. If either of you is not ready to talk about where you stand with the other in the presence of a third person, you are not ready to begin mediation.

HOW LONG WILL IT TAKE?

*T*he quick answer to the question of how long mediation will take is that it will go no faster than the time needed for the "slower" of you to make decisions. That person has to figure out what decisions need to be made and what he or she requires— in terms of parenting, property, money, and so on—to begin a new life.

Most people want to get through mediation as quickly as possible, but it is important that you take enough time to reach an agreement that neither of you will regret in the future. For most couples, four to six meetings over two or three months is sufficient. The amount of time between sessions is up to you as well.

HOW MUCH WILL IT COST?

*M*ediation is typically far less expensive than adversary representation. Mediation fees are charged on an hourly basis and generally run from $100 to $350 an hour. In addition to the time spent in sessions, mediators charge for any additional work which the parties require done outside the sessions (e.g., writing summary letters of meetings and drafting the separation agreement). A full mediation in which there are substantial disagreements to be resolved typically costs between $2,000 and $5,000. Of course, as with other aspects of the process, the amount of time spent in mediation is controlled by the parties, so the process can be considerably slower or faster, depending primarily on the parties' ability to deal with each other.

SEPARATION OR DIVORCE

*F*or some people, there is little difference between separation—living apart from each other—and divorce, while others are interested only in separating and are not even *thinking* about divorce. And for some couples, one member wants a divorce while the other wants only a separation. From my perspective as the mediator, these discrepancies are not impediments. The only requirement for beginning mediation is that both of you be ready to talk about separation decisions.

The product of mediations in my practice is a separation agreement regarding economic and custody arrangements and the distribution of property. The agreement, drafted by the mediator and signed by both parties to the separation, will be a binding legal contract that governs your future relationship. If you reconcile, you can tear up the contract; if you decide to remain separated indefinitely, the contract will be in effect for as long as you choose. And if either or both want to proceed with a divorce, one or both of you can submit the agreement to the court to be made into a court order, as enforceable as if the judge had made the decisions. Although a judge would technically have the power to reject the agreement, such cases are rare.

CRITERIA FOR MEDIATION

*S*o far, I have been describing the process somewhat from the outside. Now, let's talk from the inside. There are four inter-related criteria that are indispensable to mediating successfully. If you both meet them, you should be able to go forward with prospects for success. But *each* of you needs to meet all four:

- The motivation to mediate
- Self-responsibility
- The willingness to disagree
- The willingness to agree

1. The Motivation to Mediate. Most, if not all, people who enter mediation have a mixture of motivations, both altruistic and self-serving. But whatever their particular reasons, *both* parties must be motivated for mediation to work. If you are considering mediation to help you end your marriage, it will not be enough for only one of you to be interested in mediating. If in answer to the question "Why are you here?" one of you feels, "Because my spouse wanted me to be," we're going to have to look deeper to see if you have your own reasons to participate.

Nor is it enough if your friend, therapist, or lawyer thinks you ought to mediate. You need to think about why mediation makes sense for *you.* If one of you is not willing and motivated to be together in the same room to face the realities of your situation, then mediation, as it is generally practiced—and as I practice it—is doomed.

A variety of motivations lead people to mediate. Some clients want to *avoid the adversary system*—save money, speed up the separation, or stay away from adversarial lawyers and the legal system. Others are intent on retaining control of the decision making. Still other couples want to minimize hostility between them and set up a way to deal with each other in the future. And some, despite their decision to end the marriage, want to help each other ease the pain of the separation.

Often, as the process develops, some motivations surface that have been hidden, while some that seemed important at the beginning fade. For example, when Norman and Alice first sat down to mediate, Alice was aware only that she wanted to get a divorce as quickly as possible. But after she and Norman resolved in my office the question of which of them would move out of the house, she became aware that the two of them might actually reach a meaningful agreement together. To feel that neither of them had "lost," she realized, was very important to her. Once Alice became aware of this motivation, we all had a fuller picture of why she was there. This, in turn, evoked a similar feeling in Norman. While identifying this motivation didn't point to a specific resolution of their disagreement, it did help us find the way to the resolution.

Not all the motivations are so helpful or beneficent. Some people choose mediation in the hope of getting a better deal than they think lawyers could get them, or out of a desire to perpetuate a power imbalance that favors themselves. Some enter the process seeking to assuage the bad feelings engendered by their decision to separate; in effect, they are willing to throw in the towel, hoping to buy peace by leaving all the decision making to the other spouse. Such motivations, if left buried, can derail the process.

When Simon and Ellen entered mediation, Ellen expressed the hope that Simon would be generous with her. This meant to me that she was assuming he would be making the decisions. When we explored that further, Ellen acknowledged that she was afraid Simon would be upset if she registered her disagreements, and she didn't want to do anything that would create more pain for Simon than he had already endured. As the discussion progressed,

Ellen made clear her preference that they try to make their decisions together. She simply hadn't thought about that as a possibility.

2. Self-Responsibility. If motivation is the fuel to the process, self-responsibility is the recognition that *both* members of a couple are at the wheel of the decision-making process. Each of you must be willing to take responsibility to participate fully in the process and for the outcome.

Self-responsibility has three parts:

- You each need to do what is necessary to understand your situation thoroughly.
- You each need to understand your own priorities—your needs, your plans for the future, what is important to you.
- You each must be willing to stand up for yourself, and face whatever conflicts arise. This doesn't mean you can't enter mediation unless you've had success in expressing or resolving your disagreements on your own. But it does mean you must be willing to form your own opinion and express it.

As mediator my task is to illuminate the situation without prejudging or distorting it. This means, for example, that if one of you has been entirely in charge of the family finances, I will help you see that and recognize the implications for your mediation. I will do my best to distill and explain my understanding of the economic, practical, emotional, and legal dimensions of that information. In addition, you may find it necessary or useful to hire experts—such as accountants, appraisers, financial planners, to provide technical information and clarify specific issues. For example, if one of you is going to buy out the other's interest in the house, you may want to hire a real estate appraiser to determine its fair market value.

Assuming responsibility for yourself can be a difficult task. If you enter the process wholeheartedly, you may discover that you are facing very basic questions, such as what you want to do with your life. This process of self-assessment can be daunting, particularly if you have had no experience in living on your own. But while experience with being responsible for yourself is useful, willingness to figure out your personal responsibilities is indispensable.

In separation decisions, the stakes are high: You are deciding on no less than what each of you needs to make your own life function. It is this that makes honesty so important. Both of you must know or have the capacity to decide what you really want and need to go forward with your lives. I would consider working with anyone, even people actively dealing with such problems as alcoholism, drug addiction, or spousal violence. But if such problems prevent or interfere with the couple's ability to make decisions or prevent them from clearly identifying and stating their own needs, the protection offered by a lawyer would make more sense than mediation.

3. The Willingness to Disagree. The willingness to stand up for yourself requires a determination not only to express your point of view, but also to hold out against any decision that would impede you from moving ahead with your life. Although others may register their opinions about what you should do, ultimately you must decide on your own priorities and how your mediated agreement can best reflect them.

My clients and colleagues often find it ironic that I emphasize so strongly the willingness to disagree. "This is mediation," they remind me. "Isn't the goal to agree?" For me, it is crucial that in embarking on mediation, you realize that you may be entering some very bumpy territory.

Very few people are comfortable with conflict. The tension we experience when we disagree with someone else, especially about matters as personal as our children, homes, property, and income, can be very painful. In fact, many are drawn to mediation—both as clients and practitioners—in an attempt to avoid the messiness of conflict. "As far as I'm concerned, this is just a business deal

CONSULTING WITH AN OUTSIDE LAWYER

Why would you need to have a lawyer of your own when you have a mediator? The consulting lawyer's task is to look at the situation exclusively from the point of view of your self-interest. This lawyer does not actually represent you, but helps educate you so you can make the necessary decisions—he or she is an information resource, period. Your relationship with your consulting lawyer is very different from the traditional lawyer-client relationship. You hire the lawyer to do only what *you* think is necessary on an as-needed basis. Consulting with lawyers in this way counteracts the adversarial feeling that hiring a lawyer usually entails and also allows you to control costs. The role is a relatively minor one in terms of time, input, and, particularly, control. The lawyer is not, when used correctly, an advocate for a particular position. Rather, his or her job is to provide you with the information you need to properly represent yourself.

Theoretically, once the parties agree and the mediator drafts the terms of the agreement, the mediation is complete. You do not need to consult a lawyer to make the agreement legally binding. Still, I recommend that each party hire a lawyer to review the agreement, and some mediators refuse to draft the agreement in legally acceptable form because they want to be sure that you go to consulting lawyers before you are legally committed. Were the agreement to become unraveled as a result of lawyer review (which is not usually the case), that may well be because it failed to reflect one or both of your real wishes. It's better to find out early whether your agreement really works—and if it doesn't, the consulting lawyer's perspective can sometimes strengthen it.

It is also true that if either of you hires a consulting lawyer who insists on acting in a traditional manner and wants to take over decision making, or if you pass that responsibility on to your consulting lawyer, the mediation process can be easily undermined. So it is essential that you stay in charge and that you find a lawyer who is comfortable with your doing that.

that needs to be worked out," one client put it, signaling a distance from the start. Or as another expressed the underlying urge to self-protection, "One thing I want you to know is that I want this to be peaceful. We've already been through enough pain."

Some mediators will collude with the parties' desire to avoid conflict, neatly sidestepping potentially upsetting areas. But to try to avoid conflict in mediation is to lose the clarity, resolve, and self-determination that lie at the heart of the process.

The greatest danger is not you and your spouse getting into a fight that leaves you unable to move forward. The worst that can happen then is that you will be out the time and money invested in mediation. It would be better to find yourselves in a stalemate than to reach an unfair agreement favoring one of you over the other. In that case, the disadvantaged spouse winds up either living with a bad agreement or trying to convince a judge to overturn it, which can be extremely difficult. So in a sense it is safer to disagree than to agree, particularly if one has doubts. Paradoxically, the ability to disagree opens up the possibility of agreement. As an educator friend put it, talking about her experience with young children: You don't have a real yes until you have a no.

4. *The Willingness to Agree.* The final requirement is the willingness on both your parts to work toward mutually acceptable decisions. On its face, this may seem obvious, but in my experience it is the failure to meet this criterion that has derailed many a mediation. Consider Barney and Linda. In mediation with me, an agreement was in sight when Linda blurted out, "I know this agreement is going to work for me. I just can't stand the idea that it's going to work for Barney, too."

Some people going through a divorce cannot bear the fact that their spouses are not going to be punished or that, quite simply, their spouses will be able to make their lives work. Linda's ability to voice that concern gave us a chance to talk about it further so she could resolve her need to punish Barney, but for others the sense of personal outrage has brought mediation to a halt.

MEDIATOR NEUTRALITY

N ow let me tell you a little of the perspective I take as I work with you. For just as there are criteria you must meet in order for this process to be successful, there are also criteria for me.

Neutrality for a mediator is different than neutrality for a judge. A judge decides the outcome; a mediator, at least in my view, should not. This stance is not only mediation's greatest asset but also its most vulnerable aspect. The danger is that one party may steamroller the other into accepting an unfair result, with the mediator powerless to do anything other than reiterate, "Well, it's your decision." That description is a cliché, but the danger is real. The mediator's understanding neutrality in a positive sense is essential to confronting that danger.

Positive Neutrality: The Heart of Mediation

While I am largely neutral as to outcome (I discuss the exceptions below), I am not neutral as to process. On the contrary, I am actively engaged in trying to ensure that each party takes responsibility for him- or herself, and in making sure that all decisions are sound for both of them.

In that sense I am very much the advocate for each of you— that is, I am an advocate for the full participation of each party, not an advocate for either one's point of view. To emphasize that distinction, I call my position one of *positive neutrality.* Positive neutrality entails my continual effort to fully understand each of you. That understanding is, for me, at the heart of mediation.

Most people in conflict feel completely misunderstood by the other side, which leads them to attack, blame, or bring pressure to drive their points home. This heavy-hitting approach elicits a counterreaction of a similar nature, and the result is a vicious, escalating cycle.

Imagine yourself in a conflict with another person in which you both want the same object. You'll notice that the natural instinct is not to try to understand the other—otherwise, the thinking goes, you'd be forced to weaken your position. My job is to understand *both* of you and to hold a perspective that includes both positions. For me, the major defect of the adversary system is that it devalues and ignores the possibility of mutual understanding. The effort of positive neutrality is paradoxical, but in a productive way. When many people think of "neutrality," they really mean "objectivity." But to understand both members of a couple at the same time, I need to be deeply "subjective," trying to stand in both of their shoes as fully as I can. Ironically, I find that this effort at subjectivity creates for me an *objectivity*—the ability to see and understand each party's point of view without either one negating the other.

If both spouses know that I understand them—and I make sure they know I'm trying—then they'll each feel that at least one other person in the room does. That is no small thing in a situation in which each person feels deeply misunderstood. Indeed, it can change the atmosphere of the conflict completely. Also, my understanding demonstrates that it is *possible* for someone else to understand each of them—*and* both simultaneously.

Positive neutrality, then, does not mean that I keep my distance from you. To the contrary, it means that I actively empathize, asking each of you why you think or feel the way you do until I am confident I understand.

EXCEPTIONS TO THE NEUTRALITY RULE

*A*ctive empathy coupled with efforts to foster self-responsible, fully informed decision making has proven to be a dynamic and effective way of facilitating agreement. But what if one party continues to dominate? Or what if no understanding is reached? This rarely happens, but when it does, are there any limits to my "neutrality"?

POSITIVE NEUTRALITY:
HOW IT WORKS

*I*n his divorce from Eileen, Hal took a strong position against paying both spousal support and child support. After listening to Hal, I could understand why, from his point of view, he didn't want to pay Eileen spousal support, but not why he didn't want to pay support for their two children. After all, he agreed that the children should live with Eileen, and he earned much more money than she did. An observer might have said, "He's being outrageous. Why not tell him so or tell him that a judge would certainly think so?" The answer was, I needed to understand his point of view and why he felt as he did, even if I didn't necessarily agree with it.

It's natural, when we disagree with someone, to want to counter strongly. I have that reaction all the time when I see parties take positions that seem unreasonable, but I choose instead to follow the impulse toward empathy. "Even with someone like Hal?" you might ask. "Won't he feel confirmed in his position because you've supported him?" I understand that concern, but I believe that the effort at understanding actually reduces the danger.

All three of us realized that Hal's view could not prevail in the mediation unless Eileen acceded to it, and she did not. She saw his position as "outrageous" and did not hesitate to say so. But even in the unlikely circumstance that Eileen had been tempted to go along with Hal's position, she might well have changed her mind as she reached within herself to explain what she needed for herself and the children. In this way, my empathy could stimulate new understanding while providing important information.

Consider the alternative. If I had told Hal I disagreed with him, would that have helped? I don't believe so. In fact, I believe it would have made him entrench himself more deeply. Ironically, understanding and acceptance would permit him to change.

Active empathy is essential but by no means trouble-free. The most common impediments I have found are these:

- One spouse resents the time I spend trying to understand the other and tries to interfere.
- One spouse, fearing the other's reaction, limits what he or she will reveal.
- I simply fail to understand —owing either to miscommunication or to my own blind spots. This failure to understand is perhaps the most dangerous barrier, because it isolates one of the parties from the process.

If I couldn't understand Hal's reasons for wanting to withhold child support, he could have withdrawn and found another mediator—if Eileen had been willing; he could have said nothing and tried to move forward anyway; or he could have expressed his feeling of being judged or misunderstood.

Only if he took the third route would I have been able to see my error. Furthermore, his willingness to do this would have been a true expression of his autonomy—perhaps his first—and it could have changed the entire course of the mediation.

Although understandable, Hal's most dangerous option would have been to say nothing. The best way around any barrier is to make what is happening explicit. If anyone in the room does that—no matter who—options are produced. In Hal's case, after some gentle probing he finally realized that he had taken his position on child support because Eileen's decision to leave him made him feel completely powerless. Once he said this, his view changed and we were able to have the kind of dialogue necessary to reach a solid agreement.

There are two circumstances in which I assert my opinion: if you are about to reach an agreement that is so unfair I could not in good conscience write it up, or if you are about to make an agreement that a court would deem illegal. For example, in one instance, Betty was preparing to agree to give up spousal support without having the faintest idea how she would meet her expenses from the income of her business, and she would not deal with my repeated attempts to get her to articulate how she could get by, instead simply insisting that she wanted an end to the process. I ultimately registered my concern and refused to draw up the agreement. I reminded Betty and Ralph what I explain to all couples at the start: "The ultimate decision belongs to you, and I will defer to you *unless* the decision so completely conflicts with my sense of fairness that I am simply unable to accept it. This reaction wouldn't prevent you from writing up the agreement on your own, however, or hiring another mediator to draft the agreement. But I would make clear to you my concern and why I viewed it the way I did. I have to tell you, I have reached that point."

We went on with our dialogue until Betty recognized that her needs were as important as Ralph's. Together, they agreed that she would receive support from Ralph *if* her business failed to provide her with sufficient income. In these and other respects, Betty started to look out for her own interests, and the ultimate agreement became a balanced one.

As to the second area where I express my opinion—an agreement made by the couple that would be unacceptable to a court— most judges permit couples wide discretion in making their own decisions, even if those agreements differ from what the judge would decide. But there are a few areas in which a couple's decisions would be unacceptable—for example, if they were to agree that one of them would never bear any financial responsibility for the children, I would tell them that no judge would accept that decision. It would still be up to them to decide whether to change the agreement.

BRINGING REALITY INTO THE ROOM

*E*ven though I will not tell either of you what you should do, a critical part of my job is what I call "bringing more reality into the room"—that is, making sure you have all the information you need to make solid decisions. To be fully informed, you need practical economic and legal data, guidelines as to the potential consequences of the options being considered, and feedback on your interactions as they appear to an outside observer.

Joel and Erin, for example, came to mediation after twenty-five years of marriage. All three of their children were grown. Once we had gathered all their financial information, Erin arrived at a session with a creative plan for settling everything by cashing in her pension. While the plan was workable, it also posed some risks for Joel. My job was to reinforce Erin's creativity while explaining the plan and its consequences fully to Joel so he could make an informed decision.

Joel needed to understand what kind of investment he might make with his share of the pension proceeds that would both protect the principal and provide him with sufficient income to meet his monthly expenses. He also needed to be able to evaluate this point in the context of their other property to determine whether he was getting his fair share. Finally, he needed to understand how Erin's proposal fit within the law. But in helping Joel understand Erin's proposal, I was doing more than explaining. I was monitoring his willingness to assume responsibility for forming his own opinion, and observing his understanding of the decisions he faced.

If this willingness on my part to assert my view seems to conflict with the goal of leaving decision-making responsibility with the parties, that is only because it does. My goal is for both parties to make decisions together only when each truly understands his or her needs and these are being met.

An Inside

Look at

Mediation

Now **it's time to look** at what actually happens during the mediation process. In this chapter, I describe how a mediation generally progresses.

LAYING THE
GROUND RULES

Because traditional patterns of approaching conflict are so fixed and often so limiting, in our first mediation session I not only explain the mediation process, I also set up some basic ground rules for working together. Because most people think in terms of litigation in resolving legal disputes, and because the adversary system has the power to compel compliance, to a lesser or greater extent the law is always in the background. Four of the ground rules, then, are intended to help you understand how mediation is related to that system.

1. Litigation must stop. You must agree to suspend or postpone any litigation during the mediation. If you have hired lawyers to represent you before entering mediation, you need to instruct them not to proceed with the adversary process as long as you are mediating. In those states that have a waiting period before a divorce can become final, by agreement you can "start the clock running" by filing whatever papers are necessary to begin divorce proceedings, but even these papers or any other necessary interim agreements must be tailored to ensure that they do not confer an advantage in court on either of you.

2. Both parties will disclose all necessary information and produce relevant documentation. Litigation entails a formal discovery process, with sworn statements and other legal protection to disclose all relevant information, but no such compulsory process exists in mediation. The success of mediation rests in the willingness of each of you to come forth with all information.

To protect you both, the final mediation agreement should explicitly state that the agreement is contingent upon your full and truthful disclosure. If Carrie later discovers, for instance, that Max failed to disclose his ownership of a sailboat in the mediation, she will have the right to go to court either to overturn the whole agreement or have him pay her for her share of the boat.

What is really at issue here is how much trust is necessary and appropriate between the parties in a dispute. In reality, it is not easy to tell if the rule of full disclosure has been broken, so this ground rule alone does not guarantee openness. One clue to its effectiveness in a particular mediation is the relative openness of the parties in registering their concerns about the ground rule itself. If both members of a couple are willing to be open about "soft" as well as "hard" information—their plans for their lives and their children, where they want to live, their work and assets, their new relationships—the process will work far better than if they stick strictly to the numbers. The answers to these questions are as critical to the process as the identification of bank accounts. However, this ground rule is difficult, if not impossible, to enforce, so it is essential that both clients and their mediator reach a real understanding—not merely a superficial agreement—about the importance of openness.

3. No information obtained in mediation—either written —or oral, is to be used in court. In the event that you do not reach an agreement in mediation and end up going to court, you must understand that the mediation process is confidential. The mediator can't testify against either of you in court. Some states have formalized this agreement into a mediation privilege, which prevents mediation information from being used in court. States with no such privilege will honor your agreement, if you make one, to keep either of you from being penalized for openness.

What this means is that if in mediation one of you discloses the existence of a secret gold mine in Arizona, your spouse can't refer to that conversation in court, and the mediator can't be called into court to attest to it. Unless you agree otherwise, though, you are each free to talk to anyone you want to, including a lawyer, about what is said. And a lawyer could still check the mining records in Arizona to prove in court the existence of the mine, so the protection is by no means complete.

4. It's part of the mediator's job to inform you of how your case would probably be decided in a court of law (and about the legal consequences of any decisions you make). As I see it, if the law is unclear, it's my job to explain it as fully as possible without taking a position about any aspect of it. However, as I discuss elsewhere, mediators vary widely on this issue, from those who believe that the law should play no part to those who believe that the law should determine the outcome.

ESTABLISHING NEW KINDS
OF INTERACTIONS

*T*he next set of ground rules is intended to facilitate a shift from an adversarial way of dealing with each other to an approach based on more openness and understanding. The adversary model is not limited to the courts, lawyers, and the law. It is pervasive in our culture, and we carry around within ourselves many aspects of that system when we think about or experience the dynamics of conflict. Take a moment to remember a disagreement you had with your spouse or someone else. If you analyze your respective stances, there's a good chance you'll find them rooted in assumptions basic to that adversary culture.

For example, if you tried to convince your spouse that you were right and he or she was wrong, you were, in effect, behaving as if only *one* of you could be right. On the other hand, maybe your spouse simply gave in. Or perhaps one or both of you tried to avoid dealing with the conflict by pretending it didn't exist.

All three responses are typical adversary-type interactions. These are not bad, but they are limited in their ability to solve problems. In fact, in conflict, most couples develop patterns of interaction that have the effect of prolonging, exacerbating, or sidestepping the conflict rather than resolving it.

To alter these patterns, both participants and their mediator need to make a conscious effort. The following ground rules laid down during the initial meeting are designed to establish new patterns.

All three meet together throughout the mediation process. Some mediation approaches favor "caucusing," whereby the mediator shuttles back and forth between the two parties. Caucusing is highly controversial; the spectrum ranges from those mediators who regularly caucus with each spouse, eliciting and keeping secrets, to those who will never meet with anyone alone, ever.

My strong preference is always to meet together. Only if it

proves impossible for someone to speak freely am I willing to set up separate meetings with each spouse. But in those instances I hold no secrets. The whole idea is to ensure that all the relevant information becomes available to both of you.

How do we do that? Through communication. Talking. Listening. Not infrequently, the words are loud and angry. At other times they are quiet, poignant, and filled with meaning. It's part of an unfolding process that takes its form from the life experience of both parties. Sometimes I talk; sometimes the two of you do, and all the time we are gathering information or discussing a possible agreement—whatever the concrete task—we are communicating. And when you ultimately reach an agreement that honors each of you it will be through communication.

There is no one way to describe *how* people work through their differences and reach agreement. Generalizing about the process fails to capture the reality, and exceptions always arise to each generalization. Still, recognizing and understanding certain "conflict dynamics" can help some couples communicate more effectively.

I look at communication through two separate lenses, one focused on *content* and the other on *dynamics*. *What* the parties are communicating about is the content; *how* they are communicating is the dynamic. Though the dynamic is the more subtle, it is just as important to watch and understand. In fact, my work frequently focuses on the dynamic of the conflict, rather than the content.

Many couples are locked into ineffective communication patterns, and by the time they have decided to separate, even these have often broken down. To compound matters, people frequently enter mediation with serious misconceptions. The first, as already mentioned, is that I will actually be the one to make the decisions. "Can't you just tell us what we should decide? After all, you've been through this before." When I decline, the reality of self-responsibility sinks in. "You mean I really have to reach agreement with *him?*"

The second common misconception is that mediation is supposed to be conflict-free, and that all expressions of frustration should be avoided in favor of some "proper" way of proceeding. Sometimes one spouse uses that idea to inhibit the other's expression, but often both spouses share this view. And from what I've seen, many mediators collude in this limiting mindset. As I see it, conflict is almost always an inevitable part of the mediation process. The goal is to move beyond it, but the path is almost always *through* the conflict.

The two spouses share responsibility for the mediator's fee. This rule has symbolic importance—it reflects the fact that the spouses are sharing the investment and that the mediator is working for both. Nevertheless, from the mediator's perspective, the division need not be equal; nor is it important who writes the check. It is the ultimate sharing of the responsibility that's at issue. Sometimes this means that each party pays his or her share out of a separate or joint account as we go along. Other times one person pays and is credited at the time of the division of the assets and debts.

The clients themselves may set other ground rules. For example, during their marriage, Oscar had continually given in to Judy. When a dispute occurred, Judy would always prevail. But when they entered mediation and began to understand that they needed to change their way of interacting, they established their own ground rule: Neither of them would interrupt the other. As small as it might seem, that rule enabled Oscar to assert himself and Judy to allow him to do so.

Setting the ground rules occurs in the first mediation session, which lasts approximately two hours. In my practice, at the end of the first session, I prepare a written agreement to mediate that summarizes the ground rules established so far. Although we can alter the ground rules at any time by three-way agreement, the signing of the written agreement to mediate captures our understanding and formally begins the mediation.

GATHERING INFORMATION

*A*fter everyone agrees to proceed, the first session closes with each party understanding what he or she needs to do to gather the information necessary for making decisions. The information you need breaks down into three categories:

- Children
- Assets (what both of you own), liabilities (what you owe), and cash flow
- Your own future plans

1. Children. In this area, you will need to answer some difficult questions: Where does each of you think the children should live? Where should they go to school? Is it very important that they maintain continuity with their friends, and if so, how can that be accomplished? What kind of relationship will each of you maintain with the children? What kind of back-and-forth arrangement between you and your spouse will work best for each of you?

Sometimes the answers will not be clear at first, but it's important that each of you begin asking the questions. Depending upon the ages of the children, it may be important to have direct input from them. Sometimes a plan that makes great sense to the parents ignores crucial information, such as the children's rhythm in going back and forth between the parents' homes. At this stage, you need to agree on how to elicit this input. Do the two of you want to sit down together with the children, meet separately with each child, each have separate conversations with the children, or have a third party talk to them about their preferences and report back to the two of you? With children, as with finances, there is often an implicit, if not explicit, understanding between spouses that one of them—and only one—is the expert. Mediation may be the first chance the "non-expert" has to identify and air his or her own views. Is the "non-expert" still looking to the other to shoulder responsibility for information on the children or finances?

2. *Assets, Liabilities, and Cash Flow.* You'll both need to make written lists of everything you own, its value, when you acquired it, whose name appears on any ownership papers—in short, the details on every separate piece of property (excluding household items), debts, or accounts. Regarding cash flow, the goal is to figure out a way to make the family resources stretch to cover two households. Each of you needs to determine how much money actually exists and then how much you will need to lead your life as you envision it.

For some people, creating a budget is a simple task; others have trouble with it, especially if their spouses have handled the household finances during the marriage. In any case, this job becomes an opportunity to really evaluate your priorities, and it must be done. Forms are provided to help simplify the task.

3. *Your Own Future Plans.* Clarity about your plans is essential. Many people want to postpone figuring out their future plans until they know what the financial decisions will be, but this can become a question of the chicken or the egg. The more you understand about what you want to do with your life, the clearer you will be about the decisions you have to make.

With the collecting of information, mediation is given its first real test, and the issue of whether each of you can be self-responsible may appear in sharp relief. Is each of you disclosing all relevant concrete information fully, as you agreed at the start? Do you both understand that information? Are you each thinking realistically about your own plans for the future? And, critically, do you each understand the assembled information sufficiently to make the necessary decisions? If not, are you willing to do what you need to do to gain that understanding? If these questions cannot be answered affirmatively, the whole process can be derailed.

The initial agreements about disclosure and self-protection can help you stay committed to the process as you face these difficult questions. Having the same knowledge base allows you and your spouse to deal with each other as equals. And now, during this information-gathering period, may be the time to bring in consultants, if you think you need them. You may want to meet with a child psychologist to discuss custody or a financial consultant to go over a budget or analyze your assets.

BEGINNING THE RESOLUTION PROCESS

W ith the information gathered, we are now ready to address the conflict. But what is the conflict? It's critical at this point to determine precisely what the parties disagree about. It is my practice to work with the spouses to identify areas of agreement and disagreement. This may sound simple, and sometimes it is, but more often this step is complex and full of surprises.

Consider Art and Mary, who both assumed at the outset that their case would be easy to resolve. "Well, maybe we should start with the house," began Art, "and who will live—" That was as far as he got. "The house is easy," Mary interjected. "There can be no disagreement there. I need it. The kids are going to be with me and they need it. A court would award it to me. Art surely agrees. We can go on to the next issue." At this point I came in: "It takes two to agree. It only takes one to disagree. Unless both of you feel we have an agreement, I assume that for now that this is an area of disagreement." "You're damn right," Art told me, to Mary's obvious surprise, and now the abstractions about two-party agreements started to take on a starker reality.

Once you have identified the issues, you can start with the first. But which is the first? Again, the two of you decide. No single particular order of issues will work for every couple. While it might sound insignificant, deciding together where to start can bring home the message of self-responsibility and mutuality in decision making. But even though most mediations address one issue at a time, neither of you will likely be in a position to evaluate fully the resolution of any one issue until all issues have been resolved. Sometimes people will resolve one issue, then resolve a second, and then find themselves going back to rethink the first in light of the second. While this may not feel good, it is progress.

OPENING THE LINES OF COMMUNICATION

*I*magine for a moment two metal springs that have become entangled together. A movement in one starts a reaction in the other, which in turn is followed by a counterreaction. Often couples are so intertwined that it's hard to know where one person begins and the other ends, and it's no easy matter to disentangle. To communicate, they first need to be separated.

Certain patterns of entanglement recur frequently:

- One person tries to control the other through threats, intimidation, blame, coercion, ridicule, or persuasion. For example, Phil tells Harriet that unless she gives up spousal support, he will quit mediation. Harriet feels intimidated.
- One person devalues his or her view to accommodate the other. Steve acquiesces to Jean's need to live in the house for as long as she wants by deciding that his need to have a house of his own is unimportant.
- One person is unwilling to engage the other. Arnold continually puts off responding to Nina's demand that they use their joint bank account to pay off their debts.
- The spouses have divided their expertise between them. Joe is more comfortable with managing family finances, while Janet has made most decisions regarding the children.

The goal is to help you find ways to communicate that are not limited by these patterns. That is no easy matter, particularly when these patterns are reinforced by traditional social gender roles.

You might assume, as many people do, that spouses can't really depart from these entrenched habits. And indeed many individuals and couples spend years of hard work in counseling or other settings trying to change these patterns. I'm not suggesting that mediation can produce the same thing quickly. But ironically it is often the decision to separate that allows the change—you no longer need to find a way to live together, so you can risk new ways of telling each other the truth. And the presence of a third person sitting in the triangle also helps spur different ways of interacting.

Couples who manage to break old communication patterns can achieve a level of understanding they have never had before. It's in this way that sudden, dramatic shifts can occur to break a years-long stalemate. Not infrequently I see spouses become willing and able to deal with each other in their divorce in a way that was impossible in the marriage. This may have a bittersweet quality, but it is almost always a significant experience for those who attempt it, and can have an enormous healing effect. Providing the opportunity for couples to have this experience is one of my sources of personal satisfaction.

To help disentangle them, I work with the couple in two ways. First, I ask them to be aware of the pattern—to temporarily focus on process rather than content. When I ask them how they communicate, they become actively involved in untangling the knot themselves. For example, with Joe and Janet described above, Joe had been responsible for financial matters in the marriage and Janet had made all child-rearing decisions. When they acted as a team during the marriage, this traditional pattern might have "worked," but when they decided to separate, each faced the need to develop the other half of the equation. When they began mediation, they were still locked into their "marriage mode" of communicating. Janet was fearful of Joe's reaction and therefore understated the amount of money she needed to live. And Joe, to keep Janet from feeling depressed, decided to conceal from her some of their debts, hoping that he would figure out a way to handle them later. Both Janet and Joe had grown used to thinking that the money Joe controlled in the marriage belonged to him; neither wanted to figure out what belonged to whom, and neither had thought out how to relate to the children in the future. These ways fit their marriage but blocked their ability to feel separate and to form independent opinions. But because the patterns were so familiar and ingrained, Janet and Joe were surprised to learn they existed at all.

Sorting out these entanglements may be the hardest and most critical work I do during the whole mediation. My understanding of Janet and Joe's patterns of interrelating had to lead to *their* understanding. Only that recognition could allow them to act as autonomous and *equal*—and willing to respect each other's emerging views even when they disagreed.

This ability to step back from the fray and notice what is going on can be invaluable when the going gets rough. If you avoided dealing with conflict when you were together, you may both find it upsetting to openly disagree with each other. Without the benefit of distance, when you get very upset or angry with each other, it's easy to feel that someone is doing something wrong or that the mediation process is not working. But if you develop an ability to watch yourselves, you might be able to see that you are passing through an uncomfortable transition to a more productive (if initially less comfortable) way of dealing with each other.

My second technique for disentangling is the flip side of identifying the limiting patterns—namely, suggesting productive alternatives. For example, during the information-gathering stage, I ask each person in turn to provide the relevant information while the other party refrains from interrupting, and often their versions differ. The "asserting" party may be talking to me, but obviously the other is listening, possibly more closely now than before.

If both people are able to identify what is important for them, we have accomplished two things. First, the person expressing the thought benefits by clarifying their own thinking. For example, when Rita was able to tell Josh that by asking for spousal support she had no intention of punishing him, but that she simply needed it, she remarked, "You know, that's really true. I've never said that before, even to myself."

A second benefit is that the listener is forced to *hear,* if not understand, the statement. The listener may want to criticize, object or even agree. But if the spouses can simply allow each other to assert without reacting, blocked communication can begin to flow. Many couples can do this, and the more they practice, the more I can recede. Now they have actually moved into a mediative mode. This is perhaps the most satisfying irony of mediation: By moving apart to become more independent of each other, the two have found a way to better understand themselves and each other.

THE POSSIBILITY OF EMPATHY

Once the exchange begins, there is the chance to go deeper. Not only can the two understand each other's point of view, but they may even come to recognize their underlying connection. In short, they may even begin to *empathize* with each other. This empathy is at the heart of what I work to facilitate.

This does not mean that I *push* the parties toward empathizing—obviously, the result would not be empathy. Indeed, my primary objective is only to assure each person that his or her voice will be heard, at least by me. But as each person while listening to the other tentatively spends a moment in the shoes of the other, a field of understanding begins to open. The differences are not eliminated, but each person's needs are acknowledged. Now and only now can the two say, "We differ. So how can we respond to those differences?" With three people in the room looking at the same picture and wanting to find solutions that work for the whole family, the spouses have a chance not only of solving the problems but of finding a reference point for dealing with each other in the future.

MOVING BENEATH THE CONFLICT

*M*ost people in conflict focus on the content of their disagreement. Dealing with the conflict at the concrete level is necessary, but if the disagreement is serious, dealing *only* with the particulars usually leaves both sides feeling dissatisfied.

At the concrete level, the mediums of exchange are measurable and tangible: money, property, and time. At this level, what one of you gets, the other has to give up. Often, since both spouses perceive that they want the same thing, they adopt a fighting stance, marked by aggressive, defensive, or other strategic maneuvering designed to throw the other person off balance.

If the spouses remain in those postures and deal with the conflict only at the level of "who gets the house," resolution will be difficult. In fact, the result will probably be a trade-off in which both will compromise. So if the two of you both want to buy out each other's share of the family home, you might end up selling it to a third party. Within the adversary setting, the conflict can and often does remain at that level. One or the other gets the house, or the house is sold, and the parties measure their success in dealing with the conflict by the result.

But beneath that concrete level is a second level—that of *needs* and *interests*. When I ask each person what getting the house would represent to him or her, frequently we are all surprised. He or she might say the house means security, affordable housing, a source of money, or convenience to the family or friends—but this may never have been articulated before.

Penetrating to this second level does not automatically make the conflict go away. But it does give more room to allow possibilities to emerge for each person. Frequently, as these options emerge, the dynamic between the spouses changes significantly. Instead of being at each other's throats, acting as if only one of them can win, they are apt to realize they have a number of possible options. At this level, the differences between their needs and interests can actually serve as a path to innovative solutions.

LIFE DIRECTION

*E*ven below needs and interests lies another level where the conflict connects with a sense of the direction of each party's life. Most of us only reach this level, which has to do with our values and goals, during a crisis—for example, when a loved one dies or during a divorce. When we do, we often experience a fair amount of emotional pain and confusion. Sometimes my clients explore this level outside mediation—on their own or with a counselor—but occasionally they discover a sense of the direction they want their lives to take during the course of our work together. I am often touched by people's willingness to open to this level and the importance to them of doing so.

When they are working at this level, people come to a new understanding of what's most important to them. This reorientation can be more real and reassuring than, for example, having the house—or it may put the question of who gets the house in a completely new context. At this level, we gain a broader view of the conflict, one that allows even more room for a creative resolution.

Although there's often resistance, the deeper mediation goes the more options are expressed and the more solid is the base upon which solutions will rest. And the depth of the process depends, I think, on the mediator's ability to understand the conflict *without* encouraging the parties to compromise their positions. Still, his or her ability to do that will not guarantee that the disputants will be able to do the same.

Moving more deeply from one level to another can feel risky, and the process of resolving each and every issue can begin to seem all-consuming. But the reality is that on the deeper levels of the conflict, the same needs and interests underlie all the separate issues, so resolving one usually is the key to resolving all. For example, if Alicia's need for financial independence from Victor underlies her desire to sell the house and split the proceeds, that same need will appear again when they turn to the issue of spousal support or alimony. So if I can evoke both Alicia's and Victor's needs and interests and even deeper choices about life direction, we might be able to come up with a resolution that encompasses them all.

It is not essential to reach this level or for spouses to understand each other empathetically to achieve a satisfactory resolution of their dispute. Some do; many do not. But as a mediator, I find that the promise of these connections opens up the process in surprising and rewarding ways.

MAKING DECISIONS

*L*et me sum up the process as described so far. With my help as a neutral party, the two of you have:

- identified the conflict
- each asserted your point of view
- at least heard, and perhaps even understood, each other.

We have probably had between two and four meetings to reach this point. The work now is to actively make decisions, but the next question to resolve is: On what basis—or according to what criteria—should the decisions be made? Possible bases for decisions are the following:

- *The law and its underlying principles*
- *Each individual's own sense of fairness*
- *The identified needs and interests of all concerned*

- *The relationship between the mediating couple*
- *Any prior agreements between the two*
- *Personal criteria with special significance for the couple, such as religious or community beliefs and standards*
- *Practical and economic realities*

1. The Law and Its Underlying Principles. I start with the law not because it is the most important factor but because, until its charm is dispelled, it is seen by many as so predominant that it blocks all other factors from sight.

In a litigated divorce, law is the primary standard. Some mediators either explicitly or implicitly make law the norm in mediation as well, trying informally to approximate what a court would do. At the other end of the spectrum, some mediators take the position that the law is irrelevant to mediation and encourage the parties to ignore it altogether. My own view lies between the two. I consider it essential that each of you understands the law and its role in your thinking, but the weight you want to give it is completely up to you.

I have several reasons for this approach. First, the law is part of the reality. Even if you ultimately decide not to make the law the basis for your decisions, understanding how the law might apply gives you a more complete picture. Many people see a court decision as a standard—if not of what is fair, then at least of what they could have expected from the adversary approach. Second, ignoring the law entirely can make it more of a presence than if it has been discussed. As an unacknowledged alternative, it can loom over the whole process, stifling personal expression and creative decision making. Finally, being informed about the law is necessary for the agreements to be legally binding.

But the strong emphasis on law in our society means that people in mediation are often far too heavily influenced by what a judge would decide, forgetting that they have the right to make their own rules and base their decisions on their personal views.

In effect, they frequently see the law as an external authority that nullifies their personal power to decide together what they think is best. But in fact, within a very broad range, they are free to make their own decisions, regardless of how a court might decide. Indeed, that *is* the law. That's why although I consider it important to inform the parties about the law, I also try to dispel its power.

In mediation, I explain not just how a court would decide the spouses' case, but why. The very impersonality of the law has value for people who are looking for some sort of public standard as they struggle to reach decisions. Knowing how society might view your case can be a valuable reality test, and by understanding the principles behind the law, you can test them against your own values.

Finally, to give my clients power over the law, often I ask them *when* they want to hear about how their case would likely be decided in a court. Some people find it easier to hear the law early on. For instance, Gerry and Phyllis wanted to get the law "out of the way" so they wouldn't be so anxious about where they stood legally. But others prefer to hear the law *after* they have thought the issues through and made tentative decisions so they can compare their own conclusions with those a judge would reach. So when Edward and Mary Ann heard that the legal support guidelines would give Mary Ann less support than they had agreed upon, Edward was surprised but actually felt affirmed by what, under the circumstances, had felt right to both of them, and they stuck with their decision.

In sum, the law can have as much or as little power in mediation as you want to give it. If you understand this, the law becomes simply *one* factor among others that are helpful in determining how you will make your decisions.

2. Fairness. Many people come to mediation intending to make their decisions on the basis of their personal sense of fairness. But separation, upsetting and confusing as it is, can obscure that sense of justice—what seemed fair in the context of a marriage looks very different in the context of a divorce. Looking for an anchor, some people rely on the law to embody fairness. For others, I must admit, fairness doesn't exist. "Life isn't fair, the separation isn't fair, and talking about fairness is just another form of manipulation," said one husband, and he meant it. Still, most people have a deep internal sense of fairness that can help them make mutually acceptable decisions. One of my jobs, as the neutral outsider, is helping each of you first identify and then articulate your sense of fairness and then apply it to the conflict at hand. This process can be enormously empowering and an important part of the healing process.

3. Needs and Interests. I have already made clear how the spouses' needs and interests are critical to the decision making, but the needs and interests of others—for example, children—can be important reference points for decision making, too. If you have children who are minors, you must be willing to distinguish your own needs from theirs and to understand that certain decisions that might initially appeal to you and/or your spouse might not work for the children at all. For example, while it might be convenient for each of you to have the children with you on alternate weeks, the frequency of the back-and-forth might be too much for them.

Others besides children could be affected as well—for example, stepchildren, relatives, friends, and co-workers. In a litigated settlement, these people would have no legal standing and would be unlikely to have an influence, but mediation's flexibility can give voice to their concerns. For example, your children's relationship with their grandparents could be important enough to you and your spouse to influence your parenting agreement.

4. The Relationship. Separation might feel like the end of the relationship, but even for those people who will never see each other again, it rarely is. However you choose to interact in the future, in mediation your past and current relationship can provide guidance for decision making. Dana and Sam, for example, have a deep desire to honor the best of their past relationship while saying good-bye. Randa and Doug put a high value on divorcing with mutual respect. Colleen and Ross know they will be interacting in the future—not only because they share children but also because both are working artists in the small international world of ceramics. In all such cases, the parties' ability to refer to their relationship—past, current, or future—may provide them with a perspective that changes their attitude toward a disagreement or gives them insight into what solution will work best.

5. Prior Agreements. Any agreements—from casual understandings to written contracts—made before or during the marriage could affect the decision making. Even non-binding prenuptial agreements are useful reference points now. For example, Stan and Gloria agreed that Gloria would quit her job to have a child— and the implicit understanding between them was that Stan would take up the financial slack, even in the event of divorce.

Of course, the decision to divorce can raise questions about the meaning of a prior agreement. For example, Helene and Al both stood to inherit a good deal of money. Al's legacy came under his control shortly after they married, at which time both agreed in writing that all inherited money was to go into the marriage pot. Helene was not to inherit hers until she was thirty-five, and she asked for a separation at age twenty-three. Both couples had to grapple with the prior agreements in making their current decisions.

6. Personal Criteria. The standards of your community, religion, or any other group you belong to might also affect your agreement. For example, if John is Catholic and Lynn Jewish, how much concern will each give to the other's tradition, particularly regarding their children's future?

The challenge from my point of view is to uncover all such factors, no matter how hidden. The more these variables are brought out and aired, the more possible it is to create a solution that accommodates them.

7. *Practical and Economic Realities.* An agreement has to be practical—so reality plays a large role in decision making. For example, Lorraine decides to give up spousal support because she views it as unfair—but she still has no other immediate source of income. How is she to launch a single life? Or consider the reverse. Herb is quite willing to pay Hannah a high level of spousal support but has no real capacity to generate it.

Each individual has to look hard at and comprehend his or her own economic reality—assets, expenditures, tax obligations, and potential sources of money and goods. Reality testing is one of the services I provide. I bring to bear my experience with other couples, as well as all my personal experience and common sense, to help the couple anticipate any obstacles to implementing the agreement. For example, taxes are frequently overlooked in the rush to dismantle the household and move on, and introducing the tax implications can totally change the financial consequences of a couple's decisions. Or it may be necessary for me to help a couple think through the child-care arrangements, particularly if neither has had experience in living alone.

The challenge is to offer reality testing while still remaining neutral on the issues. My rule of thumb is to cite particulars—examples and comparisons drawn from real life—and let the couples draw their own conclusions.

DEVELOPING OPTIONS

*T*he task in the home stretch is to develop options. The most effective way to do this is to make sure all three of us, the mediator and both members of the couple, have seen every side of each issue.

At this point, I will ask both of you to brainstorm—"Give me every idea you have about how to resolve the conflicts." The object is to tap the spouses' own inner resources, not mine. Eventually I may introduce my own ideas, but waiting until they have expressed theirs reduces the danger that they might defer to me.

Often the best solutions come after everyone in the room has concluded that all possibilities have been covered, so I try to discourage evaluation of any particular option until the well is dry. Critical thinking tends to dampen the atmosphere necessary for inventing and exploring new ideas. For example, Elaine and Maury seemed to have identified all of their options with regard to their home—they could sell it, buy each other out, or own it together for a period of time—when Elaine had the idea of giving it to the children. Although ultimately the two did not opt for this alternative, discussing it had a significant effect on the whole agreement.

At this stage, most people believe that there's a pie to be divided and that the more you get the less is left for the other. This notion cannot be completely eliminated, but even a slight adjustment in thinking can dramatically change what's available. Before the pie is divided, there are often ways of *expanding* it so that there's more to go around. Ultimately, the pie still has to be divided, but if it can be expanded first, then both of you could end up better off.

How can the pie be made bigger? Again, brainstorming can uncover the answer, this time for any and all ideas on how to reduce expenses and improve the quality of life for both of you as you go your separate ways. In this phase, I jump in with both feet, contributing any ideas, particularly related to the law, that you might not know about.

For a rather simple illustration, if Henry and Selma agree to sell the family home, they do not have to pay capital gains taxes on the sale if either or both buy new residences costing as much as the sale price of the home within two years of the sale. In another example, Janice and Craig were trying to work out a way to share child-care expenses. They both had flexible work schedules but were too tightly focused on the financial aspect to see the benefit of dovetailing their schedules. From my neutral position, I was able to see that they could each spend more time with their child and reduce child-care expenses simultaneously.

But after we have expanded the pie, we still need to divide it. During this part of the process, it is important that each of you refrain from committing to any decision until you feel you have sufficiently weighed the alternatives. And once it is clear which option works best, you each need to overcome the anxiety of actually making a decision. Sometimes one spouse is nervous about how life will work after divorce, and sometimes one spouse is subconsciously trying to prolong the process to avoid the inevitable sadness that accompanies the formal dissolution of a marriage.

REACHING AN IMPASSE

*I*n some cases, however, couples on the brink of a decision reach a true impasse. In such situations, there are several possible responses. First, it's important for all involved to admit that they're stuck, to make sure all agree on this at least. Sometimes I have believed a case to be stuck but upon sharing my perception have learned that I was wrong. Also, there are times when simply talking about being stuck reveals the way out of the problem. One couple I worked with found their way around an impasse just by reaffirming the importance of deciding together.

Some couples need to let time pass to move beyond the impasse. Just because the mediation is on hold does not mean your lives must stop, and in fact your outside activities can change your perceptions of what is important to you. Lydia and Peter disagreed on spousal support so they took a three-month hiatus between mediation sessions, during which both got a clearer sense of what their work futures looked like. They translated that clarity into an idea that moved us forward.

Sometimes, too, a consulting lawyer, an accountant, or another adviser can throw a new light on the situation. For example, Bob and Jody owned property affected by a maze of prohibitive local zoning ordinances and neither wanted to sell, but a real estate adviser devised a way of dividing the property that worked both for them and within the zoning laws.

Some mediators view an impasse as a time to push both parties toward compromise. My view is that if both are willing to live with the tension of irresolution rather than concede an important issue, new ideas can emerge. In fact, these stalemates often present opportunities, because they can inspire you to dig deeper inside for what is most important to you. The greatest danger at an impasse is that someone will capitulate and make compromises he or she will later regret.

FINALIZING THE AGREEMENT

Once you reach agreement, I will draft it in a form acceptable to a court. This draft lists the specifics of the decisions plus standard clauses that ensure the agreement will be carried out. Some mediators draft a less formal memorandum of agreement.

Next, I urge both of you to review the draft with your consulting lawyers. This is a chance to get a fresh look by someone who can help test the agreement against the law to make sure you are adequately protected. Lawyers in this role sometimes pick up significant issues that were not sufficiently addressed, enhancing the mediation process.

But be warned: Some lawyers do not know how to support their clients in mediation. Used to making all the decisions for their clients, they are uncomfortable in any other role. It is possible for such a lawyer to look at any agreement from a one-sided perspective, poke holes in it, and tell you you could do better.

A few years ago I ran into Madeleine, a former client. Her consulting lawyer, acting much as a traditional adversary, had advised her to terminate mediation, and she had followed his advice. She told me she regretted that she had. Three years and $50,000 later, she had ended up with a result that was much worse for her. At the time, I had done what I usually do—said that I believed we were making progress and left the decision about continuing to my clients. Now, to protect the process from being undermined, I discuss with you beforehand how you might best use your consulting lawyer to enhance mediation. Increasing numbers of practitioners are becoming familiar and comfortable with the consulting lawyer role.

After the lawyer review, the three of us meet to make any necessary changes. While this revision phase often goes quickly, sometimes there is a lot of going back and forth before everyone is satisfied. And occasionally, if a new central issue arises or if one of the parties expresses ambivalence or dissatisfaction, the agreement can start to unravel. At this stage with Evan and Hilary, Evan's anticipated raise failed to come through, and because many of their decisions had been based on the extra income, the whole agreement had to be reworked.

The challenge at this point is to keep the atmosphere open. Two sources of tension that have been present all along can come to a head. The first relates to the measures of flexibility and predictability the agreement will permit in future economic arrangements. If both spouses value predictability, they will lock in the financial deal and sacrifice flexibility. If they both value flexibility—arrangements that may change in unspecified ways as their children grow or their incomes ebb and flow—they will sacrifice predictability. The problem arises when the parties favor different values. For example, Don wanted to know now what his entire financial obligation would be to Pam, but Pam was entering the job market for the first time in fifteen years. She wanted to know that the agreement could change if things didn't turn out for her as she hoped. Our task was to strike a balance between enough predictability to satisfy Don and enough flexibility to satisfy Pam. By agreeing to pay more support than Pam may have required under a more flexible scenario, Don made it possible for Pam to agree to less flexibility.

A second source of tension can arise over how specific the written agreement must be. No matter how specific the agreement, some issue is likely to crop up in the future that is not completely covered, something that no one anticipated or could have anticipated at the time. But even with that assumed, legitimate differences can and do come up over how much to provide for in the agreement. For example, Elliott agrees to provide for the children's college education but wants it to be a matter of trust, not spelled out in the official separation agreement. Jane, on the other hand, wants to be sure that Elliott will provide for the kids' education because she knows she will be lucky just to make ends meet. She won't feel secure until the issue is covered in writing. So begins a new round of discussion.

Often it becomes clear at this stage that one—or both—of the parties has a deep-seated resistance to signing written agreements. Elliott might be afraid of promising to provide for tuition costs, even though he agrees in principle, until he knows how much they will be. The remedy here is not to sidestep the issue but to make the wording of the agreement a question to be decided in itself.

If the parties agree to leave certain issues open or to renegotiate aspects of the agreement later on, the document should spell out how and when the parties will address them. Elliott and Jane agreed that in three years—unless Elliott were earning a certain salary, which would automatically commit him to paying—they would sit down together to nail down the specifics of funding the kids' college education. They also agreed that if they were not able to resolve the issue, they would mediate before they would go to court. Other couples in similar situations have reached agreements calling for more fixed resolutions that would obviate the necessity of any future negotiations.

The separation agreement you will sign is a binding, legal contract. Once signed, it can remain as a contract, in which case it will be as enforceable as any other legal agreement, or it can be submitted to a court, where it will be made into a court order in the form of a judgment of divorce. One of you, your mediator, or one of your consulting lawyers can then prepare the papers necessary to proceed with a divorce.

AFFIRMING WHAT HAS HAPPENED

*B*efore the ink on the agreement is dry, there is an understandable urge on the part of the mediator and parties alike to say "That's it," stand up, and walk out. But many couples want to take the opportunity, with my encouragement, to acknowledge to each other what has happened—that they have strived to come to terms with the past and plan for the future in a way that works best for each of them and their children. And they have done so through a process by which they asserted themselves while respecting each other. If the three of us have been able to do that successfully, we are all grateful.

CHOOSING A MEDIATOR

*I*f you are interested in trying mediation, it's important that you choose the mediator with care. In most states, there are no legal restrictions preventing anyone from acting as a mediator, nor is any license required. The Yellow Pages, local social service referral networks, friends who have been in mediation, therapists, clergy, or lawyers supportive of mediation are all potential sources of names. But be prepared to look outside your community for someone who seems promising. Mediation is too new and ill-defined to conform to an objective standard and you may encounter "mediators" whose ideas of the enterprise differ sharply from your expectations and from the descriptions in this book.

You'll probably be able to glean enough from the grapevine to decide whom to call, but don't expect to have a one-on-one conversation with the mediator—any mediator who values impartiality knows how crucial the first contact can be, and will either remain inaccessible unless both of you are on the line or try to minimize contact with you so as not to create a relationship with one party that could result in misunderstandings later on. But a query to the office assistant should be sufficient to determine whether the mediator is taking on cases, what the fees are, a rough estimate of the number of sessions typically necessary to reach agreement (in my office it's four to six), and whether the mediator will draft the separation agreement and help prepare any necessary court papers.

Because there are many different approaches to mediation, both of you should have a clear idea about what you need from a mediator. One purpose of this book is to help you form that idea. Still, to find out whether a candidate can really meet those needs, it will be useful to think of your first meeting as a sort of interview. You may want to go prepared with a list of questions. Here's a sample list that will help you clarify the person's orientation:

1. Why did you become a mediator? What do you see as your goal for a mediation? What you can find out here is the mediator's personal and philosophical orientation, and you will have a chance to measure your own goals against his or hers to determine your compatibility. You will also have a chance to find out how open the mediator is willing to be about him- or herself. It is very difficult to enter into a process that calls for you to reveal very personal information if you don't feel that the person you hire is able to relate to you on a personal level.

2. What kind of commitment do you need from us to agree to mediate? Mediators who demand a commitment to the process should be viewed skeptically—this may indicate that they are inexperienced or want to overcontrol the process. Trust an answer that allows you to leave anytime you are dissatisfied with the process. The truth is that no mediator can compel you to stay against your will, anyway.

3. Will you want to meet separately with us? If so, why? And if so, would you hold secrets? The answer to these questions will tell you about the mediator's comfort in dealing with conflict between you. Mediators who insist upon separating the parties usually do that because they aren't able to handle the conflict when the parties are together. And if they hold secrets on top of meeting separately with each of you, they are likely to assume the role of arbitrator, not mediator, at least in your eyes if not in theirs.

4. *Are you familiar with family law? Will you tell us how you think a court would decide our case? How important is the law to you?* The role of law in mediation is critical to the success of the process. What you should be looking for here is a mediator who is well informed about family law and at the same time doesn't want the law to dictate your outcome.

5. *How would you deal with stalemates?* The response to this will tell you whether or not the mediator has a coercive approach. You want to make sure he or she will give you and your spouse enough room to explore your disagreements thoroughly so you don't settle for a shortcut solution that might not last.

6. *How do you feel about our using consultants, including consulting lawyers? Would you talk directly to our lawyers?* Beware of mediators who will talk directly with your lawyers, or mediators who discourage you from consulting lawyers or other technical experts at all. With the former, you run the danger of having the lawyers and mediator control your outcome, and with the latter, you run the risk of ignoring realities that must be faced.

7. *How do you see your role in our communication with each other? What is the place of our feelings in this process?* This will weed out mediators who are exclusively result-oriented and don't understand the importance of the two of you dealing directly with each other. The answer to the second question will indicate the mediator's comfort with the subjective as well as the objective dimensions of your situation.

8. *How do you feel about our talking to each other about our conflicts outside the mediation office?* Again, here you are looking for a mediator who will give you a balanced view that respects both your primacy as decision makers and the dangers that can arise from your dealing with each other without someone else present.

9. *How much mediating experience do you have?* It is important that the mediator have enough experience that you don't feel

like guinea pigs. But also beware of the mediator who implies that he's seen it all—you don't want him to peg you as this or that type.

In deciding on a mediator, by far the most important criterion is whether or not you both feel the candidate can understand you and your issues. Any discrepancy on this question—a yes from you, a no from your spouse, or vice versa—does not bode well.

You'll also get a sense, during that first session, of what it's like to be in the same room with your spouse discussing the particulars of separation. Are you both ready to do the work to make the necessary decisions? Do you feel as if you need the protection of lawyers to speak for you, or are you willing and able to speak for yourselves? If you're troubled by these questions, don't be afraid to ask the mediator for an opinion.

Consider the candidate's particular style. Is the person:

- at the "muscle" end of the spectrum (taking on the decision-making role)
- at the laissez-faire end (too committed to the parties' right to decide to intervene in any way)
- or somewhere in between?

The danger of picking a mediator at the "muscle" end is that you are actually choosing a process much closer to arbitration than mediation and will run the risk of being dissatisfied with a result chosen by an outsider. The risk of the laissez-faire mediator is that the stronger or more manipulative of the pair might be able to maneuver the other into an unfair agreement without the mediator blowing the whistle. The questions above will help elicit the candidate's mediation style, but ultimately it will be up to the two of you to agree on the kind of mediator you are comfortable with.

Most mediators come from a background of law or psychology, but those who have fully embraced mediation know that both the psychological and legal dimensions of the issues are important to the process of mediated conflict resolution.

Many lawyers who have become mediators have worked hard to develop sensitivity to the personal and psychological dimensions that cut close to the heart of the process. Many psychologist/ mediators understand the importance of the external and concrete aspects of the issues—including the law—and are totally competent to help guide the parties through the maze of economic, tax, and legal issues that will crucially test the finances of the agreement. And many who have neither background have mastered the intricacies of both.

THE GENDER OF THE MEDIATOR

*O*ne more question arises time and again: What gender should the mediator be? There is no way to generalize about this—many male mediators have a style that reflects the traditionally "feminine" values and many women understand and employ "male-oriented" ways of attacking problems. However, this question cannot be dismissed out of hand. For most couples, two-thirds of the people in the divorce mediation will be of the same gender. If the "odd one out" feels overwhelmed or outnumbered, this could have an important impact on the course of the mediation. It's important, therefore, to pay attention at the outset to how, if at all, the gender of the mediator affects the comfort level. Co-mediation with a cross gender team of mediators is also an option which can alleviate this problem to some extent, although the relationship between co-mediators is critical to whether this will reduce or increase tensions.

In the end, the choice of a mediator is as much intuitive as it is rational. If you both sense you can trust this person and that he or she can help you reach an agreement, then you've found the right mediator. And if the process works, you'll be able to look back on mediation as a great accomplishment: With help from a third person, you will have found a way—together—to separate.

PART TWO:
THE CASES

*I*n this section of the book, you will be reading a sampling of what happened in twelve mediations that together I think exemplify what goes on in mediation. Each of these cases is unusual in at least one respect. There are a fair number of people who come to mediation and go through the process without a great deal of difficulty. I have intentionally omitted describing such cases, because they reveal less about the process than the more problematic ones do. Each of the following cases illuminates an aspect of the process that is significant to understanding both the limits and the possibilities of mediation. For instance, it is a myth that people who have strong conflicts shouldn't mediate. I have included many examples intended to dispel that myth. I have tried to give you a sense of what each spouse was going through, at least from my perspective, as well as how it affected the work that I was doing with them. Because each case is meant to demonstrate a particular aspect of the process, I have condensed the descriptions of the cases to highlight the issue at hand, often focusing on one particular session in what might have been a four-to-six-session process.

Going through a divorce is not easy for anyone. It is painful, confusing, liberating, frightening, and in all events, stressful. The intensity of the experience can evoke feelings and behavior that in normal times we don't experience or at least have under control. Sometimes they appear suddenly or in exaggerated form. Our fear alone can distort our perceptions, make us unnecessarily over-reactive and overprotective, cause depression, exhaustion, self-doubt, outbursts of anger and blame, and destroy our will to go on. In reading these cases you may find yourself repelled by one spouse or both, or particularly sympathetic to one or the other. If you can manage to feel sympathetic to both at the same time, you will have arrived at a position that I work very hard to achieve in each case and which I try to help each spouse reach as well.

In reading the cases, you will also notice that the same issues repeat themselves, at least on the surface—dividing the assets and liabilities, including what to do with the house if the couple owns one; parenting issues, if there are children; and support for a spouse and/or children. You will also notice that each mediation is unique, even if it initially appears to be similar to another. The uniqueness of each situation derives from the personal history of the couple, each of whom has brought to the relationship his or her own family history, values, fears, assumptions about marriage and divorce, and aspirations.

In one or more of these cases, you may find yourself, or people who seem familiar. If you're thinking about mediation, this book will give you the closest experience to a dry run. Its aim is to help you understand mediation's benefits as well as the obstacles that need to be overcome to make the process work.

N O T E

All of the following case studies are based loosely on mediations I have done over the years. In each case all names, identifying characteristics, and circumstances have been changed to thoroughly protect my clients' privacy and the confidentiality of the mediations in which they participated.

TO MEDIATE

OR NOT

TO MEDIATE

SUMMARY

Mediation is not for everyone, and part of deciding whether or not to mediate involves the disputants delving deeply into the motivations that brought them to my office. Because the success of the process rests on the parties' willingness, despite their conflict, to go the distance required to reach a mutually acceptable agreement, that willingness must be genuine—otherwise, it's easy for the process to break down. Martin and Claire's case dramatizes the profound importance of this initial stage to the effort as a whole. Of particular interest is Claire's struggle to shed the role of victim and to assert her needs in forging the agreement.

I **received a call** from a man named Martin one afternoon. He said that he and his wife, Claire, were stuck with a disagreement they couldn't resolve and wondered if mediation could help. I told him that the intensity of their disagreement had no bearing on whether or not mediation would be workable, and that the real question was were they willing to work together to find a good solution? Martin immediately wanted to describe their situation, but I cut him off, explaining that the process would have a better chance of working if I heard the facts for the first time when we all met together, since I make it a practice not to begin a relationship with one mediation client alone. Martin seemed put off by my response, but agreed to come in with Claire.

My first impression of Claire was of an articulate, bright, sensitive woman in her late thirties. She wore a brilliantly multicolored smock from India and purple sandals, and her long, graying hair was in a braid down her back. Claire's eyes were clear, her focus direct. The roundness of her face and body suggested a soft, maternal warmth, and I was surprised later when I learned she had no children.

Though she looked healthy, when she walked across the room she seemed to shuffle. In the last several years, as she would tell me, she had developed headaches that had only been aggravated by medical treatment. She was now so disabled that she could no longer focus her attention for long or perform any strenuous physical activity. She had not worked for the past three years. Before that she had worked for a variety of nonprofit organizations in low-paying administrative positions. Claire still had dreams of becoming an artist but little confidence that she would be able to support herself in that effort.

Martin, in his early forties, was a folk singer with enough of a following to keep him busy on weekends. He taught guitar and piano to aspiring musicians during the week. If Claire was round, Martin was square. His long black hair was pulled back in a ponytail, revealing a turquoise earring in one ear. He was dark-skinned, handsome, and friendly. He wore a freshly pressed black shirt and neatly creased jeans. I wondered who did the ironing.

When I begin a mediation, I usually start by attempting to find out what brought the couple to mediation. The variety of responses to this simple question still surprises me. Some people want to tell the whole story of what happened in the marriage. Others want to reveal as little as possible. Martin and Claire were willing to give me a little background, but mainly they wanted to get right to "the heart of the problem." They were too anxious to listen carefully to an explanation of the mediation process. While it is essential in the first session to give the parties a sense of how the process works, the nonverbal creation of a warm, open atmosphere is equally important, so I was willing to postpone my explanation. The room is intended to be a place safe enough for people to say what is on their minds and in their feelings, a place where a certain level of trust can develop.

In his opening remarks, Martin got right to the point. He said that he had become increasingly disenchanted with the life he shared with Claire, and eight months before had suddenly left her to live with another woman. Martin was still living with this new woman and Claire had remained in their house. For Claire, just being in the same room with Martin was very stressful. Before we could begin to talk about what mediation was, she needed to say how hard it was for her to be there. Turning her chair toward me and away from Martin, Claire addressed me directly. It was clear that it was difficult for her to look at Martin. It was almost as if she were making an effort to shut him out of the room.

> ***Claire:*** Martin's leaving was a great shock. I have been working very hard not to be victimized by my situation. I still don't understand what happened. I know that I can play the role of the rejected woman and have everyone feel sorry for me—my friends do. But I don't enjoy being pitied.

She fought against that with the help of an extraordinary wit, which ranged from self-deprecating humor to devastating sarcasm, the latter inconsistent with her motherly demeanor.

PINPOINTING MOTIVATIONS FOR MEDIATING

*I*n explaining the mediation process to Martin and Claire, I compared it to the litigation option, in which each of them would hire a lawyer. Many people automatically compare mediation to going to court, but since only a small percentage of cases are ever heard by a judge, the fairer comparison is to lawyers negotiating a resolution. There are two major differences between mediation and a negotiated settlement: the directness of the communications and the basis of the decisions reached. In negotiation the parties communicate through their lawyers; in mediation they communicate directly. In negotiation the law is the exclusive basis for their decisions; typically, lawyers negotiating with each other refer primarily to their predictions of what a court would do in trying to reach an agreement. In mediation, although the law is consulted, the primary reference points are usually the parties' personal priorities and their sense of fairness.

Ultimately, the major decision the parties have to make before they can mediate is whether they are willing and able to work together to make their decisions jointly. Once I had explained the mediation process to Martin and Claire, I asked them how they felt about proceeding.

> *Claire:* If I could afford it financially, I'd leave this to a lawyer to work out for me.
>
> *Mediator:* How come?
>
> *Claire:* Let me count the ways. First, you said that the goal of this process is to reach an agreement that is fair to both

of us, and frankly I couldn't care less about reaching a result that is fair to him. Second, he has a live-in adviser, a businesswoman—a corporate raider, would you believe? A man snatcher and a corporate raider.

Martin: She doesn't know anything about law.

Claire: Mostly though, I find being with him extremely painful, and dealing with what we have to talk about here is doubly painful.

Mediator: So the prospect of having to work this all out together here may not be something that makes sense for you.

Claire: I don't really have any choice.

Mediator: Why not?

Claire: I can't afford to hire someone to do this for me.

Mediator: A court would probably require Martin to pay at least a good portion of it, if you couldn't afford it.

Claire: Besides, I don't like lawyers. I don't trust them.

Mediator: You trust yourself more?

Claire: Yeah, although everyone tells me if I do this, I'll get screwed.

Mediator: Would you know if you were getting screwed?

Claire: Of course.

Mediator: Then the only way you could get screwed here is if you agreed to it. If there's no agreement, you can and probably will have to go to lawyers or a judge.

Claire: What makes this process a particularly unpleasant prospect is being here with Martin. I find it very hard to be around him, since I am still working hard to free myself of my attachment to him.

Mediator: You don't have to do this now. You could make some preliminary decisions and then put the rest off until you feel ready to deal with each other.

Martin: No way. *I'm* ready to do this now, and if we don't do it here, I'm going to have a lawyer get going on it.

Mediator: I appreciate your sense of urgency, but it is also important that you see the effect of what you're saying.

Martin: What do you mean?

Mediator: I think it's much harder to mediate when you feel coerced into it than when you choose it more freely.

Martin: Well, it's time we get this done. We've been separated for eight months and nothing's happened.

Mediator: So, from your side, it already feels late. But notice that from Claire's side, she feels pushed. It's not a question here of one of you being right and the other being wrong. It is a matter of finding a way to do this under circumstances that give you the best chance of making it work. My experience is that this process works better when you both feel ready.

Claire: I think I'd rather get it over with sooner than later, too. All I was saying is that it's hard to be in the same room with Martin.

Mediator: Suppose it were only up to you, Claire, assuming legal fees were not an issue. What would you do, mediate or have lawyers do it?

Claire: I can't ignore the money, and I really appreciate your having a sliding scale, so I guess we might as well get down to it here. But I don't have much hope that it will work unless I give in.

Mediator: Because that's the way you've operated before?

Claire: Yeah. He's a stubborn son of a bitch.

Martin: Give me a break. You've been calling all the shots.

Mediator: So each of you feels as if the other has more of the power. That makes sense to me, just given our brief interaction and your situation. What do you need from each other to make this process work better than some of the decision making you've done up to now?

Claire: I need Martin to be willing to respect my way of doing things, even if it's not his way.

Martin: I am not about to capitulate to you. I feel guilty enough about what's happened. I'm not going to make myself more miserable just so you don't feel so bad.

Mediator: So when she says she wants you to respect your differences, you hear that you're supposed to give up your viewpoint?

Martin: Yeah.

Mediator: What do you need from Claire to make this work?

Martin: For her not to be unreasonable.

Mediator: My hope is that you'll both give each other enough room to have differences without either of you having to give up anything important. That will mean living with the tension of disagreeing. If you're willing to stay with that tension, I can be helpful. I won't see one of you as right and the other as wrong. I assume that both of your points of view can exist simultaneously and not cancel each other out.

Most couples play out the basic patterns and power struggles of their marriage in the mediation room. As we talked, I became aware of some resistance on Claire's part to recognizing that she had any alternatives other than to give in to Martin. I had a hunch that this was how she related to Martin during the marriage—he dominated; she acquiesced. If my hunch was right, she may have become used to this dynamic, and even used it in her own way to gain power. The "victim," consciously or unconsciously, retaliates against the oppressor by making him feel guilty or suffer in some way.

But if Claire could say no to mediation knowing she had other options, she could also say a strong yes to mediation. It was clear to me that choosing to mediate could help her escape this pattern. It could affirm her strength, ease her feeling that she had been victimized, and reduce her power to make Martin feel guilty. I wasn't sure whether those possibilities were clear to her, but if they were, I wanted to convey the message that Martin had a choice as well. It was important that he not feel coerced into reaching an agreement that compromised his wishes either. By exploring with both their options *not to* mediate I was attempting to evoke their real motivation *to* mediate.

I wanted to help Martin see that trying to force Claire to mediate would ultimately be self-defeating. If she could claim he had forced her to mediate before she was ready, she would later have reason to blame him not only for the divorce but also for a failed mediation. But the fact was, though Claire was playing her cards close to the chest, she wanted to resolve the dispute as much if not more than Martin. Martin was so blinded by his own impatience that he could not see this, and I knew that he would not see it until he released the pressure on Claire.

My intention at this beginning stage was not to disrupt the balance of power between Martin and Claire but to uncover their motivations to mediate so I could help both myself and them assess the mediatability of their case. In addition, if motivations have been articulated, they can serve as important reference points during the confusion and difficulties that arise later.

In the beginning most people tend to express motivations that are "safe," revealing little of themselves and their vulnerability.

Examples might be a distaste for lawyers, an attempt to save money, and a desire to get things over with quickly. Further along the continuum toward more openness, other, less self-protective motivations emerge—for instance, a desire to avoid the bitterness of the adversary process, a desire to retain the power to decide rather than handing it over to lawyers or judges, and a desire for privacy.

Some people turn to mediation *after* meeting with a lawyer and learning that the litigated result would be far below what they believe to be fair. They hope to better their chances of getting a fair result in a more flexible process.

The most powerful motivations to mediate can be the least tangible. The desire to preserve the best of the disputed relationship and to protect its positive aspects from erosion by the personal and economic difficulties that often arise in a divorce runs deep for many.

It can be an enlightening experience for the parties to hear their spouse's motivations. Each usually has only a partial idea of why the other is there. A more complete picture of the spouses' real reasons can help both appreciate the mix of feelings a divorce usually evokes. This understanding can make it easier for both people to cope with the tension of their differences.

With Martin and Claire, I wanted to alleviate Claire's sense that she was being coerced into mediation so that both could identify their deeper motivations. I suspected that the hardest part of the process for Claire might be dealing with any feelings of closeness with Martin; her need right now was to protect her emotional well-being by putting distance between them. At a deeper level, I felt it was important for Claire to be able to stand on her own two feet in dealing with Martin. I could also feel the possibility of a continuing friendship between them after the divorce. But right now, even after an eight-month separation, I sensed that Claire needed time to "catch up" with Martin emotionally. I was concerned for her. She was clearly under a lot of stress and was struggling to keep from becoming victimized by her situation.

Claire's physical problems compounded her difficulty, and I knew it would be important that in her desire to get on her own feet she not blind herself to the very real limits on her capabilities. She would have to find her own way without reacting to Martin's demands so much that she lost sight of her own needs.

Martin's motivations for beginning mediation had their own complexities. On one hand, he felt guilty that he had left Claire. On the other, he was anxious to get on with his life and was, with reason, concerned that their case could drag on indefinitely if they went the way of lawyers and courts. Yet he genuinely cared about Claire—that was unmistakable. He didn't like the situation she was in any better than she did. And Martin was vulnerable to losing sight of his own needs in this process, too. Out of his concern for Claire, he could end up in a caretaking position that would keep him from moving forward with his life.

IDENTIFYING THE BASIC DISAGREEMENTS

*T*wo weeks later, they returned for the second session, having gathered their financial information.

> ***Claire:*** We bought our house three years ago for $90,000 with a down payment of $30,000, most of which came from money I saved before we married. As a result of the increase in real estate values in our area, the house is now worth about $150,000.

> ***Martin:*** There was $10,000 that came from my earnings, and I've been making the mortgage payments since we bought it.

> ***Mediator:*** When was the money for the down payment earned?

Martin: Since we've been married.

Claire: It's actually hard to say exactly where that money came from. Martin's books are very sloppy. I made some of that money. And even though Martin's been paying the mortgage, I've been taking care of the house.

As we explored this information, it became clear that disagreements over two separate issues had to be resolved: the house and spousal support. The specific questions regarding the house were, when would it be sold, and how would the proceeds be divided? As to support, the question was, how much would Martin pay Claire and for how long? In the middle of the session, I pointed out that the two issues were interrelated and asked them which issue they would like to work on first.

Martin: Well, I'd say the amount of spousal support is pretty well established. I've been paying the monthly mortgage, insurance, property taxes, and loan payments. And I'm willing to do it for a little longer.

Mediator: How do you see this issue, Claire?

Claire: I don't want to receive support from Martin any longer than I need to, but everything in my life is up in the air right now, so I don't know how long I'm going to need it.

Mediator: Is the present level of support satisfactory to both of you?

Martin: I don't mind paying what I'm paying. The question is, how long do I have to pay it?

Claire: I agree. I can get along all right with what he is paying now.

Mediator: So for you, Claire, it's hard to answer the question of how long without knowing what will happen with your career, and this depends to some extent on your health, right?

Claire: Right. But I also want to sell the house, so it will depend on that, too—on how much I get and when it sells.

Mediator: What can you tell us about your work plans for the future?

In response to this question, Claire looked at me as if she had just been assaulted, her cheeks flushed, eyes widened, an expression of shock on her face. Martin shot me a knowing glance with a hint of a smile.

Claire: Look, I'm not prying into Martin's life. Why does he get to pry into mine?

Mediator: You're uncomfortable with how we're going about this. How would you like to do it?

Claire: I don't know. I'm just sick to *death* of Martin's persistent questions about my work plans.

Mediator: Since it's you who needs the support, I think you are the one who should be defining your need here. That's why the focus is on you. But this isn't the only way of going about it. It's only Martin's strong desire to get this issue settled now that pushes us to decide the future of support. A court, for example, wouldn't require you to figure out at this point when support should end. In fact, it's probable that a judge would only set a time for review. Then at that time the judge would look at what had happened in the interim to determine whether and when spousal support should end or at least be reduced.

Claire: Listen, I know this man, and if we don't get this settled now, he will make my life miserable. I don't want to go through that.

Mediator: So you feel compelled by Martin to get this all resolved now?

Claire: Yes, but postponing the decision would be easier for me. Maybe I won't need the support for very long. I just can't tell now.

Mediator: This does set up a tension here, because to protect yourself from coming up short in case your life doesn't go as well as you hope, you need to ask for a longer period than you might actually need.

Claire: Oh, this is awful. I just don't know how to do this. [Breaks into tears]

Martin: [Looking pained] I don't either, but I think we have to have more information from you, Claire, in order to figure it out. As I have told you before, I think you should talk to a career consultant and I'm willing to pay for it. That would give us a more objective basis for looking at this.

Claire: [Angrily through her tears] I've told you before and I'm going to tell you again. I'm not about to have some jerk who knows nothing about me, my life, or my values tell me what he thinks I should be doing. I've never led my life that way before and I'm not about to start now.

Martin: [Sighing in frustration] You sit there like some kind of queen. You don't have a job. You won't talk about your plans. You won't even see someone who could help you because you have too goddamn much pride.

Claire: [Enraged now] Pride! I lost that when you humiliated me eight months ago.

Mediator: Is this what you want to be talking about?

Martin: Absolutely not. What do you suggest?

Mediator: We can pursue this further to identify your disagreement more sharply and then look at what's behind it. Or we can move to other issues, which could shed some light on this one, and then return to it.

Claire: I'd like to talk about the house.

Martin: Yes, okay. I think we need to agree as to what my share of the house is worth and how I'll get paid if Claire wants to buy me out.

Claire: [Struggling to regain control of herself] I'd agree to give you about fifteen thousand dollars or about a third of our equity, but I can't give you the money until I sell the house.

Mediator: When do you plan to do that?

Claire: I don't know. I think I might be ready to put it up for sale in the next year, but I think it would take about a year to sell it.

Martin: [To me] I think you'd better tell her I could force a sale of the house right now *and* receive half of the proceeds.

THE CORE OF THE MATTER

*T*his was a very charged statement. In using the word "force," Martin was at least indirectly threatening Claire with going to court. Why would he do that? People threaten others only when they fear they will not get what they want. So they reach out for a way to exert pressure on the other person. What was it that Martin was seeing slip through his fingers? My guess was a quick resolution—Martin wanted to get on with his new life.

But a quick fix that didn't account for the uncertainties in Claire's future ran completely counter to Claire's stated goal, which was to extricate herself from the role of victim. To be a victim, one must have a persecutor. If Claire reached an agreement without thinking through her financial future, she could end up feeling victimized by Martin after the divorce. But out of frustration or the fear that he wouldn't get what he wanted, he was trying to pressure her to conform to his desires. Both positions were understandable and each conflicted directly with the other.

Claire's Options: Claire was in a bind, but she had several options. We spent several minutes identifying and assessing each in turn. She could succumb to Martin's pressure and continue to play the victim, giving up her own needs. Only one benefit could come from this: She could feel free to blame Martin and anybody else who supported him—including me—for her failure to move on.

A second option would be for Claire to disregard Martin's desires entirely and flatly deny him what he wanted. This route had two possible outcomes: a stalemate, or Martin's concession to Claire out of guilt, fear, or frustration. With either possibility, Claire would be breaking out of her role as Martin's victim.

But neither alternative was actually in Claire's best interest. A stalemate would be counterproductive. On the other hand, if Martin agreed to her demand, she could discover that the result was not what she wanted at all, but rather an expression of her desire to keep Martin from getting what he wanted. Blocking his progress might give her a sense of power and increase her self-esteem, which would be preferable to her remaining a victim. Still, it would leave both of them unsatisfied in the long run. And in effect it would prove to be completely without value, for in operating in reaction to Martin, Claire would still be controlled by him.

A third option was for Claire to figure out what she wanted and assert her desires. Then, not only would she be likely to emerge from the process with more strength and a clearer idea of her direction, but she would have less reason to oppose Martin in his efforts to achieve his own goals. This choice would give Claire the chance to exert her power, but in a different way than a fight would do. Most of us make significant life decisions in conformity with or reaction to what others expect us to do rather than going through the difficult, confusing, and lonely process of deciding what we *really* want for ourselves. To reach that point is to feel the strength of true self-knowledge and self-determination.

Martin's dilemma: Though Martin's suffering did not approximate Claire's, he too was trapped by the victim-oppressor pattern. As long as he wanted to exert control over her, he was playing into the problem. And his life was also on hold until hers straightened out. But while Claire seemed to have a pretty clear picture of their pattern of relating—she was seeing a therapist at the time, which undoubtedly helped her gain some clarity—Martin seemed much less aware of or interested in it. Claire seemed to see that the pain of aloneness could be a chamber through which she could pass to a new sense of herself. But without feeling distress analogous to Claire's that would motivate him to observe his pattern carefully and commit to the hard work of change, Martin was in danger of simply gliding into a new version of his old life.

MEDIATION
AND THE LAW

As mediator, I had a delicate task to perform. Martin's last remark—"I think you'd better tell her I could force a sale of the house right now"—opened two central issues that had been waiting to rear their heads: my own role in the mediation process, and the role of the law. The understanding between us from the beginning was that I would remain neutral regarding their final agreement unless what they decided seemed so unfair to me that I could not in good conscience draw up the contract. Under no circumstances would I serve as an advocate for either party. If either of them found they needed the protection of an advocate, then it would be better for them to leave mediation and hire a lawyer to carry on negotiations. Still, as a human being, I could not honestly call myself a detached witness. My main role in sorting through the options and proceeding toward an agreement was to monitor the process with respect to *fairness*.

I already knew I could not let Claire agree to her first option, acceding to all of Martin's demands. That such an agreement would be unfair was as obvious to Claire as to myself. To be fair, the agreement these two finally reached would have to permit Claire to decide on and execute her plans for her life.

The agreement would also have to be measured against the law. Part of my job was to predict what the law would decide in their case so they could use that as a reference point in making their own decisions. Not only do the parties need to understand the legal context of the decisions that they are making for practical reasons, but they can also use it to develop and articulate their own sense of justice.

But the law is more than just a reference point in the mediation process. By continuing to mediate, the parties are implicitly deciding, sometimes from moment to moment, not to turn the case over to their lawyers. And throughout mediation, their understanding of the law and their decision to depart from it can be an empowering experience. But the option to stop and turn to lawyers is always present.

The trick for the mediator is to find a way to bring the law into the process without intimidating the parties into giving up their personal sense of how to resolve their dispute. I do this by trying to educate them about not merely the court decision in their case, but also the principles that would inform that decision. In that way they can measure their own sense of what's fair against the principles of justice that inform the law and society's sense of what's at stake in their dispute. I act as a neutral friend who happens to understand how a court would view their situation.

One hitch makes this job difficult for me: The law often is much less clear-cut and much more subjective than most people recognize. Judges base their decisions on their *interpretations* of the law, and lawyers can never be sure what a judge will do in a particular situation. All I could hope to give Claire and Martin was a neutral but educated guess as to how a judge would decide their conflict over the sale of their house.

This would be very delicate. As I interpreted the law, I would have to watch myself for any tendency to favor Claire in an effort to help her feel more powerful. On the other hand, I didn't want her to feel coerced by the law into going along with Martin—and thus betraying her own sense of fairness. Then we would have a double whammy to fight: her tendency to feel as if she always had to give in, and her inevitable conclusion that her personal sense of justice was in conflict with the law, a bitter notion that could weaken her further. If this happened, I would probably terminate the mediation as it would clearly be leading to a destructive end.

So it was imperative that I remain neutral in delivering the law to Claire and Martin when in fact I wasn't neutral at all. I was very much against a destructive outcome.

THE FATE OF THE HOUSE

I stepped into the mine field opened by Martin's threatening invocation of the law this way.

> **Mediator:** So you'd like to talk about how a court would look at your situation?
>
> **Martin:** At least as far as the house is concerned, I think Claire should know that I'm being very generous.
>
> **Mediator:** How about you, Claire? Do you want to talk about the law now or would you rather wait until later? It's

important to me that we have that discussion at some point, but only when both of you are ready.

Claire: Frankly, I'm not much interested in hearing about the law at all.

Mediator: How come?

Claire: You said that the two of us will decide things here. We're not in court, at least not yet. If we go to court, then I'll hear plenty about the law.

Mediator: So you'd prefer to not know the law at all.

Claire: I suppose we need to hear it at some point. You did say that the agreement would not be legally solid unless we knew what the law was. Do you think we should hear it now?

Mediator: What's important to me in doing this at any time is that regardless of what the law says, neither of you gives up your sense of what's fair. And you also need to know that although I'll give you my best opinion, there is some uncertainty in the law, so I could be wrong. That's another reason why you shouldn't defer to my opinion if it differs from what seems right to you. So knowing that, do you want to hear it now?

Claire: Yes.

Martin: All I want Claire to know is that I could force a sale of the house now and get half of the proceeds.

Mediator: That's not my opinion of what the court would do. First, the question of *when* a court would order the sale would depend upon when your case came to trial, and in this county it would take at least nine months before a judge would likely hear it. It is true that at that point you could force a sale, but only if Claire couldn't make an offer to buy your share that the judge considered fair. As for the rest of it, it is not at all clear that a court would order the proceeds to be divided equally.

Martin: Yeah? Well, read this.

Martin pulled out of his papers a photocopy of a very recent California Supreme Court decision. I usually know the updates in the law before my clients do, but this time I was caught short. I read the published opinion carefully. The California Supreme Court had decided in a case similar to Martin and Claire's that the proceeds of the house should be equally divided when both parties had purchased the house as joint tenants even when some of the down payment came from one of the parties' alone. Martin and Claire had bought their house in this way, with $20,000 of the down payment coming from Claire's pre-marriage savings. On the surface, it seemed as if Martin was right. But as I read further and reflected, I saw substantial differences between the two cases.

Mediator: Let me try to explain. For the last several years the courts here have been trying to clarify the question of how to treat a family residence when people divorce and the house is in both names. A few years ago, the law was clear. Unless you had an understanding or agreement to the contrary, if the house was in both names, you each would get half regardless of where the money came from to purchase it.

But a couple of years ago, the legislature decided that that law was unfair and changed it to read that upon the sale of the house each of you should be reimbursed any separate money you put in for the down payment or into improvements before dividing the rest of the proceeds. Still, it's not altogether clear whether that law would be applied in your case, because at least one court has decided that this reimbursement law might violate the guarantee in the United States Constitution that no one's property can be taken from them without due process of law. Since that challenge, the courts have been distinguishing between houses bought before and after the reimbursement law was passed, using the purchase date to determine whether the new law will be applied. Since your house was bought after the reimbursement law was passed, Claire would probably be entitled to be reimbursed for her contribution. The published opinion you brought in, Martin, was based on a purchase date that preceded the reimbursement law. So reading this opinion doesn't change my mind that the reimbursement law would be applied to your situation. Before either of you reacts to what I have said, do you both understand?

Claire: More or less. I've never had a lot of respect for the law, and seeing it flip-flop like that tells me that nobody has a very clear sense of what's right. So it doesn't seem very relevant to me.

Martin: You've explained the law as *you* understand it, but I was given this opinion by a lawyer who told me that this was the law. So who am I supposed to believe?

Mediator: That question goes right to the heart of mediation. Trust yourself after listening to everyone. Does it seem to you that what I'm saying makes more sense or less sense than what the lawyer said in interpreting the case you brought in?

Martin: Frankly, neither of you make much sense to me.

Mediator: What part of what I said doesn't make sense?

Martin: Why would it make any difference when the property was bought?

Mediator: If you bought the property before the reimbursement law passed, you would be entitled to half of the property. But in passing the law, the legislature would, in effect, be taking away some of your property without giving you a chance to fight it. And the Constitution doesn't permit that. That's what the challenge to the reimbursement law says.

Martin: So if we bought the property in 1983 instead of 1985, then I'd be entitled to more, is that what you're saying? So the legislature took away money from me by passing the law.

Mediator: Yes, but they actually passed the law before you bought the property. So at least theoretically, if you had known the law at the time, to protect your half interest, you would have known that you had to enter into a different kind of arrangement.

Martin: But I didn't know we were going to get a divorce.

Claire: And if you had, you probably would have gotten me to sign a paper giving you half.

Martin: That's not the point.

Claire: What *is* the point here? Do you really think you're entitled to half the value of the property after I put in most of the down payment?

Martin: I never said I thought it was *right* that I get half. I only wanted you to know I was trying to be easier on you by not insisting on my legal rights.

Claire: Look, I don't need you to try to go easy on me. I just want what's fair.

Martin: Then don't put me in the position of having to support you endlessly. I want an end to this and I want it decided now.

We'd hit bedrock—support was the issue that lay under the matter of the house. However support was resolved, the house would fall into place.

THE QUESTION OF SUPPORT

Mediator: Do you want me to explain how the court would decide support?

Martin: This is the most important part to me. I don't care what the law says.

Claire: But we have to find out sometime. I am interested in knowing how long support would go on.

Mediator: If push came to shove and you decided that you *couldn't* decide at this point how long support should go on, there's little or no chance a court would decide now when support would end. The very thing that concerns you, Claire—the uncertainty of your future, particularly your work life and your health—would also concern a court. So a judge would be sure to order temporary support now and would probably set a time for that decision to be reviewed.

Martin: [Agitated] Hey, Gary, I thought you were supposed to be neutral. It seems to me you're aligning yourself with Claire, and I don't like it.

Mediator: I'm sorry you feel that way. But what I am trying to do is what I think you both asked for—to give you as clear an indication as I can about how the law would apply to your situation. I don't want either of you agreeing to something without understanding the legal context of the decision. I'm also trying to ensure that neither of you feels pushed into a decision you could regret.

Martin: Good luck, because I'm going to regret any decision that doesn't settle everything *right now*.

Mediator: That's clear enough to me. And if Claire agrees to that, too, then there will be no problem. But if Claire doesn't want that, it's important that both of you realize that on the issue of support, she has the legal power to put off deciding the question. You could get a court to decide the question of the amount of temporary support almost immediately, but not the termination date.

Martin: I think that stinks.

Mediator: How come?

Martin: Because we don't have kids. There's no reason in the world we should have to continue to be bound together financially. I need to know when I can quit sending Claire money, and I need to know it *soon*.

Martin had nailed it. In the matter of support, I was once more in danger of becoming Claire's advocate. Martin already felt alienated. The only thing worse would be if Claire began to perceive me as her advocate and fell back into a passive role, leaving me to deal with Martin. For me to play Claire's advocate would be implicitly suggesting that she was too weak to protect herself and robbing her of the chance to stand up for herself against Martin, thus sabotaging the whole mediation process.

Yet there was also the opposite danger—that Claire would continue to play the victim by capitulating to Martin's wishes. That could spell disaster not only for Claire but for Martin as well: If she caved in now, she could go to court later to have the mediated agreement overturned on the grounds that she had been unaware of her legal rights or pressured into the agreement at the time. I realized that although it was necessary for both to understand Claire's legal rights, by emphasizing what a court would do, I might be inadvertently encouraging them to view such a conclusion as the "right" one, even if neither saw it as the best.

To add one further twist, if my efforts to ensure that Claire understood her legal rights resulted in her agreeing not to exercise those rights, then the conversation we were having now would probably jeopardize the possibility of her chances of having the agreement overturned at a later date. From that perspective, it could be said that what I was doing now was more in Martin's interests than Claire's.

This kind of step-by-step analysis is absolutely imperative to my remaining in the middle. With the momentum of the conflict constantly propelling the two disputants toward confrontation, an important part of my role is to define the disgreement precisely. The delicate part is remaining objective while still being empathetic enough that both parties feel I understand them and care about what happens.

Deciding whether a person whose position is favored by the law is personally strong enough to stand up for his or her position in the mediation process is one of the most difficult assessments I need to make. With Martin and Claire, I was concerned about Claire's victim history and the very real obstacles she would face in her effort to become self-supporting. Her way out of the victimization pattern would be to articulate her needs for support precisely. It was essential that if she agreed to a termination date for spousal support she do it because it felt right to her and not because she was intimidated by or wanted to conciliate Martin. It was equally important that the date, if she gave one, be realistic, and that she would be able to manage or have contingent plans for surviving financially after support ended. I certainly did not want to be an agent of Claire's self-destruction.

For Claire to independently agree on a realistic date for termination of support could be an extraordinarily liberating and powerful act, a way of declaring her own independence and autonomy. So it might well be in her own best interests to do the very thing that Martin wanted her to do. I hoped that by my injecting the law, Claire would feel enough power to decide how much money she could realistically expect to earn and when she could become self-supporting.

Although it was not clear to Martin yet, the worst thing that could happen at this point would be for Claire to succumb to his pressure on a termination date and thus remain dependent not only in her own eyes but in the eyes of a judge. That would keep both of them locked into their old pattern. The key to Claire's liberation would be Claire herself, and that is why it was so important for me to avoid a position where I was perceived as her advocate. Turning the spotlight on Claire was what we all needed to create the hoped-for balance between us.

Mediator: [To Claire] What is your view of this?

Claire: Frankly, I have mixed feelings. I know that if I don't agree to a specific date I'll pay the price of Martin's resentment. I don't want that. I know that we'll probably not be friends, and I'm not sure I would want that even if Martin did. But I sure don't want him to get any angrier.

But I also think that it would be helpful to me to be able to cut the cord that connects me to him. I need to do that for my *own* good. I don't *want* Martin to take care of me—he was never particularly good at it anyhow, and it's not really worth it to me to have to count on him. He'd always be hassling me about getting a job or a better job. I know that whatever I decided to do wouldn't be good enough for him, and I don't want to have to answer to him any more in my life. I've had enough of that. Still, I have to be sure that I'm going to be able to make it financially. And I just don't know what's going to happen in that regard. Some days I think I can do it. Others I feel lucky to be able to get out of bed.

Mediator: So what you would like is to have enough support from Martin to get you through this transition. It would make sense, I think, to look at various possibilities of what might happen: What's the worst that could happen to you? What's the best?

Claire: I'm not sure I want to do that. What I know is that I'll probably sell the house within the next year and buy a smaller place. I'll have to pay some taxes if I do that, but it would still give me some cash. If I knew I could count on the money from the house sale and have help from Martin *until* it sold, well—I guess I'd probably be willing to give up support beyond that point.

Martin: [Bursting out] That would leave me with nothing!

Claire: No, you'd still have your health, your business, and your relationship with what's-her-name. And that's a hell of a lot more than I can say for myself.

Martin: I wouldn't even get back the money that I've put into the house. And I've been paying the mortgage since we bought it.

Claire: I know that, but look, you say you want me to be financially independent. If you really don't want me knocking on your door, you have to give me a head start.

Martin: I'd be totally screwing myself if I agreed to this.

Mediator: How so?

Martin: The house is the only asset I have in the world outside of my paycheck. I don't even have any money in savings. Besides, she'd never get anything like this in court.

Mediator: That's true. And you wouldn't get the termination date. I think from your point of view, Martin, the question is really how important it is to you to get a termination date. I imagine that neither prospect at the moment is appealing: giving up your whole nest egg or paying out support indefinitely.

Martin: You're damn right.

Mediator: But you might consider that there are some real advantages to you in Claire's proposal. I would suggest that you sit with it a bit before you decide.

We ended the session on that note. Martin's impatience and sense of urgency were signals to slow down the process. I was afraid that he might now make a decision that he would later regret, so I was glad that our time was up before he had an opportunity to decide. When the parties are moving quickly toward a solution, my function often is to slow things down. If people have an opportunity to deliberate, their feelings frequently shift. Time is an important test of the solidity of a decision. I was not surprised when Martin came into the next session with a variation on Claire's proposal.

Martin: Here is what I am willing to do. I'll give up all of my interest in the house if you give up support. And I'll lend you $750 a month between now and when the house sells, if you pay me back with interest out of the sale proceeds.

Claire: Hell, no! I'm not about to pay you a dime of interest. You're not a bank. And *no*, I don't like the idea of the support money being a loan.

Mediator: Why doesn't this seem fair to you?

Claire: Damn it, he's acting as if we were never married.

Martin: What do you mean? I don't go around giving away my property, everything I have, to my business associates, you know. Giving up my share of the house is a huge concession. It's $45,000. [This was based on the house's present value of $150,000, reduced by closing costs and the mortgage balance of $60,000, divided by two.]

Claire: [Slowly] It's actually more like $25,000, if we followed the law. And I assume I'll be paying the taxes on the gain. That could cost $15,000. I do appreciate your being willing to give up your interest in the house, but making the other money a loan with interest feels awful.

Martin: Then get the money someplace else. [Long silence] Okay, look. I'll give you the $750 a month without interest, if that will make you feel better, but I want that money back. I've already been paying you for the past eight months.

Claire: Okay. [Strongly] But we'll only make the loan retroactive to four months ago and I want you to get all of your stuff out of the house within the next week.

Martin: Consider it done.

Claire: And I don't want *her* coming over to help you, either!

Martin: Yeah, all right.

DOUBLE CHECK

C laire got up and walked over to the window with her back to both of us. Martin seemed to sink deeper into his seat and breathed a sigh of relief. They had an agreement, but I still wasn't sure if it was mutually fair or realistic. I needed to find out.

Mediator: We need to be sure that this agreement is going to work for both of you, not just now but in the long run. So I need to ask you some questions to check that out. My main concerns are with you, Claire. [Claire shot me a look as if I were intruding on her.] What happens to you if your life doesn't work out as you hope? What happens if you don't get better, or if you get worse?

Claire: I'm not worried about the medical bills. They're covered by my insurance.

Mediator: But how will you pay your expenses?

Claire: I don't know. I guess I'll be okay until the house sells with Martin lending me the money. And then when the house sells, I'll have that money to live on. That will be at least fifty or sixty thousand dollars after I pay Martin back and pay taxes, the mortgage balance, commissions, and closing costs. And after that, I don't know. I might rent a house for a while or buy a smaller place. I guess I don't think that should be Martin's problem. But I'd still feel better if the money he gives me until the house sells isn't a loan.

Martin: It has to be a loan to give you incentive to sell the house quickly.

Claire: [Snapping] You back off. It's hard enough dealing with Gary's questions.

Mediator: And what happens if you can't sell the house for a long time? Or if you run through the house sale proceeds before you get a job?

Claire: I don't think that'll happen, but if it does, I don't think Martin should have to help me just because he's obligated to.

Mediator: Do you think he would help you if he weren't obligated?

Claire: Maybe, but it's not healthy for me to think that way. I need to think positively. I know what you're getting at, but I think that what he proposes, but without the interest, is reasonable. I think it'll work.

Mediator: You sound only half-convinced.

Claire: Maybe sixty percent.

Mediator: Is that enough to make an agreement?

Claire: Yes, I think it is.

Mediator: That's going to feel better or worse in the few weeks between now and when you sign the agreement. I don't want you to sign it if it feels worse, or even if it doesn't feel better.

Martin: What about me? I'm giving up all my property.

Mediator: I think that when you have this agreement reviewed by your lawyer, that person will advise you that you've probably done better financially than if you were to go to court. Under a judge's decision, your obligation to pay support would be open-ended and Claire would also be entitled to half of the value of your business, whatever that amounted to. Since you don't have any savings to fall back on in case you get sick and can't work, this is a big consideration. It's also true that if Claire were to remarry quickly, then from an economic standpoint you'd have paid more than you are legally obligated because support would end upon her remarriage.

Martin: That's right. And I've been paying the mortgage since we separated. Except for the mortgage, we're now debt-free. And—I didn't mention this earlier because I didn't want to ruffle Claire's feathers—but if she gets into trouble, her mother would help her out.

Claire: I told you to *back off.* You know how hard she is to deal with. If that's what you need to say to yourself to assuage your guilt about what you've done to me, then say it, but it's not true. My mother doesn't have the money to support me, and she wouldn't do it even if she had it.

Mediator: [To Martin] As I implied, Claire's lawyer is probably going to discourage her more strongly from accepting these terms than yours will you.

Martin: That would ruin all the work we've done to get to this point.

Claire: I know it. Martin, I know I'll stick to this agreement if you agree that I don't have to repay you the money you are lending me.

Martin: I won't do that. It's too open-ended, and I need to get something out of the house sale.

Claire: All right. I guess I'll go along with it.

Was this the victim operating again? How did Claire really feel about the agreement? I wasn't sure. Sometimes she seemed to be solidly advocating her position, and other times, not. It was a borderline situation for me. Whether I would draw it up was my next decision—I had been clear from the beginning that I would not draw up an agreement that I felt was unconscionable.

On the one hand, it seemed that Martin had won. Claire had given up support—so in the one area they disagreed upon most strongly, she had given in. On the other hand, she would be getting at least $25,000 to $30,000 or more in exchange for the right to any support and whatever interest she would have had in Martin's business. She undoubtedly would have gotten more money if she had had a lawyer negotiate for her, or at least the security of knowing that she could look to Martin for support, but she would be free of any scrutiny of her life by a judge or Martin. It also appeared to me that during the process, she had moved away from her place of victimization and toward a position of strength. If her health held out and she landed on her feet, I concluded, this would work well. If not, she could end up regretting this agreement. I didn't know whether we were finished or not, but drew up the agreement feeling that this was not so unfair that I would inject my opinion. And it was clear to me that they both understood what they were doing. It had taken us four sessions to reach this point.

When I sent Claire and Martin each a draft of the agreement to review with their consulting lawyers, and they sent me back copies marked up with minor changes, Claire enclosed a note saying that she was relieved it was over and that the agreement felt right to her, even though she felt under pressure to sell the house quickly. Her lawyer did not support the agreement, but that hadn't changed her willingness to commit to it.

A few months later, I ran into Claire. She looked wonderful, happy, and healthy. When she saw me, she came right over. "It all worked out well," she said. "Selling the house felt like getting rid of a great burden, and I never would have done it if I hadn't had to. As it turned out, the week after we signed the agreement, I got an offer on the house for $15,000 more than we thought it was worth, so I didn't have to borrow any more money from Martin. And I found a job designing greeting cards. It gives me a chance to be creative, the hours are flexible, and the pay's not bad." Then, looking at me, she winked. "And you know, my headaches have almost gone away."

WOULD I LIE TO YOU?

SUMMARY

*J*ust as there can be no mediation without a willingness to agree, there can be no mediation without honesty. This case shows the fundamental necessity for full disclosure in conflict resolution, and demonstrates practical strategies for addressing and dismantling deceit.

Louise learns the extent of Kurt's deception the hard way, and it is her very struggle to expose his lies and confront him with them that becomes their path to agreement. Also explored are the differences between uncovering the truth through mediation and through litigation.

Kurt and Louise arrived in my office looking as if they had just stepped off of a television sitcom set—they were your typical American suburban couple. Attractive, well-dressed, healthy, and forty, Kurt wore a well-cut brown tweed sports jacket, tan slacks, and a moss green and blue striped tie. A few years younger than Kurt, Louise was tan and trim, her auburn hair cut short and casual. She wore a yellow tennis dress with a matching jersey jacket for her postmediation tennis match and carried a large red Guatemalan bag into which she dug at the beginning of each session for her notebook and pen so she could take notes on our discussions.

They came to me after a year of marriage counseling. Louise had decided to end their fifteen-year marriage and Kurt was still having a great deal of difficulty accepting the fact that it was over.

In our introductory session, Kurt appeared to me to be unusually forthright and vulnerable, blaming himself for his failure as a provider and husband and actively seeking to understand what he had done to end up so unhappy. Louise seemed far less engaged in the process. Whereas Kurt would spill out volumes of information in response to any question, Louise would hesitate to respond to what seemed to me even the simplest. In general, she appeared to be distrustful of Kurt, mediation, and me. I was puzzled by this.

Kurt owned a small advertising firm. His success, erratic at best, resulted in his making $75,000 one year and $10,000 the next. Louise had inherited more than $150,000 from her father during the marriage, of which $50,000 had gone into the purchase of the family home and $40,000 remained in a joint bank account. The rest had been spent to help raise the family's standard of living during the marriage. The couple had two children, ages five and ten, raised primarily by Louise.

Outside of the bank account, they had the house, which was now worth almost $450,000. They owed $150,000 on the mortgage. Kurt was anxious to sell the house right away, because with him in a rented apartment and Louise in the house, they were spending more than they were bringing in.

In the first working session, Kurt presented all of this information. He also told me he had put $30,000 of his before-marriage
earnings into improving the house. During the marriage, he had
made all of the financial decisions and controlled all of the couple's assets. Louise had begun to design tennis clothing and was
trying to develop her own clothing design business, but it had yet
to produce any substantial income beyond its expenses.

TRUTH . . . OR CONSEQUENCES

*I*n our second session, Louise wore another tennis outfit and
Kurt a handsome gray pin-striped suit. Kurt proposed that
when the house was sold, Louise's inherited $50,000 be returned
to her and he be reimbursed the $30,000 he had put in for
improvements. After that, the remaining proceeds would be split
equally between them. When Louise asked him for some documentation of this $30,000, Kurt agreed to provide her with it
immediately. Louise also asked Kurt to provide her with an
accounting of his income in the four months since they had separated. Kurt responded that he had only $10,000 in the office
account, just enough to pay his monthly overhead. Louise registered some skepticism. With no hesitation, Kurt invited her to look
at his books and Louise said she would. They then talked about
making agreements subject to verification of Kurt's assertions.
Louise said that it made more sense to her to verify the information first.

> ***Mediator:*** What's the difficulty with going forward as if
> the information were correct?
>
> ***Louise:*** I'm not comfortable with that.
>
> ***Kurt:*** I'll tell you. She doesn't trust me and she wants
> everything to go her way. Where's the common ground?
> Where's the trust?

Louise: You're right. I *don't* trust you. You've always kept our financial information secret from me. I went along with it, but I'm not going to anymore. It's your sickness. Produce the information first, and then we'll talk about what the agreements might be.

Kurt: It's true. My successes and failures in this business have been extreme, with much more of the latter than the former. I was afraid that Louise would lose respect for me if she knew how badly I was doing, and I was right—she has. I've repeatedly apologized, but now it seems that she just wants to beat my brains out.

Louise: All I can say is I want to see the records first.

Kurt: Fine.

We spent the rest of the session arranging for Louise to inspect Kurt's books and his other records. Louise was obviously frustrated that Kurt had been in sole charge of finances during the marriage. Now she was attempting to right that wrong. I was impressed by her insistence, although in Kurt's behavior I saw none of the usual clues that suggest misrepresentation or concealment, such as impatience, hesitation, or balking.

Lawyers often criticize mediation for the informality of its mechanisms for discovering information, particularly as compared to adversary representation. The formal methods used by lawyers require all information to be sworn to as true, under penalty of perjury. Each lawyer is permitted to interrogate the other's client in the presence of the other's lawyer and a court stenographer, who provides a written transcript of the exchanges. Additionally, each side has the opportunity to obtain written answers from the other to questions relating to the issues.

The lawyer critics argue that the informality of mediation permits one party to hide relevant information to the detriment of the other. It is true that if both people do not have the same information, the process inevitably becomes skewed. But it is also true that the formal disclosure mechanisms of litigation do not guarantee the discovery of all relevant information. If someone is willing to lie to the government on his or her income-tax returns, he or she could succeed in withholding or misrepresenting information to a spouse's lawyer. Furthermore, the atmosphere of noncooperation and resistance common to litigation, where each lawyer's emphasis is on client protection, often leads to guarding information that could be used strategically by the other side to gain the upper hand.

In mediation, the assumption that the parties are cooperating with each other can allow one person to take advantage of the atmosphere of openness. This is a particular risk if the more open person is unsophisticated. Yet the direct contact between the parties and the informality of the atmosphere often stimulates spontaneous interaction, making it potentially harder to hide information than in the more orchestrated adversarial proceedings. In addition, the mediator can use personal experience and review the written documentation to gauge the honesty of the situation. The parties can also ask their own technical advisers and/or consulting lawyers to review and verify the information gathered.

What kinds of information are we talking about disclosing? There are three distinct categories:

1. "Hard" or objective information, usually verifiable, such as how much money there is in a bank account or how much real income after expenses is available for personal use. Hard information can require subtle and sophisticated analysis by outside consultants.

2. Concrete, subjective information that has enormous bearing on the fairness of an agreement—for example, whether one of the parties is intending to move or remarry. This information is easier to obtain under more cooperative circumstances than in a stilted or hostile atmosphere.

3. "Soft" information. This comprises the interests, needs, and desires of each party—for example, to arrange co-parenting or distribute assets or cash flow, knowing each spouse's personal priorities is often the most important of all, and this knowledge can only be obtained where there is at least some trust and cooperation.

It was clear that Louise had some historical reasons to distrust Kurt. But to me his behavior and attitude in mediation indicated complete cooperation and openness. If Kurt had been determined to hide information from Louise, I reasoned, he would probably have had an easier time of it through advocates, who would have been out to protect his interests. But he was acting as if he had nothing to hide and his history of deceit was a thing of the past. Although I had requested that Kurt produce his records for me as well as for Louise, my primary reason was to test his openness to such a request. When he had unhesitatingly agreed to produce them, I felt reassured that they would be consistent with his spoken words.

When the two arrived the next week, I was struck less by their clothes than the obvious tension in their faces. Louise began.

> ***Louise:*** I'm not sure why I am here today. [Looking at me] I feel unsupported by you. Even though you asked to see Kurt's records, it was clear you thought it was unnecessary, and I felt that you were just humoring me. But it turns out that not only did Kurt lie to me while we were together, but he has continued that pattern, even in our last session here. I went down to his office and went through his books and found out that instead of $10,000 in his account, as he said last session, he has $50,000.

I looked at Kurt.

> ***Kurt:*** It's true. I was worried that Louise wouldn't agree to sell the house if she knew I had that money. I've apologized to her and I think she knows that I'm truly sorry. It will not happen again. I say that on the honor of

my father. Louise knows that it's been the truth whenever I've said something on the honor of my father.

I was really surprised. Why had he told her a lie that was so easily discoverable? Had he thought she wouldn't actually check his books? Or had he believed that she wouldn't be able to read the books and discern the lie? Or had he really *wanted* her to find out?

When Louise discovered his deceit, what a mix of feelings she must have had! On the one hand, she would have experienced some relief and a boost to her self-confidence in discovering that her suspicions were well founded. But she must have felt rage, too, at seeing that Kurt had continued to lie to her. I didn't see how she would be able to continue in mediation, knowing that Kurt could deceive her again, regardless of what he said.

I was angry with Kurt. I felt that his actions betrayed not only Louise but the mediation process and myself as well. Even if Louise *were* willing to go on, I didn't know if *I* would be. Maybe the lie she had uncovered was just the tip of the iceberg. Even if it were the only lie, how could she—and I—know? Certainly we would be fools to take Kurt's word for it. The priority now was to help Louise assess her position and then to support whatever decision she made. But if she decided to continue in mediation, I needed to be sure that Kurt would not use this process to rip her off.

RESPONDING
TO DECEIT

Mediator: [To Louise] You certainly proved that it was important to see the books. It was wise of you to trust your experience. You're right. I was deceived by Kurt's openness. So, given your discovery, why did you decide to come back today?

Louise: I'm not sure. I find all the possibilities scary, but I know it's important not to play out again what I played out in the marriage. I think I feel more in control in mediation than I would in turning the case over to a lawyer. That would be like turning my finances over to Kurt. I want to deal with him face to face. I *know* this man. I know our pattern and I know it's time for me to be in charge of my life. I'm telling both of you right now, I want written and objective verification of all further information. Kurt, I'm simply going to assume that you're lying. That's the only way for me to proceed.

And there's something else I need to say. As much as I know that he is a deceitful shit, he is also the father of my children, and we are going to have to be able to work out a number of problems together. At least, I know that it would be better for the kids if we could. And another thing. I am unwilling to compromise at all about what I need for my life to work and what I need for the kids.

Kurt: And you do believe me when I swear on my father's honor, don't you? I've never gone back on that.

Louise: I don't know. All I do know is that if I assume you're lying, it will be hard to be deceived again.

Kurt: You know I wasn't going to hide that money from you forever.

Louise: Right, just until we had negotiated an agreement.

Louise's statement was powerful. She was both assuming responsibility for her role in the deception and putting an end to it, and in the process declaring her limitations and needs. She had just turned what many would have called a disadvantage of mediation into a statement of her personal strength. But had Kurt misrepresented other things she hadn't yet discovered? What steps could she take now to find out? To run down the balance in the office bank account was one thing, but finding more subtle misrepresentations would require an accountant.

Mediator: I understand why you don't trust Kurt. The main question now is whether you need to hire an accountant to examine the office books or other records further.

Louise: I don't want to spend the money to do that.

Mediator: What if you were to discover that there was more money hidden in those books that you didn't see?

Kurt: Wait a minute. That's not true. Sure I've lied. But you know everything now, and I resent what you're doing to me. It feels like you're trying to punish me.

Mediator: I'm not trying to punish you but I understand how you feel. If I felt I had just come clean, I might feel persecuted too. The problem is that although I *am* neutral toward the two of you, I'm not neutral about the truth. So I feel that even though it will be up to the two of you to make your decisions, I need to ask these questions. It would be unconscionable for me to allow the two of you to work out an agreement based on lies.

Kurt: I think I understand what you're saying. I need a practical solution.

Mediator: It's up to me to do what I can to assure the integrity of the process.

Louise: And I want to get on with it. I don't care if there *are* other lies, because I'm going to keep my mind on what I need from our settlement. If I get that, I don't care what other lies there are.

Louise had found her strength. She was the clearest person in the room, in full control. The only danger I could see was that she might become unrealistic about her future needs; I didn't want her to underestimate them in her desire to get out of the marriage. The danger for me was that I could become so enthusiastic in my support for the truth that I could lose my neutrality. Kurt had picked up on my moralism and was feeling judged. Could I support the search for the truth without condemning him?

> ***Louise:*** Regarding the house, I want to be reimbursed for my contribution and then split the rest of the proceeds from the sale.

> ***Kurt:*** What about the money I put into improving it from my separate funds?

> ***Louise:*** Where's the documentation?

> ***Kurt:*** I didn't keep the records, but I swear that I'm telling you the truth, on my father's honor. It would be unfair not to give me credit for it.

> ***Louise:*** I won't do it. And I think that's fair, even if it is a penalty for your secrecy.

> ***Kurt:*** Well, I don't. A lot of the payments were made in cash, and I put cash into our account.

> ***Louise:*** And you never said a word to me about it. No, that's it. I don't care whether it's true or not.

FORGING A PRACTICAL
SOLUTION

Kurt knew that he had been hoisted on his own petard. His secrecy and deceit were Louise's raw spots, and Kurt knew that she would not change her mind; he conceded the point. The major remaining issue was child support. They had agreed upon a cash buy-out of spousal support, but Louise also wanted regular monthly payments for child support. Kurt wanted instead to pay for the extraordinary expenses—such as private school, camp, and medical and dental bills.

In registering their points of view, both were trying to draw a line and hold to it. We needed to look underneath their positions to understand what was going on.

Mediator: [To Kurt] Why do you want to do it this way?

Kurt: The kids will be with me half of the time. Once the house is sold, Louise will be getting the lion's share of the proceeds [the repayment of her inheritance and the spousal support buy-out] and I won't be in a position to buy a house for at least a year and a half, *if* I can get my business to produce. If I can't, then I'll be stuck with having to pay the taxes on my share of the proceeds, and—

Mediator: What does this have to do with the question of whether you make regular child support payments or pay the major expenses yourself?

Kurt: It'll work better for my cash flow.

Mediator: Any other reason?

Kurt: None that I can think of. What do you think?

Mediator: It would also keep you from having to pay Louise directly. But maybe even more important, it would leave you in control of the major decisions affecting the children.

Kurt: You're right about not paying Louise directly, but I'm not so sure about the other. I think I just want to make sure the kids get all the advantages in life that I can provide for them.

Louise: Don't you think that I want that too, Kurt? If we are going to continue to parent together, we're going to have to make these decisions together. That's not going to be up to you alone. You have to trust that I have their best interests at heart.

Kurt: But you don't trust *me.* You think I lie to you about everything, but you ask me to trust you. How about a little trust in return?

Louise: I *do* trust that you want what's best for the kids. But I don't trust you around money. Maybe if we start to work together effectively, I'll start to trust you around money.

Mediator: [To Kurt] What's it like to hear that?

Kurt: I've never really trusted anyone in my life, particularly with money. We do need to be able to trust each other's intentions with the kids, and I do trust Louise. I guess maybe it does make sense for us to make all aspects of decisions concerning the children together. [Kurt starts to cry] This is really hard for me. Please help me.

Louise: [On the verge of tears] Okay, we have to make a new start with the kids. I have never questioned your love for them. I trust that.

Kurt agreed to monthly child support payments and within the next hour, they had settled the details of the agreement. Kurt turned to Louise. "Now that we have worked all of this out," he said, "I want you to make a gesture of good faith by reimbursing me the $30,000 of my own money I put into the house."

Louise: Not a chance.

She smiled, and he smiled, too. "Can't hate a guy for trying" was how he ended the session.

IMPLACABLE, IMMUTABLE, INFLEXIBLE

SUMMARY

*T*he issue here can be summed up in a cry mediators and family lawyers hear a great deal: "Spousal support over my dead body!" My job here is to help redress a radical power imbalance: All the power lies with Nick; Marie is compliant, accommodating . . . and desperate. Their unfolding drama shows how important it is to uncover the feelings and needs that lie behind a disputant's stance in order to move beyond a stalemate.

Neither intelligence nor intuition was needed to recognize that Nick was extremely reluctant to be in my office. He had canceled three appointments that his wife, Marie, had set up for them. A flat tire, a dental appointment, and an Oakland A's game had been the excuses. Knowing that, I had been surprised when he appeared, and I was even more surprised when he met me with what appeared to be genuine warmth and sincere apologies. Receding gray hair and a generous mustache adorned his handsome, open face, and he smiled as we shook hands. A clean blue shirt with his name on the pocket identified him as the service manager at a large local car dealership and did not conceal his burly chest.

I was not surprised, however, when Marie responded first to my question directed at both of them: "What brings you to mediation?" The first person to speak usually turns out to be either the person who is the more interested in mediation or the person who has habitually spoken for the couple. In Marie's case, her response clearly was for the former reason. A plumpish woman in her late thirties, Marie had a vitality that seemed to be emerging after having been under wraps for some time. She worked part-time teaching learning-disabled kids and spoke carefully and slowly. She appeared to be measuring each word for its effect on Nick. She also spoke deferentially, like a respectful child speaking to an adult, her large dark eyes seeking my approval.

> ***Marie:*** I want a divorce and I want to get it in the most painless way possible. The idea that we could come here and work with one person is a lot more appealing to me than each of us hiring our own lawyer and doing battle.
>
> ***Mediator:*** How about you, Nick?
>
> ***Nick:*** [Stiffening, his smile disappearing] I'm here because Marie suggested this. I'm not interested in a divorce at all, but everyone tells me that if Marie wants it, I can't stop it.

Mediator: Do you think there's any chance of saving the marriage?

Nick: That's not up to me. It's up to Marie.

Mediator: If it *were* up to you, would you try to save the marriage?

Nick: We did go to one session with a marriage counselor, but it was clear to all of us that it would be a waste of time to try to save the marriage. Marie wants me to be a different person, and I can't do that.

Mediator: [To Marie] Is that the way you see it?

Marie: Yes, it is. Our marriage has been like our parents' and like our grandparents'. He's the boss; I'm the servant. He's a good man and I respect him but I don't have a life of my own. He makes all the decisions—I even ask him who to vote for. I want to change, but I can't do it in this marriage. But I don't want us to end up as enemies. I want to work out something fair for us and our two children. [They had a twelve-year-old daughter, Eleanor, and a ten-year-old son, Max.]

Nick: Well, I don't understand what she's talking about. It's this women's stuff she hears on TV. I think it's crazy for her to just end the marriage, and I can't see how I'm going to get a fair result out of this process.

Mediator: I understand. So, one of the things you'll need to consider in deciding whether or not to go on is whether you want to participate actively in a process that will lead to the end of the marriage. If you don't, then it won't be a very good idea to continue with the mediation.

Nick: [Raising his voice and emphasizing his points by moving his arms and pointing at Marie] As far as I'm concerned, if she wants a divorce, I'm not going to try and stop her, but she's not going to get everything to go her way. She wants me to move out of the house now. I want you to know that I'm not budging from that house until we have a written agreement that spells out everything. I don't have to leave the house, and I *won't* until it's all worked out.

Mediator: It's true that a judge would not order you out of the house unless you had done something that endangered Marie or your children. But it's also true that it's difficult to make all the necessary decisions before you separate, such as the distribution of your property, assignment of responsibility for your debts, maintenance of cash flow, and creation of a co-parenting agreement.

Nick: So be it. *I'm* not the one who wants to make all of this happen. And I want you to know one other thing. I will not mediate unless Marie agrees first to give up spousal support, no matter what else happens. If she wants the divorce, then she can have it, but I'll be damned if I'll pay her a *cent* toward her support.

Mediator: So you have very strong feelings about that.

Nick: It's not just a feeling. It's a principle. I won't pay any spousal support, and that's it. And I don't care what the law is, either. She can go to court and get a judge to order me to pay spousal support, and I won't even hire a lawyer. I'd rather go to jail than pay spousal support.

Nick's stance was extremely powerful, so powerful that I doubted whether mediation would work. I didn't see how Marie would be able to stand up to either his refusal to move out of the house before a full agreement had been reached or his precondition to mediation—that Marie give up spousal support before any other issues were decided.

Coupled with his willingness to self-destruct—for example, to go to jail—if he didn't get his way, either position could overwhelm Marie. His refusal to move out would bring to bear on her the extreme psychological pressure of living with Nick after having decided to live apart or moving out and either uprooting the kids or leaving them behind. His insistence on her agreeing to give up spousal support before mediating the other issues and his willingness to go to jail could put Marie in a position of either conceding the issue of spousal support or facing a nasty—and potentially hopeless—fight. If Nick would really act on his threat to go to jail before paying spousal support, Marie would lose no matter what she did. And if Marie believed his threat, she could lose even if he was bluffing.

ELICITING BOTH VOICES

Nick's position was coming across loud and clear. My challenge was to make sure Marie's point of view came across, too, and to maximize her sense of choice. I couldn't allow her to concede on the issue of spousal support before we looked at the whole situation—such a result would go against my major criterion, fairness. Of course, if Marie didn't really care about receiving support, her concession would make sense . . . as long as she had enough money to survive without Nick's help. One of our first goals, then, would be to assess the financial situation. More difficult but equally important, as I saw it, was to elicit Marie's sense of fairness in the face of Nick's potential intimidation.

With Nick, the challenge would be to help him appreciate Marie's reality. This would not be simple—if my hunch about them was right, Nick's failure to do this was undoubtedly well ingrained in their relationship, so I had to be careful not to delude myself that this would necessarily occur. On the other hand, I knew that a decision to separate can enable people to say and hear things that couldn't be expressed within the context of marriage. Ironically, if Nick could really come around and appreciate Marie's point of view, he might be taking an action that, taken earlier, could have saved the marriage. But it was probably too late now.

THE REALITIES BELOW THE VOICES

*H*elping Nick see Marie's point of view would mean empathizing with him, trying to understand how it felt to be so desperate, so pained by the end of the marriage, that I would feel forced to take this extreme position. I had to try to get closer to his many fears, his uncertainty, and his sense that he lacked control over his own destiny. If I could do that, it was possible Nick would become more interested in the power of understanding than the force of coercion. It would be quite a challenge.

With Marie, I wanted to maximize her sense of her own freedom. She actually had a couple of different options:

- With respect to the house, she could gain some breathing room if she were willing to move out of the house and wait to see whether Nick's stance was simply a negotiating strategy. If it were, she could call his bluff, but if it were a sign of his desperate state, it was likely to subside in intensity with time.
- If Marie were willing to treat Nick's choice of jail over paying support as a bluff, then—regardless of whether it really *were* a bluff or not—she could weaken Nick's hold over her and assert her own strength.

Further, she wouldn't be risking her chances for support by calling Nick's bluff, since she could still go to court and get a spousal support order from a judge. The freer she felt to leave mediation and to exercise her legal rights, the greater was the chance that mediation might work for her. Why not skip the mediation and go straight to court? To do that would be to lose any leverage she might have to force him out of the house.

DEALING WITH COERCION

*O*verall, then, the goal for both was to open the dialogue by neutralizing Nick's coercive power over Marie and giving her the opportunity to assert herself fully. As to *how* to achieve that goal in the face of Nick's entrenched position, I had a number of choices:

- I could refuse to accept Nick's condition, even if Marie agreed to it. In other words, I could ask him to choose between ending the mediation (at which point Marie could take her case to court) or continue on without coercion. This could be enormously effective if I were able to do it firmly, yet softly enough to keep mediation open.
- A second option would be for me to caucus with each party separately once the mediation had progressed. The point of doing that would be to ensure that Marie's concerns didn't get lost in the trialogue—that she wasn't holding back out of fear of Nick's reaction. But if in the caucus some new concerns did come out, it would be difficult to integrate them into the process without me seeming to be Marie's advocate. That danger is inherent in the caucusing option and is a strong argument against it.
- The third option was to try to bring out Marie's concerns through a two-way conversation with her while Nick listened. In this way I could focus the discussion on the

area that seemed to be the least exposed and help Marie assert herself without speaking for her. Meanwhile Nick would be privy to the information if Marie felt trusting enough to divulge it with him present. The advantage would be that I could become the bridge to direct communication between them without having to contend with Nick's power.

The disadvantage to this option would be that despite her trust in me, Marie might be unwilling to say what she really thought in Nick's presence. If that were the case, we would have the appearance of mutuality but in fact no real accord. Also, Nick might feel ignored and therefore alienated from me. Since he was suffering so deeply, my empathetic support of him would be particularly important. If Nick trusted me, after all, we might be able to communicate at the level of pain that was triggering his intransigence. I certainly didn't want to risk shutting the door on that.

- A fourth option would be to put off dealing with Nick's stance until later in the mediation. After all, no agreement made now would be binding until they had agreed on everything. Perhaps Nick would cool off and soften his view as the mediation progressed and he became more aware of Marie's needs. Moreover, I would then have more time to develop a connection with him, which might make him more receptive to a strong stance by me or a strong assertion from Marie. Waiting made a great deal of sense to me, but I knew the disadvantages were considerable. First, by permitting Nick's strong position within the mediation, I would be in effect reinforcing it. This might well encourage Marie's deferential inclinations. The second disadvantage was even more grave than the first—it would mislead both of them into thinking I thought mediation held promise for them. In fact, I considered it unlikely that Nick and Marie would be able to reach a fair agreement.

One more thing bothered me, and ultimately led me to the next step: Had Nick expressed himself fully, or if Marie accepted his position on support, would he take the same all-or-nothing stance on the other issues? To keep the mediation open, I needed to find this out.

Mediator: [To Marie] What's it like to hear all this?

Marie: I know that Nick is very angry and very upset.

Mediator: That's apparent to me, too. But what's your response to his assertion that he would go to jail rather than pay support and his insistence on a full agreement before moving out?

Marie: I guess I will have to get along without spousal support and put up with him in the house until we've worked everything out.

Mediator: How come?

Marie: Because that's what he is insisting upon.

Mediator: And if he weren't insisting upon it?

Marie: He knows I want him to move out of the house now, but since I can't force him out, I'll have to live with that, won't I?

Mediator: You don't have to accept what he wants if you don't want it. That doesn't mean you're going to get what you want, but if you have a disagreement, my job is to help the two of you find solutions you haven't thought of and help you both make sure your points of view are expressed and heard.

Marie: If he wants to stay in the house and I want him to get out, what other solutions can there be?

Nick: If you want the separation so much, you can get out.

Marie: I'm not about to do that.

Mediator: How come?

Marie: Because Max and Eleanor are there and they need me. I don't want to upset their apple carts too much. They don't even know we're going to separate.

Mediator: So you feel you have to stay in the house for their sakes?

Marie: That's right. But it's very hard on me to have Nick there, too.

Mediator: I would imagine it would be hard for both of you, particularly after having decided to separate.

Marie: This is a very stubborn man. When he digs his heels in, it's impossible to budge him. I *know* that.

Mediator: Then you need to decide whether you feel strongly enough to disagree with him here and make some decisions that make sense for all of you, or whether you think that's hopeless.

Marie: I don't see what good it's going to do to disagree with him if he won't change his position. We'll just be stuck.

Mediator: That's how it feels to disagree with someone. At first, you feel that either you have to go along with them or you're stuck. But if you are both willing to make the effort to get past that point and find solutions that respond to both of your concerns, then we can create something else.

Marie: But isn't this a question of whether he moves out or not?

Mediator: When you frame it like that, yes. But there are other ways of framing it. You both find it unacceptable to move out of the house. So if we take that as a given, we need to find solutions that allow you both to feel that you won't be giving up something important. We need to look *beneath* your stances. For you, the stability of your kids in the house seems to be the priority. I don't know what it is for Nick.

Nick: I don't want to give up any of my legal rights, which I would if I moved out. If we have a full agreement, then it's okay.

Mediator: And suppose there were another way to ensure that you wouldn't be giving up your legal rights during the time you were working out an agreement. Would that satisfy you?

Nick: Yeah, but my lawyer says there isn't. So I'm not going to do something else.

Mediator: So we need to find some agreement that provides for the stability of the kids and doesn't erode any legal rights of either of you. Suppose there were a way in which the two of you could have more separation and yet not officially move out of the house? Would that work?

Marie: Yes. I'd prefer he move out, but if there were a way to do that, it would help a lot.

Mediator: How about you, Nick?

Nick: Maybe. I'm not moving out, but what do you have in mind?

Mediator: There are several options. You could try to find ways of not being in the house at the same time. That might mean getting an apartment that you stay in alternately. Or each one of you could stay with a friend temporarily while we go through this.

Marie: You could stay with your friend Joseph.

Nick: No. You could stay with Linda.

Mediator: Those are possible solutions. The key is to find solutions that work for the kids and don't leave either of you feeling legally weakened. Maybe you could think of others.

Marie: That's very helpful. I think we need to think about this more and see what we can come up with. But what about the issue of spousal support?

Mediator: From my perspective, we don't need to resolve that right now. It's more important for you *not* to assume that you won't get it just because Nick doesn't want to give it. The process is the same. We look at your overall cash-flow needs in your new situation and try to figure out ways to make it work.

Nick: I don't give a damn what you say. I'm telling you right now I will not *ever* give her one dime of spousal support, come hell or high water. That's it.

Mediator: And I take that as an expression of the very strong feelings you have right now. To me that doesn't necessarily mean you'll continue feeling that way throughout this process, particularly when we look at some of the other issues that need to be resolved. Clearly something very important to you underlies the statement, and if you decide to go ahead with this process, we'll have to get clearer about that as we work together. It may be that the two of you *will* end up with an agreement calling for no spousal support. But I don't know that now, and I don't assume that is what will happen. You, Nick, have to decide where that fits in with your overall priorities, and Marie has to see how important this issue is for her. Then we'll see. It's important now for Marie *not* to assume that there will be no spousal support.

Nick: I thought you weren't supposed to take sides.

Mediator: I don't think that's what I'm doing.

Nick: I said that under no conditions would I pay spousal support, and then you come back and say that I will. If that's not taking sides, I don't know what is.

Mediator: I didn't say "will," I said "might." This is not an issue that either one of you can decide on your own. There has to be agreement on everything if this process is going to work. And agreement doesn't mean that if one of you says something will happen, the other agrees because he or she feels there's no other choice.

Nick: I thought that your job was to be neutral.

Mediator: It is. Frankly, I don't care whether you reach an agreement that calls for spousal support or not. What I do care about is that all decisions be mutually satisfactory to you, and not the result of one person's decision. If you care about the spousal support issue a lot and Marie doesn't care, then there probably won't be spousal support. But I will not accept an agreement that calls for no spousal support simply because Marie is afraid to disagree with you. So I *am* neutral about the outcome, just not about the process. You need to feel equal here.

Marie: I certainly don't feel equal to him. He's stronger than me.

Mediator: If you feel you can't or are not willing to learn to stand up to him here, you shouldn't mediate.

Marie: But I don't want to end up having lawyers fight it out and then end up with us hating each other.

Mediator: That's possible, and it's also possible that you could find lawyers who could negotiate with each other effectively without creating hostility. And you could even be creating long-term hostility through mediation if you end up with an unfair or unworkable agreement.

Marie: So how do we decide?

Mediator: You both need to think about what I've said today, and then decide whether you feel you can go through this process. Marie, you have to decide whether you are willing to register your disagreements with Nick, particularly when he seems adamant about something, and hang in there when you disagree until you get to something workable. I think you did that with the question of separation. Nick, you need to decide whether you can stand being in a process that will lead to divorce, something you don't want, and can accept an agreement that works as well for Marie as it does for you. If I were you, Nick, I could imagine feeling so powerless and frustrated by her decision that I couldn't make the other decisions together. You won't find satisfaction from feelings of revenge or from the sense that you're in sole control here. So you both need to think about whether this is the way you want to go.

Nick: I'm willing to do this, but I want you both to know that I'm not going to pay a dime of spousal support.

Mediator: If you both decide to go ahead, we'll need to explore and understand that statement more fully.

On that note, we ended the session. When the two returned for the next session, they had worked out a plan for occupying the house in turns, which involved them alternately staying with friends.

BREAKING THROUGH
AN ESTABLISHED PATTERN

*M*arie and Nick's only assets of significance were the house and separate pensions each of them had from work. Each readily agreed to give the other half of what their pensions had accumulated during the marriage. They had bought the house ten years before for $200,000; now it was worth about $300,000, subject to a first mortgage of $70,000 and a second mortgage of $40,000. Nick's job as service manager provided him with about $70,000 per year. Marie's three-quarter-time teaching job earned her about $25,000 per year. Besides support, the main issue to be resolved was how the house would be disposed of.

> *Mediator:* I'd like to get an idea of each of your priorities with regard to the house and support.

> *Nick:* You mean child support, not spousal support, right?

> *Mediator:* I know that's how you look at it. I don't care what words we use now. Perhaps "cash flow" would be the best term.

By using the term cash flow, I was hoping to take the charge out of the issue and focus on the practical reality of how much total income they had and what their total expenses would be rather than the "morality" of spousal support.

> *Nick:* All right. I just want to make it clear where I stand.

> *Mediator:* By that, I take it that your highest priority in all this is not to pay spousal support.

> *Nick:* How'd you guess?

Mediator: Pure intuition. It's what makes me such a great mediator.

Nick was unable to suppress a smile.

Humor is an important mediation tool for neutralizing tension. It has the effect of both changing the parties' perspective and conveying a message of trust. In this case, by joking with Nick, I was conveying to him that I really did understand him.

Mediator: How about you, Marie? What are your highest priorities in all of this?

Marie: The only thing that really matters to me is that we protect the kids as much as we can from any trauma. That means that they should be able to stay in the house, rather than having to go through the trauma of moving. I would like to be able to stay in the house with them for seven years, until Eleanor graduates from high school.

Mediator: And then what would happen?

Marie: We'd sell the house and split the proceeds.

Mediator: How do you know that it would be traumatic for them to move to another house?

Marie: I've never talked to them about this directly, but they have both said how much they love that house so many times that I know uprooting would be very hard on them. All their friends live in the neighborhood, and if we moved, we would never be able to afford to live near there or even in the same school district. It would really be horrible for them to go through that kind of a change.

Nick: That's total baloney. I can hardly stand listening to such drivel. They wouldn't have any problem handling a move. The real problem is *you*—*you* don't want to move.

Marie: That's not true, and you know it. All you can see is what you want to see. Both kids are having problems in school. That house is very important for their stability.

Nick: Come off it, Marie. The only real problem they have is that their mother is so overprotective they don't have a chance to live their own lives.

Mediator: So the two of you have different points of view about this. Marie, I particularly appreciate your willingness to disagree, because you seemed afraid to do that before.

Marie: Well, I don't think Nick really understands the kids.

Mediator: What do you think he doesn't understand about them?

Marie: He doesn't understand how afraid of him they are.

Nick: [In a booming voice] What kind of talk is that? My children are not afraid of me!

Mediator: That may be true, but would you be willing to hear why Marie might see that differently?

Nick: I don't think she knows any better about what is happening with the kids than I do.

Mediator: That may be true. But would you find it useful to understand how she came to her conclusions?

Nick: It depends upon what she has to say.

Mediator: I can imagine feeling that way if I were you. I'd like to suggest that you listen to her and accept what you find valuable and don't worry about the rest.

Nick: All right.

Mediator: Marie, are you willing to tell Nick why you think the kids are afraid of him?

Marie: I don't want to upset him any more than I already have. I'm afraid of his reaction.

Mediator: What do you think could happen?

Marie: For one thing, he'll get even angrier than he already is with Max. Max would much rather be taking violin lessons than playing on the soccer team.

Nick: [Throwing his hands in the air] That's exactly what I mean. Marie's afraid he's going to get hurt playing soccer. Max sees his mother's concern and so he tells her what he thinks she wants to hear. The only one who wants Max to take violin is Marie.

Marie: [To me] This is exactly the problem. Every time I try to tell him what's really going on, he just says I'm wrong.

Mediator: Let's find out. Nick, is there anything in what Marie has said that you find valuable?

Nick: Nope.

Mediator: Really?

Nick: Well, it's true I want him to play soccer. I love that game. And I don't think it's such a bad idea for him to be doing something that pleases me.

Mediator: Even if he doesn't want to be doing it?

Nick: No. I wouldn't want him to play soccer unless he liked it, and I think most of the time he does. And I sure don't believe Marie's right when she says he'd rather play the violin.

Mediator: Okay. But do you think that there might be some truth to Marie's point that Max doesn't like soccer?

Nick: Maybe. Maybe he's not as crazy about the sport as I am and maybe sometimes he doesn't like to say things that he thinks I won't want to hear. But he does the same thing with Marie.

Mediator: Maybe he doesn't want to play soccer *or* the violin.

Nick: At least I'm direct about wanting him to play soccer. Marie, she manipulates Max into thinking that he really wants to play the violin.

Mediator: Do you think there's anything to that, Marie?

Marie: [Her voice softening] Maybe, but I think it's really important that he be exposed to music.

Nick: And I think he needs to be part of a team with boys his own age and learn how to take a few knocks.

Mediator: Right now, I'm beginning to get a sense of how it feels to be Max, caught between what his father wants and what his mother wants.

Marie: [Starting to cry] I don't want to do that to him. That's what my parents did to me.

Mediator: What would you like for him?

Marie: I'd like him to do what he wants, but I don't think he's old enough to know that yet.

Mediator: It might be important to find out the answer to that question. What's this conversation been like for you, Nick?

Nick: I don't want him to feel caught between us, either. I'm sorry if that's what's happening.

Mediator: Do you think it is?

Nick: It's real possible.

Mediator: [Looking at both] I think that we've defined a major shared concern about Max. What do you think we should do about this?

Marie: There are other signs that he's having problems. And I think this is a hard time for Eleanor, too. I'd like them to meet with the school counselor a few times.

Mediator: Nick, how do you feel about that?

Nick: That's all right. But I think we both should talk to them first. And I don't want to send them to a psychiatrist. [Marie nods in agreement.]

Mediator: That's not the suggestion. It's clear that we could benefit from some more concrete and specific information about the kids' needs. You agree that you need to talk to them together. Another possibility is having them talk to the school counselor. Then we will have more information to work with. But let's look at this from a different angle right now. Suppose for a moment that it turned out that you were agreed that the kids didn't need to be in the house. Would you still want to stay there, Marie?

Marie: Yes, I would. I can't imagine living anywhere else. I've looked around at places I could afford if I got half of the sale proceeds from the house, and I can't stand the idea of living in places like that.

Nick: Now you know what it's like for *me*. And you wanted to kick *me* out of the house.

Mediator: Wait a minute. Please let me pursue this for a minute. Then we can get back to your reactions, Nick. If you're afraid you might forget them in the meantime, it's fine to jot them down, but let's stay with this for a bit. So, Marie, regardless of what might make most sense for the kids, it's important for you to be able to stay in the house.

Marie: Well, yes, that's true, but it's no less important for the kids.

Mediator: I understand that. But it is more powerful, at least for me, to know that staying in the house is a personal priority for you, too.

Marie: I don't see them as separate from each other.

Nick: Listen, I really don't care if staying in the house meets Marie's needs or not. *She* wants the divorce. *She* can't have everything. I have just as much right to stay in the house as she does. And if I can't stay there, she shouldn't be able to, either.

Mediator: Do you really want to be able to stay in the house?

Nick: No, but I don't think she should be able to stay there.

Mediator: Try saying this to Marie, if it fits: "I want you to feel as miserable as I do."

Nick: Yeah, that's right. I do.

Mediator: So maybe the goal we talked about in our first session—that we might work out a solution that makes both of your lives work—might be the worst thing this process has going for it, as far as you're concerned.

Nick: If you can figure out something that will give us both what we want, I won't oppose it. But frankly, I think that's impossible.

Mediator: We'll see. Maybe you're right, but let's at least lay out the situation and look at it. Marie, your highest priority is to be able to stay in the house. Nick, yours is to be in a position to minimize your financial obligation to Marie.

Nick: I want to be able to buy a house that I can live in

indefinitely, and I want to do it now. I don't want to have to wait to do that.

Mediator: And how much will it cost to buy the kind of house that you could imagine yourself buying?

Nick: About $200,000.

Mediator: So you'd need a down payment of about $40,000.

Nick: At least. And the only way we can get that kind of money is by selling the house. It's the only asset we have.

Marie: Then I guess that's what we'll have to do.

Mediator: What do you mean?

Marie: If Nick is unwilling to postpone selling it, what choice do I have?

Mediator: We're back to our first session. I haven't heard Nick saying he's opposed to postponing the sale. What I've heard is that he needs $40,000 to make a down payment on another house. But on your side, I've heard you say that your highest priority is to stay in the house, both because you want to and, in your view, because the kids need to.

Marie: Yeah, but Nick doesn't seem to care about that.

Mediator: But you do.

Marie: Of course—not that it seems to count for much.

Mediator: In your eyes?

Marie: No.

Mediator: Well, if staying is important to you and we don't find a way to meet your needs, we won't have an agreement—unless you want to be miserable. Even though you and Nick disagree, you don't need to capitulate to his wishes.

Nick: Wait a minute. My lawyer told me that I can force the sale of the house. And that's what I am going to do.

Marie: Do you see what I mean?

Mediator: What I see is that at the first sign of disagreement you assume you won't be able to get what you want except at Nick's expense. And you assume that if one of you is not going to get what you want then that person is you.

Marie: That's right. That *is* what I assume.

Mediator: And you, Nick, assume that in this instance the law will determine the result of the disagreement. Your lawyer told you that you can force a sale of the house, and you're counting on that as the outcome.

Nick: That's what he said.

Mediator: All right, let's clarify the law first. The law is relevant here, but it doesn't necessarily determine the decision you'll make. And as a matter of fact, if we refer back to the first session, Nick made it clear that he didn't care *what* the law said about spousal support—he doesn't consider it fair to pay spousal support and so he won't do it. That was not an irrational statement, even if a judge might think it was. That was a statement based solely on his sense of fairness, which is our most important reference point in mediation. Now we're onto another issue, and again the law has something to say about it, and again you have to decide how important the law is. In this situation, a court would probably order that the house be sold. If a court did order a sale of the house, that would probably be at a trial, which would be at least nine months from now. The time it would take to find a buyer and close escrow would probably add another six months.

Marie: So the law is on his side.

Mediator: As to this issue, probably. Just as it is on your side with respect to spousal support.

Marie: So what it comes down to is that either he gets to buy a new house or I get to stay in our house for now.

Mediator: That's what it looks like. But you both seem to assume that if it comes down to that, Nick will win.

Marie: That's right. I don't want to be hassled by him after this is all over just because I wanted a divorce.

Mediator: But suppose we could find a way for you to stay in the house and Nick to buy his house now?

Marie: That would be terrific. But where is he going to get $40,000?

Mediator: Maybe if you refinanced the second mortgage on the house, you could borrow an additional $40,000. Since interest rates are lower than what you're paying now, you'd end up increasing your monthly payments on that only slightly.

Nick: That would be all right with me if she paid both mortgages and there was no spousal support.

Mediator: What do you think about that, Marie?

Marie: How would I afford it?

Mediator: Good question. What's your answer, Nick?

Nick: That's *her* problem. She wants the divorce and she

wants to stay in the house. How she pays for it is her business.

Mediator: [To Marie] What's it like to hear that?

Marie: It really makes me angry. I'm willing to try to find a solution that works for him, and he's not interested in finding a solution that works for me. He just wants me to suffer.

Nick: Why should I have to pay for *you* to stay in the house?

Mediator: But you're asking Marie to finance your share of the mortgages and the down payment on what I assume will be a house that would belong to just you.

Nick: I see what you mean. Okay. I'll pay for the share of the second mortgage that would go for my down payment. But then I'll be paying that mortgage and my mortgage on my own house, too, so *I'll* be paying for two mortgages.

Mediator: We need to look at what the monthly expenses will be for the four of you in that situation. At the prevailing interest rates, let's assume right now—we'll need to get clearer when we know the specifics—that, given the two mortgages we are talking about, the monthly payments will be $1,600 per month for Nick's new house and another $400 per month for his share of the second mortgage. Then Marie's monthly payments would be the $550 on the first mortgage and another $400 per month on her share of the second. With an after-tax income of about $1,700 per month, that would leave Marie with about $750 per month to live on. Nick would be paying $2,000 per month for housing with an after-tax income of $4,500 per month. So he would have $2,500 to live on.

Marie: How can I live on $750 a month?

Nick: You can get a full-time job. That would give you another $600 to $700 per month.

Marie: You know that it doesn't make sense for me to do that until the kids are older. It was your idea that I work part-time so that we wouldn't have latchkey kids.

Nick: They're old enough now so you don't need to be there. Half the time they go to their friends' houses after school anyway.

Marie: But it's particularly important now that they have me there.

Mediator: So one option might be for Marie to work more, although at least from her perspective, there are problems with that. We will need to get more information about how the kids see this. What other options are there?

Nick: I don't know. It's her problem.

Mediator: Right now, it's our problem. Once we work out the agreement, *then* it's her problem, although if it has to do with the kids, it will be a joint problem. I need both of you to be thinking about this.

Nick: She can always sell the house. Then the problem will go away.

Mediator: You want her to give up her highest priority.

Nick: I don't care. I just don't want to end up having to pay the bill because she wants to stay in the house.

Marie: If you would pay the second mortgage, I think I could make it.

Nick: I'll tell you what. I'll loan you the money for the second mortgage and you can pay me back when the house sells.

Marie: It's still your house, too, you know. Don't you expect to pay anything for a house you still own?

Nick: No. You get to live there rent-free, so you should have to pay the expenses of the house.

Mediator: But as we sit here, none of us has any ideas for how Marie can do that, except to give up the house or borrow from you.

Marie: Then what do we do?

Mediator: Either come up with another alternative or work with what we've got. So far, if Marie is going to stay in the house, Nick is the only source of money we can think of that seems viable to Marie. We still need to talk about how long Marie would have to live in the house before selling, and we haven't talked about the amount of time the kids will spend with each of you or how their expenses will be paid.

Nick: We've already agreed that we'll each spend half time with the kids. I'd like to have the right to do that, but I also know that it might take a while before we are ready to do it, so we can build up to it. On these matters, I feel flexible. I'm also willing for Marie to live in the house—as long as the kids are there and provided I don't have to pay any taxes from the sale of the house. My accountant has explained that if we wait more than two years from the time I buy a new house or move out, then there will be taxes.

Marie: This is the first I've heard of that. I want to be able to stay in the house longer than two years, but I'm not willing to pay your taxes.

Nick: That's completely unreasonable, Marie!

Marie: Do you think that *you've* been reasonable? All you care about is making sure you don't have to pay me support and getting to own your own goddamn house. And you call *me* unreasonable?

Nick: Look, you wanted the divorce. And you want everything to be easy for you. Well, you're finally getting a taste of reality. Life's not easy and things don't always go your way.

Mediator: You know, I'm starting to see how your underlying needs might fit together. We need to find an agreement that one, allows Marie to stay in the house as long as she wants; two, eliminates taxes from the sale of the house; three, allows Nick to buy a house now; four, gives you a chance to work out a co-parenting relationship with Eleanor and Max; and five, keeps both households afloat with regards to cash flow and, at least from Nick's point of view, makes spousal support unnecessary. Anything less than that is going to be disappointing to at least one of you.

Marie: Do you really think we can accomplish that? So many of the elements seem to be contradictory.

Mediator: To tell you the truth, I don't know, but if each of the three of us is willing to give it some thought, maybe we can.

On that note, we ended the session. I was not sure that we would be able to come to such an agreement, but I had a few ideas. The main obstacles were Nick's unwillingness to pay taxes if the sale of the house were deferred beyond two years, his refusal to pay spousal support, and Marie's clear need for help with her expenses. The good news was that Marie was now asserting herself much more fully than when they first came in. While it seemed possible that she could revert to her old deferential ways, I felt much better about dealing with the contradictory needs and wants of these two than trying to mediate while Marie suppressed her discontent.

BREAKTHROUGH

When we reconvened, neither of them had been able to come up with a solution, and they both appeared glum. I had a couple of ideas, but they depended on whether Nick's problem with spousal support was based on principle or not and on Marie's long-term plans. Once we had exhausted their short supply of ideas, I began to ask some questions.

> *Mediator:* Marie, I want to understand better what your long-term plan is with the house.

> *Marie:* I'd like to be able to stay there at least until Eleanor finishes high school.

> *Mediator:* Then what?

> *Marie:* Then I guess I'll have to sell and move into a smaller house.

> *Mediator:* I have an idea that might help Nick with his tax problem and, if he's willing to wait to get his money, give Marie control over when the house is sold, although it would also give her the risk. If Marie agrees to buy out Nick at a set time in the future and pays in the form of a promissory note, then even though Nick doesn't get his money, his tax problem is solved. After that point, any in crease in the value of the house will belong to Marie only. When she sells the house, she pays off the promissory note. But then Marie will have the burden of the taxes.

Marie: I'm willing to do that to be able to have the house until then.

Nick: That's okay with me, but I want to be sure I have my money by the time Eleanor goes to college.

Marie: That's all right, because by then, I will have sold the house. And if I get the money sooner, maybe I'll give it to you then.

Mediator: Now with respect to support, if the two of you agree on child support, there may be a way of giving Marie the benefit of spousal support without calling it that.

Nick: How could we do that?

Mediator: As long as you are a co-owner of the house, if you pay the second mortgage directly to the bank, you can deduct that amount from your income taxes and Marie would not have to report it as income.

Marie: If I had that, then I wouldn't *need* spousal support.

Nick: But I'd be paying money to help fund your life.

Marie: The *kids'* lives. They'll be there in the house at least half of the time.

Nick: Then you'll give up spousal support now and I'll pay the mortgage until you buy me out. And that will be it, except for child support.

Marie: All right, fine.

Mediator: Do you mean that?

Marie: Why do you ask?

Mediator: Nick's refusal to pay spousal support has always been clear, but I've never understood how you felt about that. Legally, you'd be entitled to many years of direct support. It's up to you to give that up, but if you do, I need to be sure you fully understand what that means.

Marie: Yes, I understand. I've talked it over with my lawyer. I guess I've always assumed I wouldn't get spousal support, so there's no great surprise about it. And his paying the mortgage will help. It's okay.

As we explored the ramifications of this further, it became clear to me that although there were more details to be worked out, such as the timing and terms of the buy-out, they both felt they had a workable framework for an agreement. I had mixed feelings about their agreement, partly because I had suggested the particulars and partly because I was concerned about how it would work for Marie in the future, particularly with respect to the taxes she would incur when she moved into a smaller house. Still, I didn't feel concerned enough to refuse to draw up the agreement. Three years later I happened to see Marie at a concert. She came over to say that she was grateful for my help and that she had never been so happy in her life. She had received a raise in pay and her kids were doing well. And she and Nick had maintained a decent relationship. He had even given her more money for some of the kids' expenses than the agreement called for. And the best news was that she had recently figured out a way to pay Nick for his share of the house, enabling her to keep it for as long as she wanted and postpone the tax problem indefinitely. It's nice to hear about cases that end up that way, especially ones that look so unpromising at the start. I wish all my cases worked out so well.

TELL ME WHAT TO DO

SUMMARY

*T*his case answers the question: What is the difference between mediation and arbitration? The distinction is simple, but its meaning for mediation is profound, since it rests on the difference between dependence and autonomy. Annie and Roger enter mediation expecting me to hear both sides and then decide what they should do—in effect, act as an arbitrator. But the principle behind mediation rests on the parties making the decisions for themselves. In this case, Annie's and Roger's gradual assumption of responsibility for their own fates is the path they take toward identifying and meeting their own specific needs in a final agreement.

Roger and Annie were South African, young, and beautiful. They came to me after working for several sessions with another mediator. Both felt things were going wrong and agreed to terminate, but neither had given up hope for the process. They spoke excitedly with thick accents. Our first session began with their spewing out criticism of the other mediator's performance. "Boy, if you're able to agree on the issues that divide you as easily and fully as you have agreed on your assessment of this mediator," I told them, "we'll sail along to an agreement."

Privately, the situation felt like a setup to me: "We have come to you, Great Mediator, but be warned: We already carry one mediator's scalp in our hands." Still, their willingness to try the process again meant something, although it didn't take me long to see that they were under a misconception about mediation.

A QUESTION OF CONTROL

Roger: We've heard that you are a fantastic mediator. That's why we're here. We want you to listen to each of us and then tell us what we should do and that will settle it all.

Annie: Please. Just do this for us quickly and then we can get on with the rest of our lives.

A fair number of people come to mediation with a similar plea. Because they disagree and can't imagine themselves moving beyond their deadlock, handing over the power of decision to a third person seems the only possible solution.

Seeking a solution in this way is not mediation; it's arbitration, a much different process, in which the arbitrator gathers the necessary information and then decides what is best for the parties.

MEDIATION OR ARBITRATION: WHO DECIDES?

*I*t is crucial that both you and your spouse understand the difference between *mediation* (in which the decision-making power is shared by the two parties) and *arbitration* (in which the power to decide resides solely with the arbitrator). Unfortunately, these distinctions are not well understood even by some practitioners, and mediation as a profession is plagued by some who call themselves mediators but actually practice arbitration.

This confusion can occur on a very subtle level. For example, some mediators believe that they can distinguish between control of the process and control of the results. In their view, the mediator should direct the process—for example, determining the order of topics to be discussed, information-gathering, speaking order, and all rules of procedure. And indeed, in some disputes, the mediator's seizing of control is the only way to move forward at all. However, it is almost always the case that whoever controls the process bears the responsibility for its outcome. In fact, it is close to impossible for most people to retain the decision-making power if they hand over control of the process. The line between substance and procedure is not as neatly drawn as many would claim.

As a mediator, I see my goal as maximizing the parties' mutual decision-making power. This means that they decide about the process just as they decide on the final settlement—unless my own sense of justice prevents me from endorsing their methods or the terms of their final agreement. My work, therefore, is to help create a balance of power that grows out of their personal relationship, not to make decisions that I then impose upon them from the outside.

Arbitration has much in its favor, because if the parties agree ahead of time that it will be binding, they are guaranteed a resolution of their dispute. It can also be both efficient and informal, and thus a good alternative to going to court. Its effectiveness depends upon the arbitrator's ability to gain a clear enough understanding to make a wise decision.

The arbitration option is particularly tempting for people who think they are right, because they are confident that their position will be vindicated by the arbitrator. Moreover, because people who feel they are right often see the other person as wrong, it is easy for them to see the process as one that will end in victory for themselves and defeat for the other. The fact that they agree to turn over their decision-making power tends to encourage the parties to skew the information they present to the arbitrator, painting their own views with a brush of righteousness and trying to invalidate the other's position. Defending one's position is a natural human tendency that is enhanced when one does not have the power to decide.

Although Roger and Annie spoke as if what they wanted was arbitration, I had the sense that they really wanted mediation. Still, I—and they—had to be sure, so I saw this point of clarification as the natural starting point.

> ***Mediator:*** Let me see if I understand what you would like me to do. You want to present all your disagreements and then have me decide what you should do, right?

> ***Roger:*** Not exactly. We want you to tell us what you *think* we should do.

> ***Mediator:*** And is that different in your mind than having me act like a judge?

> ***Annie:*** Absolutely. I do not want you to be the judge. That's why the last mediator made me furious. She ended up telling us what we should do, and then when we didn't like it, she got all huffy.

> ***Mediator:*** So you didn't really want her to decide for you?

> ***Annie:*** [Smiling coquettishly] No, only if she agreed with me.

Mediator: If you both think you're right, then you probably both assume that anybody hearing the situation will decide in your favor. But of course, that can't be true for both of you.

Roger: I would much prefer it if *we* came to an agreement, but I have no idea if we *can*. We seem hardly able to talk to each other without one or both of us going nuts.

Mediator: Still, it's helpful for me to know that if you could you would prefer to decide yourselves rather than having someone else do that.

Annie: Of course. Wouldn't everyone?

Mediator: Not really. It takes some guts to put yourself in a situation that isn't under any one person's control, and especially not under your control. The hope here is that if I can find a way to help you make decisions together, you'll do that, even if you feel that you're poles apart and don't know how you can come to an agreement. Finding out you both want to do that is the most important step in deciding to mediate. If one or both of you thought you didn't want to, I would say forget it.

Roger: But how do we know if we are able to come to an agreement? We could go all the way through the process and end up with no agreement, and then we'd just be throwing our money away.

Mediator: And you've already done that once, right?

Roger: Not really. From what you've explained, I see now that the other mediation was really an arbitration, but we didn't like it.

Mediator: Well, I don't know whether you'll be able to reach an agreement here or not, but your both wanting to is a very hopeful sign. Another question you can ask yourselves to see whether this process is likely to end in agreement is how you would each feel if we reached an agreement that worked as well for the other person as it worked for you. If that would please you, or if it would at least be acceptable, that's another positive indicator.

Annie: We do have a very hard time talking to each other in a positive way.

Mediator: That's where I think that I might be helpful: in helping you understand each other.

Roger: But won't you suggest solutions, too? I know that you don't want to be an arbitrator for us, but you've done this so many times. I'd at least like to get the benefit of your experience.

Mediator: Sure, I'll be glad to share with you any ideas I might have about possible solutions, but I want you to know that my primary effort will be to extract solutions from you. I think that you understand more about what might work for you than anybody outside.

While having this important conversation, we were also playing out the issue at hand. I was asserting myself as a neutral party and attempting to clarify a crucial first question: of whether to mediate at all. They were trying to find a way to agree to undertake the effort. In addressing the issue, we had effectively begun.

THE BASICS

*R*oger had never earned a regular living in his life. Ten years before I met them, at the age of twenty-four, he had inherited a good deal of money. Shortly thereafter he and Annie had met, fallen in love, and moved from Pretoria to California. Annie had never been to the United States before, and she had found the adventure exciting. They had had twins, Dominique and Alfred, now seven, and within four years, Roger had lost all his assets through a disastrous investment in importing Beaujolais nouveau from France. There remained only a town house, which was now mortgaged to the hilt. The romance had plummeted as the money dwindled, and Roger, as his own disillusionment with his life set in, had had a series of casual affairs.

Annie was disillusioned, too, and her bitterness had almost reached the point of desperation. The life Roger had promised had disintegrated before her eyes. She alternated between rage and a desire to get the past behind her. A handsome, petite, and spirited woman, her careful makeup didn't hide the pain in her face.

Roger had the look of someone who has done something wrong and believes he is on the verge of being found out. He sat hunched over and abject, his bright blue eyes continually darting about the room, fleetingly settling on me and even more fleetingly on Annie. Having decided a few months before we met to try to get a job, Roger had recently landed a position as a salesman for a group of French vintners. This job paid him on a commission basis only.

Roger and Annie had been separated for three months when I saw them. In their previous mediation, the mediator had more or less decided that Roger should pay Annie half his monthly earnings. Reluctantly, they had accepted and adopted this decision, and Annie had also taken a $20,000-a-year job as a saleswoman in a chic San Francisco boutique. Much to her surprise and confusion, she enjoyed her work—she had never contemplated a life for herself other than as wife, mother, and hostess at elegant parties.

Annie was very clear about what she wanted: to stay indefinitely in the town house with the twins, for which Roger would make the mortgage payments as long as she stayed; to receive a minimum monthly support payment of $1,500 per month; and to have Roger assume responsibility for payment of their approximately $20,000 total debt.

THE
RELATIONSHIP

*R*oger was clearly intimidated by Annie. She constantly interrupted him or shot glances of disapproval at him that stopped him dead in his tracks. They had a history of making arrangements that Roger would then fail to follow through on, which infuriated Annie. He never openly disagreed with her; instead he presented himself rather passively. When Roger, his eyes darting about the room even more furtively than usual, acceded to Annie's demands, I knew we were in trouble. In his career as a salesman, he had yet to have a month where he had taken in more than $4,000.

> *Mediator:* Where would you get the money to be able to live up to this kind of agreement?
>
> *Roger:* I have several possibilities, and all I need is for one of them to work. Then I could do it.
>
> *Mediator:* What happens if none of them hits?
>
> *Roger:* Then I will borrow the money.
>
> *Annie:* [Angrily] On what credit? This is what you always do. You always break your agreements because you live in a fantasy land.
>
> *Mediator:* [To Annie] Why do you think that happens?
>
> *Annie:* I don't know. He works something out and then he doesn't follow through. It happens again and again. I don't know why. Ask him.
>
> *Mediator:* Do you really want to hear the answer?
>
> *Annie:* Of course. What good does it do me to have an agreement that doesn't work?

Mediator: Right. My guess is that when Roger disagrees with you or if he thinks something else would be better, he doesn't tell you because he's afraid of your anger. I can tell you that even sitting in this chair, when you express your anger, it is fearsome.

Annie: What are you trying to do here?

Mediator: I'm trying to tell you as honestly as I can what I think happens when the two of you try to work out agreements. I might be wrong, and if you think I am, I'll let it go. But frankly, I think that I'm on to something here.

Annie: What am I supposed to do, not say what I think?

Mediator: No, it's important that you feel free to say what's on your mind. You show your anger easily. You don't show your sadness and frustration as much. Those are harder to let someone else see.

Annie: [Appearing startled] You are right. You cannot believe how devastating this has been for me. I feel trapped in this life that Roger created. It does not work. All I have left are the twins and the town house, and I am about to lose that. I don't know what to do. Sometimes I think I should just go home.

Roger: I feel so badly. I've let you down completely. That is why I agree to whatever you want. I know that whatever I do will not be enough.

Mediator: Is that all?

Roger: What do you mean?

Mediator: Are there any other feelings that you have other than guilt and remorse about what's happened?

Roger: Sure, but I don't think that it would be productive to talk about them.

I had to make a choice. Should I try to urge Roger on when the questions I was asking clearly made him uncomfortable? Or should I take his discomfort as a signal that I should back off, as I might if we were having a polite conversation? Although Annie was uncomfortable with my questions of her, I could feel a basic strength that invited me to go further. But with Roger, I had a feeling the line of questions I had begun was threatening to him. But we had made some significant progress. Doubtless, it was not really news to Annie that she could intimidate Roger, but this might have been the first time that topic had been discussed, and it might have been the first time that Annie recognized the negative effects of her power over Roger.

For Roger, simply acknowledging that he had feelings other than just remorse and guilt toward Annie was a big step—and perhaps as far as he could go right now. But I felt like a detective moving toward the close-in. I believed Annie and Roger could benefit not only from the knowledge that their communication pattern was dysfunctional but also from learning how to change it.

The question was, how to proceed? If I took charge of the situation, I would be taking the power from Roger and Annie. But if I could help them change a dysfunctional communication pattern into a functional one, not only would they be able to reach future agreements on their own (for example, regarding their children), but they would have a chance of reaching a solid agreement in mediation.

They were explicitly hiring me to help them attain such an agreement, I reasoned, so I wouldn't be overstepping my bounds by teaching them how to work together.

I needed to be careful that Roger wouldn't shut me off as he had Annie because I was raising fear in him. I knew that people often cling to their dysfunctional patterns because they are familiar, even when they realize frustration is inevitable. Becoming more open to each other requires courage and a willingness not to be limited by the past. People going through a divorce often feel so fragile psychologically that facing painful issues can be overwhelming. It is a lot to ask people to be vulnerable in any situation. But to be vulnerable in the presence of a person whom one sees as having caused great suffering is exceedingly difficult. Still, this very vulnerability can allow one to make changes more profound than those one might make during more tranquil times.

From some perspectives, the territory I wanted to delve into would not be deemed particularly profound. Certainly psychotherapists would consider that I was barely scratching the surface of the issues they uncover in their work. But for Annie and Roger, who were relatively unaware psychologically, the inner territory I was helping them uncover was well-shielded from their view.

If I could restrain my instinct to push and instead engage the parties' choice to look within, I would be operating more consistently with my beliefs about how people should treat each other. Experience has taught me that people who choose freely are usually more willing to accept the responsibility for having made the choice and to make choices that honor others.

With that in mind, I jumped in. When Roger said he didn't want to talk about his deep feelings, I asked, "Why not?"

> *Roger:* She will just get angry and it will begin again.
>
> *Mediator:* What's it like for you when she gets angry?
>
> *Roger:* I am scared. I feel like I'd do anything to stop her anger.
>
> *Mediator:* And then what do you do?
>
> *Roger:* If I can, I go away.
>
> *Annie:* No wonder we cannot make anything work.
>
> *Roger:* Why talk about this now? It seems bizarre. What's done is done.
>
> *Mediator:* Let me try to explain what I'm doing, and then see if it makes sense to the two of you to continue in this vein or proceed differently. What I'm noticing here, and

what you have reported to me, is a pattern of communicating that makes decision making together difficult. When you disagree, Annie gets angry and Roger backs off, agreeing to anything that Annie wants to keep her from exploding. Later on, Roger registers his disagreement by sabotaging the agreement, and that in turn infuriates Annie.

Roger: You've described it very well. And I think it would be very helpful to recognize this pattern if we were still together. But why do anything about it now when we have decided to get a divorce?

Mediator: There are a few reasons that I can think of for trying to change the pattern for at least the duration of this process. First, if the pattern persists here and governs the decisions you make, you'll end up with another unworkable agreement. So to get to something that's more solid, we need to break the pattern. Second, to the extent that you need to make decisions together in the future—particularly those regarding your children—it would be useful to have a more constructive way of working together. Finally, you may each find yourselves in new relationships someday where you play out the pattern or something similar again, and if you can get a handle on at least your part of how it goes off, you are less likely to fall into the same trap.

Annie: Is there another way to mediate if we do not change this pattern—as you call it—with each other?

Mediator: Yes. You'd probably both look more to me to figure out what agreements you should make. Or you might just reach an easy agreement—that's what it looked like would happen a few minutes ago—and then have to deal with it later if it doesn't work out.

Annie: When you put it that way, it looks like the only smart thing to do is to see if we can change it.

Mediator: I think that would be worthwhile. But if *you* don't, we shouldn't do it. As a matter of fact, if you do it just because I think you should do it, we're not likely to get very far.

Roger: Do you think that in the little time we have with you we can change a pattern so old?

Mediator: You've already started by talking about it. I don't know how far you can go, but I've seen others make some dramatic changes. It has to do with whether you see making the change as necessary. So far what we've done is identify what you both do. The next step would be for Roger to say what he has not been willing to say to Annie, particularly about his discomfort.

Roger: [After a long silence, looking at me] What I would have to say is not pretty.

Mediator: Do you need anything from Annie or me to be willing to do this?

Roger: Do you want to hear this, Annie?

Annie: Yes. I do. The other way hasn't worked.

Roger: I need to know you're not going to yell at me for what I'm going to say.

Annie: I know that I scare you. But sometimes I just can't control myself.

Mediator: Would there be any value for you in just being able to listen to Roger?

Annie: Yes, I'm willing to try.

Mediator: How come?

Annie: Because I would like to know what he really thinks.

Mediator: Even if you find it hurtful?

Annie: Yes. It's time for the games to end.

Mediator: [To Roger] Do you have what you need to be ready to talk?

Roger: Okay. I think I'm willing to try that. [Then, looking at Annie] I have been angry with you for a long time. I think you married me because I had money, and when the money started to go, you dropped me like a hot potato. You've turned your back on me since things started to go bad. You have not supported me.

Annie: That is not true. I supported you. I tried to help you, but you always act like everything is all right. And when you started being with those other women, I stayed with you.

Mediator: Has Roger ever said any of this before?

Annie: No.

Mediator: What's it like to hear these things?

Annie: Awful. He's very wrong.

Mediator: Maybe, but do you believe *he* believes what he's saying?

Annie: Probably, but he's wrong.

Mediator: At least from *your* perspective. But it may be that if you were sitting in his chair, the situation would look different.

Annie: How?

Mediator: Are you willing to hear more?

Annie: Does he have more to say?

Mediator: Let's ask him. Roger, are you willing to say some more?

Roger: I don't know. It's hard to say things that I know she just dismisses.

Mediator: What do you need from Annie to make it work?

Roger: I know that the only reason she is not angry now is because you are here. So I'm grateful for that. But it would also help if Annie would at least *consider* the possibility that my point of view might have some merit.

Mediator: How do you hear Roger's request?

Annie: He wants me to stop fighting and see everything his way.

Mediator: I don't think so, but I can see that that's how it feels to you to take in his point of view.

Annie: What do you mean?

Mediator: I imagine that you are afraid that if you started to look at the situation from his side, your own perception would be invalidated. That is, either he's right or you're right. That's how it feels.

Annie: Yes, that's how it feels. I *am* right most of the time.

Mediator: But the truth is that both of your views are part of the truth and they can coexist. They don't have to cancel each other out. It's been my experience that often both people's perceptions are their personal truths. If they are being honest in describing their positions, you can see how it really looks to them without having to give up the validity of the way it looks to you. So all Roger is asking from you is that you take a look at the situation from his side, not that you give up your point of view.

Annie: Okay, I will try it.

Mediator: Just try to listen to Roger as carefully as you can without having to decide that he's wrong.

Annie: I understand. I will try.

Mediator: And don't interrupt him or try to answer him right away.

Annie: That will be hard for me.

Mediator: I know.

Roger: I do, too. I could never win any contest against you. So I did not fight. I surrendered. And I think that after a while, I lost my confidence in myself. And when you would come to rescue me, I felt worse about myself, and resentful of you.

Annie: You just wouldn't face up to your mistakes. You were always hiding.

Mediator: Give him room, Annie, so he can have his full say.

Annie: I can't.

Mediator: I know this is painful for you to hear.

Annie: [With tears in her eyes] I was doing the best I could to help. I didn't know what else to do.

Mediator: What was it like to hear Roger's last statement?

Annie: It was hard, but I do believe that we both misunderstood each other, maybe right from the beginning.

Mediator: It looked to me as if you really allowed yourself to hear him then.

Annie: I did. I don't understand why we didn't have this conversation a long time ago.

Roger: When we got together, we were very young. I don't think we understood much about ourselves, never mind the other.

Mediator: What was it like for you just now, Roger, to be able to say what you felt to Annie?

Roger: It was a big relief. I felt like maybe I'm not as crazy and wrong as I think I am so much of the time.

Mediator: This is important, because it feels to me that the two of you were able to break the habits you've created that keep you from being able to talk to each other, at least for these moments. While you are in this place, is there anything else that either of you wants to say to the other?

Annie: I'm sorry we never tried to do this before. I'm sorry for me, for you, and for the twins. We've hurt each other so much that I don't think we can save the marriage, but at least now I won't go around hating you all the time.

Roger: And it feels better for me to say what I've been feeling. It's like a weight that has been lifted from me.

BREAKTHROUGH

*A*fter we had called attention to the way Annie and Roger colluded to keep Roger from expressing any negativity, Annie broke, for the moment, her habit of pushing Roger around. Once she saw that she did not have to choose between giving up her truth and accepting his, she allowed herself to become more receptive to Roger's point of view. And once he knew he could speak openly without a blast of anger from Annie, Roger found himself willing to expose himself, particularly his negative feelings, which were difficult for him to experience and express. For both, having also had this experience, they suddenly saw that it might be possible to understand each other.

This breakthrough did not guarantee that they would be able to communicate easily with each other in the future. But we had created an opening and they had accrued a little experience in speaking to each other more honestly. Sustaining this kind of communication would take more work. But this was at least a start, and from my perspective a necessary precondition to their exercising their power to make decisions.

What had allowed these two to keep from invalidating the other's point of view was their mutual desire to understand each other and their belief that I could understand both of them. For Roger to see that Annie's anger was not going to blow me out of the room gave him the confidence he needed to speak of his distrust and his resentment at being put down.

THE DIALOGUE

*M*y hope for the next session was that both Roger and Annie would look at the situation from both their own *and* each other's point of view and then begin a dialogue intended to lead to a resolution. A few minutes into that session the following exchange took place.

> *Mediator:* Now, we need to figure out how to handle the debts, the house, the cash flow for the family, and co-parenting of Dominique and Alfred.

> *Roger:* What are your suggestions? You've seen people deal with this before.

> *Mediator:* I promise I'll do that if you need it, but it would be helpful if the two of you looked at this first to see what seems workable.

> *Annie:* I've already said what I want to have happen. It's nice that we can communicate better, but that doesn't change how much money I need.

Roger: So I either need to go along with what you want or we're stuck.

Mediator: That's an important perception for you right now. What you've done in the past at this point was just give in. What we need now is for you to tell us what makes sense to *you*, Roger. For right now, disregard what Annie wants and tell us what you want the decisions to be.

Roger had shown that he was tempted to disregard his own needs. Ultimately, I wanted him to get to a place where he took both sides into consideration, but because it was new to him to focus on himself when he felt under pressure from Annie, I was trying to help him articulate his point of view. If it turned out there was no real conflict between Roger's desires and Annie's, we would have a solution. If there *was* a conflict, we'd take the next step. In all this, it was important for me not to take on the role of Roger's advocate.

Roger: I want to sell the town house because we really can't afford it anymore.

Annie: [Throwing up her hands] Shit, Roger. You're trying to take away the only thing I have left.

Mediator: [To Annie] Hold it for just a moment. I want to keep the focus on Roger now, because if we don't, I'm afraid we'll end up caught in your old pattern.

Annie: Well, I am furious to think of having to sell the house.

Mediator: That's important information, and at some point we'll need to focus on your priorities in all this. And if keeping the house ends up high enough on your list, we'll need to look for solutions that take that into account. But right now, I want to be sure that we don't lose the chance to find out what Roger wants.

Roger: Thank you for saying that, because I already found myself assuming that the house will not be sold.

Mediator: It may not be sold. But right now, I want you to look at what would happen if everything worked only for you.

Annie: And why don't you ask *me* to do that?

Mediator: Because I think you're good at doing it already.

Annie: I think Roger's going to manipulate you onto his side now.

Mediator: Then it's a good thing I've got no power here. But that isn't what I think is happening. I think we could make some real progress if you could sit back now and just let what Roger wants come out. Try not to assume that just because it's what he wants it will actually happen anymore than that would be true for you.

Annie: This is very difficult. I don't know if I can do that.

Mediator: It's new, so it will take special attention to do it. But you've already shown you could do it when you were able to listen to him fully before.

Annie: All right. I'll try.

Mediator: Now, Roger, in addition to selling the town house, what else would you like to happen?

Roger: I want to be sure that Annie doesn't take the twins out of the area.

Mediator: That's important to you?

Roger: Yes. I get really scared when Annie threatens to return to South Africa.

Mediator: So that's a real power she has over you?

Roger: That's the way it seems.

Mediator: So you want to be involved in the twins' lives. What else?

Roger: I want the debts paid off. I would like to be able to support Annie and the kids, but I can't do it fully if I have to carry the house and pay off the debts at the same time.

Mediator: I would imagine that that would be particularly difficult with your income so uncertain right now.

Roger: Yes. If I had the money, I'd be pleased to have Annie live in the house with the twins, but I feel so much pressure from that, the debts, and the support that I don't think I'd be able to handle everything.

Mediator: So if the house were sold and the debts paid off, you feel confident you could afford to pay Annie the $1,500 a month she wants?

Roger: Yes. Absolutely. I would guarantee it.

Annie: And, tell me, what if we sell the house and pay off the debts and you *cannot* pay me the support?

Roger: Then I would understand if you wanted to leave the country. It would be very painful for me, but I know that you need that much money to live all right.

Mediator: And what else do you want, Roger? Is there anything you haven't mentioned that is a priority?

Roger: If there is any money left over after the town house is sold and the debts paid off, I'd like some of the money as a reserve so I can pay support even if I've had a bad month.

Mediator: What is it like for you to hear this, Annie?

Annie: I get furious.

Mediator: How come?

Annie: [Crying] I just can't believe this. That the one thing I have he asks me to give up.

Mediator: That brings up the pain of all of your disappointments about your marriage and your life now.

Annie: Yes. And you did this, Roger. It's your fault. That stupid Beaujolais nouveau. You lost that money, and now, look, I lose everything.

Mediator: So you see that as all his responsibility?

Annie: Yes. At least most of it. There were some things I agreed with that didn't work out.

Roger: And you liked spending the money, too.

Mediator: So both of you have some responsibility for where it ended up?

Annie: Some, but it's mainly his.

Mediator: The main question here is the house, right?

Annie: Yeah.

Mediator: [To Annie] Suppose you were a judge who was out to do justice to this whole family and come up with a fair, workable solution. What would you do?

Annie: I don't know. I guess we have to sell the town house. [Starts to sob.]

Mediator: And you, Roger?

Roger: I would like to be able to save the house, too, but we just can't afford to do it.

Mediator: So it's painful for you, too, to think of losing the town house?

Roger: Yes. I never thought it would come to this, either.

Mediator: So you both feel the same pain and disappointment.

Annie: [To Roger] I never realized that you felt that way, too. It helps a little to know that. But you, Mr. Mediator, where is your great solution? You said you'd come up with solutions. How about it?

Mediator: It looks to me like selling the house may be the only realistic thing to do. You're already a month behind in your mortgage payments. Your income is less than your monthly debt payments. Unless there's a source of money out there from a friend or your parents or somebody else to bail you out, it looks like the sooner you sell it, the better off you'll be. So I don't have any brilliant solutions. What I'm afraid of is that the more time you lose in selling the house, the less money you'll have, because the debts increase every month. And you'll have some taxes to pay on the sale from any profit from your purchase price, too, unless you can reinvest in another house within a couple of years. But the house hasn't appreciated much, so that doesn't look like a major problem.

Annie: Well, I'm disappointed in you.

Mediator: I'm sorry that I can't do more. Sometimes it's better to cut your losses and move on to something else than to hold on to something that's going down the tubes. In some way, you already made that decision about the marriage. Maybe that's the decision you need to make about your home, too.

Roger: For me, as painful as it is, it's a relief now to think about doing it.

Mediator: Do you feel any relief, Annie, along with the disappointment?

Annie: [Angry] No, not really. I wish you would have come up with something better.

Mediator: Now I think I know what it feels like to be Roger.

Annie: What do you mean?

Mediator: You're disappointed in me. And you show it with a very powerful anger. What that does is to make me want to do something to make you feel better or not be so angry. You have a very powerful way of registering your disappointment.

Annie: I don't know what else to do with it. [Starts to cry] I'm not really angry with you, but I wanted you to jump in and save us.

Mediator: I appreciate your saying that. What's it like for you, Roger, to watch this?

Roger: I'm glad to see someone else taking the heat besides me.

Mediator: And Annie, what's this like for you?

Annie: I never realized I appear so powerful. I feel so weak and frustrated inside.

Roger: Join the club. [They both laugh.]

Shortly thereafter, Annie and Roger reached an agreement that called for them to sell the town house immediately, using the proceeds to pay the debts and splitting any money left over. They also agreed that until the town house was sold, Roger would continue to pay the mortgage and then would pay half of his net income as support until his income stabilized, at which point they would agree upon a specific amount. And they worked out a co-parenting arrangement for the twins that took advantage of the flexibility in Roger's schedule to give him a chance to spend more time with them. They also agreed that if Annie ever decided to move they would meet again and try to work out together how that would affect their co-parenting. And if they couldn't resolve that matter between themselves, they would come back to mediation.

As it turned out, what had appeared to be a deadlocked conflict between them was more of an internal conflict within Annie— she couldn't get herself to let go of her home. In order to see that her deepest desire was unrealistic, Annie had to confront her bitterness and frustration. She also learned to distinguish between more and less valuable uses of her anger, and that it could be a powerful tool when separated from the blame that often accompanied it. And Roger learned the importance of being able to assert himself, especially when faced with a difficult situation.

For me, I must admit I felt a pang of regret at letting go of the chance to be the great savior they had hoped I would be. These two needed me to hold the ground of reality and help them move toward accepting the situation as it was, not as they wanted it to be. And in the end, Annie and I both got over her disappointment with me, as I hoped she might someday be able to do with Roger. But that would take time. At any rate, although Annie and Roger didn't leave mediation on a cloud, it did feel to me that they both left knowing that the ground they were walking on was solid. That would have to be enough for them and for me.

IF I'M NOT YOURS, WHO AM I?

SUMMARY

After twenty years of marriage, Dennis abruptly decides he wants out. Mimi, in shock, is unable to conceive of any other life than that of Dennis's wife. When the parties in mediation have such sharply divergent views of the separation—one desperately wanting it, one desperately opposing it—the decisions made are often far from solid. In this case, I try to help Mimi understand the value of an individual identity. As I help her see the future, she gradually realizes how unforeseen changes in her circumstances and attitude could make her regret decisions made before she is sufficiently adjusted to the separation.

*I*n our first meeting, when I asked Mimi and Dennis whether they were still living together, they answered simultaneously. Mimi said yes and Dennis said no. In the beginning, he did most of the talking. Several months before, after twenty years together, he had announced to Mimi that he was bored with the marriage and it was over. Mimi had attributed this decision to a midlife crisis and tried to ignore what he said, figuring that with time the crisis would pass. She was unwilling to consider the marriage over. Classmates in high school, she and Dennis had become sweethearts in their senior year and were married at twenty. Since then, Mimi had defined herself as Dennis's wife. When their son, Jeffrey, was born, Mimi happily broadened her life purpose to include being Jeffrey's mother. He was now fourteen years old.

Until the moment of Dennis's announcement, Mimi had considered her life to be idyllic. Over the years, she had fixed up their home with care and flair. With her loom, sewing machine and paintbrush, she had decorated the apartment and dressed the family. Equal creativity went into the cooking and gardening. At first she had succeeded in ignoring his announcement, but after a while he repeated it. She pleaded with him to tell her how he wanted her to change to make the marriage work. She was willing to try anything. The problem was that Dennis wanted her to become less dependent on him, both financially and emotionally. She countered that he was betraying their original understanding—they had opted for a traditional marriage, with Dennis as the sole breadwinner and Mimi as the wife and mom. With only a high school education, Mimi quickly became discouraged in what Dennis called a "half-hearted" job search, and gave up.

Dennis agreed that he was changing their understanding, but felt he had no other choice—he was stifled, he said. Then he announced that he had fallen in love with another woman. In her despair, Mimi began therapy. During the several months before I met her, Mimi's feelings about the marriage hadn't changed, but she had discovered in therapy that no matter what happened, she would be able to go on living.

The two did not make a striking couple. Mimi's movements were slow, her body heavy and low to the ground, but her dark eyes were warm and alive and her mouth determined. Dennis was a slight, unathletic-looking man with black strands of hair swept over his balding pate. His style was conservative—he wore the same clothes at every session—and he looked like a man whose life had been the same for a long time. I was surprised to learn of the "other woman." Dennis's manner was gruff. He rarely smiled, and he snapped at Mimi regularly, as if she were an annoying child pulling at his pants leg.

The two of them owned a town house containing two apartments and a converted garage. After Dennis announced he was seeing someone else, he had moved out of their apartment into the other apartment upstairs. Mimi had gone to a lawyer known for his litigious nature who had promised her that he would get her the whole town house and a lot more. When Dennis heard about Mimi's lawyer, Dennis went to see an equally tough litigator who had locked horns many times in other cases with Mimi's lawyer. During their meeting, Dennis's lawyer had predicted that it would cost $75,000 for the two of them to go at it, and mentioned mediation as an alternative. Dennis jumped at the idea.

Mimi was ambivalent about mediation. On the one hand, she wanted Dennis back and was pretty sure that the lawyers would destroy any chance of that. At the same time, though, while a less adversarial approach might give them a chance to stay together, she considered herself no match for Dennis in respect to verbal skills, ability to think on her feet, or knowledge of finances. She was completely ignorant of the family finances and had no idea of how to go about educating herself. She had never earned any money in her life; she hadn't needed to. Mediation, with its emphasis on informed negotiation, seemed every bit as threatening to her as litigation, and I didn't feel I could reassure her into feeling any differently.

Mediator: [To Mimi] If you want to reach a financial separation agreement, there's a lot you're going to have to learn. At a minimum, you'll need to know how much money it costs you and your child to live; familiarize yourself with the assets you own and any debts that you have; and be able to formulate your future plans for yourself and your child. But that will be true whether you hire lawyers to negotiate for you or mediate.

Dennis: I'm absolutely delighted that Mimi can go through that learning process here. I don't need to be here for it, though. As a matter of fact, I'd have no objection if you acted as her lawyer and negotiated with me.

Mediator: No, I'm not willing to act in that capacity. And normally I don't meet separately with people in mediation, because the process works better when you work together. So mediation would require some patience on your part, Dennis, and your active participation in the learning process for Mimi.

Dennis: Let's get on with it then.

Mediator: I'd like to know what Mimi's reactions to this are first.

Dennis: Look, it doesn't make sense for us to leave it to the lawyers.

Mediator: I understand that's your point of view. But I'd also like to hear Mimi's.

Dennis: I speak for both of us.

Mediator: Not here you don't, and not if you want a separation.

Mimi: I'm willing to mediate if Dennis considers it the best way for us to go.

Mediator: Do you have any thoughts about this, separate from his?

Mimi: [After a long pause] Well, of course, I'm scared. I'm afraid that Dennis will take advantage of me. He's so angry with me so much of the time.

Mediator: What can he or I do that would make this go better for you?

Mimi: I need him to be patient as you said. I move slowly.

Dennis: That's why I suggested separate meetings with her. She's right. I am impatient. I want to get this over with.

Mediator: Then perhaps there's another alternative. Maybe you can both find a lawyer who would act as Mimi's lawyer and have that lawyer negotiate directly with you, Dennis. Then you two wouldn't have to meet together at all. Having the lawyer deal directly with you might give Mimi the protection you both think she might need.

Dennis: No, we might as well go ahead with this. I'll try to be patient.

Mediator: How about you, Mimi?

Mimi: I'm willing to go along with Dennis.

Mediator: That could become a major problem.

Mimi: What do you mean?

Mediator: I want you to be willing to disagree with him and make up your own mind about what you want to do. If you don't, you'll just be rubber-stamping what he wants, and I think you'll be unhappy in the long run.

I was very concerned about the degree of Mimi's dependence on Dennis. What was it all about? It seemed that no matter what was behind it, it would be a critical issue in deciding whether mediation would be appropriate. If Mimi was attempting to lure Dennis back by cooperating with him, she would never focus on her life independent of him. She needed to accept the fact of separation and its implications for her. She had already taken a significant step by seeking out a therapist and recognizing that she was going to survive whatever happened. But there were still more preconditions to a successful mediation. In the near future, she would need to decide:

- what living arrangement suited her
- what co-parenting arrangements would work best for her and their son
- how much support she would need.

But was mediation the appropriate way to go? It seemed to me it might be easier for both of them if they had their own lawyers. Then Mimi wouldn't have to deal directly with Dennis's bullying impatience and she would be able to gain some distance from him—that is, if she wanted distance. Although clearly disheartened by the recent events and distraught by Dennis's continual snapping, Mimi actually seemed to enjoy being in his presence. Did she really think the marriage could still be saved? Was she right? If she hung in for long enough, would he come around? I wondered: Was that a bad reason to mediate?

From my point of view, despite Mimi's poor self-image, she was in better shape than Dennis in many ways. Her outlook on life was optimistic; his was pessimistic. That had probably always been true and probably always would be. But her whole adult life had been spent within a reality defined by Dennis. She seemed to have no sense of herself as an autonomous individual.

The apparent imbalance between these two brought me face to face with my own strong feelings about marriage and divorce. Having gone through a divorce and married again, I am strongly convinced that having one spouse emotionally dependent on the other is unhealthy for both partners. The most successful marriages I know are partnerships of independent people who enjoy sharing their lives together while maintaining their own identities. Mimi's dependence seemed antithetical to both making her marriage work and going through a divorce. Even if she and Dennis were to get back together, I saw it as desirable for her to become more independent. Clearly Dennis wanted more autonomy himself. Paradoxically, if Mimi could let go of her dependence on him, perhaps the marriage would work. And if it didn't, then the same solution would allow her to handle her life without him.

Though this idea made sense for me, I wasn't sure whether it was right for Mimi. And what did I mean by autonomy? Did it comprise financial independence, separate friendships, and decisiveness with the child, or was it a bigger thing, a less definable but more general sense of how one sees oneself in the world? If I subscribed to the larger sense of the word, did autonomy really make sense for Mimi? Maybe, for *her*, dependence upon Dennis was actually healthy. Could I say she was wrong to try to save her marriage, whatever I thought of it? Perhaps the dependence was simply a strategy to save the marriage.

If that were the case, the strategy didn't seem to be working. Dennis was explicit in expressing his desire for a wife with a life of her own, someone he didn't have to feel so responsible for. Ultimately, then, it wasn't just a question of my own idea of a healthy marriage. Dennis wanted a divorce, so whether Mimi liked it or not, she was going to have to learn to be independent. Would mediation help her do that? Probably, if she were truly willing to change her life.

I didn't want to impose my ideas about independence on Mimi. It was hard enough for her that one of the men in the room seemed intent on forcing her to do that. What I could provide was support for her growing sense of self. I wanted to offer that without fostering her emotional dependence and becoming a replacement for Dennis. I needed to help her assess her decisions, understand their implications, and form her own independent opinions, even when Dennis opposed them. But in doing that I had to be careful not to cross the line and become her advocate against Dennis.

Mimi's independence would probably serve not only her own interests but Dennis's as well. Soon we would need to discuss Mimi's ideas about earning her livelihood, and I knew that Dennis's impatience and her low self-esteem would add great pressure to the situation. I could also see that, strategically speaking, if Dennis could back off during the short run and give Mimi the room to become strong, he'd be better off in the long run.

All told, mediation seemed an inferior choice for Dennis and Mimi, not necessarily unworkable but probably not as well suited to their needs as negotiation through lawyers. Lawyers would be able to come up with a temporary agreement that would give Mimi time to come to terms with the situation. The trouble was, both were deeply distrustful of lawyers and subscribed to the stereotype of the greedy shyster who creates fights and problems where none existed before. I knew of lawyers who could handle their situation with compassion and a minimum of hassle, but Mimi and Dennis were dead set against the idea. To them it felt far safer to continue the relationship the three of us had developed than to plunge back into the unknown again.

AN
INTERIM SOLUTION

*N*ow the challenge was to see if Mimi could separate herself from Dennis to the point where she could make her own decisions. Some short-term decisions had to be made right away—above all, how much Dennis would pay, at least temporarily, until Mimi got on her feet.

Though Dennis had moved upstairs, he had continued to pay the mortgage, taxes, and insurance on all of their property. This consisted of the two apartments and the converted garage, which they were renting out, as well as Mimi's car insurance, health insurance for the family, Mimi's therapy bills, and an additional $1,200 per month for her and Jeffrey's living expenses.

Since Mimi was not working and had no immediate prospects, she clearly needed to continue receiving this kind of help from Dennis. He earned $50,000 per year from his middle-management job in a large printing company and received rent on the garage unit, so he could afford to pay support. But he was concerned not so much with the amount of support but its duration. He wanted to know when Mimi would go to work and earn some money of her own.

> *Dennis:* Can she get away with this, not working while I work my ass off and have to fully support her?
>
> *Mimi:* It's enough for me right now to just keep my life together and take care of Jeffrey.
>
> *Dennis:* But he's with *me* half of the time.
>
> *Mimi:* That's because that's what you want. I'm willing to take him full-time.
>
> *Dennis:* And he's in school most of the day. Why don't you get off my back and get a job?
>
> *Mimi:* I'm not ready for that. Anyway, you were the one who insisted that I not work, so I have no education. You're the one who's changing our arrangement.
>
> *Dennis:* All right. I'll carry you on my back as I've always done, but if you don't get a job within a few months, then I'm going to be very angry.

It was clear to all of us that Mimi wasn't ready to give up her dependence. It was Dennis who was changing the contract, and she wasn't going to let him off the hook. So their interim arrangement seemed workable as long as Mimi was willing to accept Dennis's resentment along with the monthly check.

EX-SPOUSES/NEW NEIGHBORS

*T*he ownership of their properties seemed simple as well. Together, they owned the town house and the garage unit, all worth in excess of $600,000.

> ***Dennis:*** As far as I'm concerned, Mimi can live in the downstairs apartment as long as she wants, but I just want to make sure that ultimately the entire property stays in my family. My parents live next door.

> ***Mimi:*** I *love* the house. I've always known that I would spend the rest of my life there, and the separation doesn't change that one bit.

> ***Mediator:*** That's how you feel now.

> ***Mimi:*** And that's how I'm always going to feel.

> ***Mediator:*** I wish I knew how I was going to feel in the future.

> ***Mimi:*** What do you mean?

> ***Mediator:*** I want to open your thinking to the possibility that your feelings might change. You're going through a big change, from husband and wife to co-parents and neighbors. I'd be surprised if that were easy.

> ***Mimi:*** It certainly has been hard watching that woman parading in and out of the upstairs apartment. And Dennis just strolls into my apartment whenever he wants. I don't like that.

> ***Dennis:*** If you weren't such a snoop, you wouldn't see who comes to my place. But I spend most of my time alone. I like being alone.

Mimi: You flaunt that woman. It's hard for me and it's not terrific for Jeffrey to see her leave in the mornings either.

Dennis: I don't flaunt her, for God's sake. You spy! But as for my strolling into your apartment, it's still my house as much as it is yours.

Mediator: Do you want to be able to enter the downstairs apartment whenever you want?

Dennis: No, but you have to understand. The apartment downstairs is much bigger than the one upstairs. I'm living in about half of the living space that Mimi has, with no room for storage. I have to be able to store my tools. And I have to store some other things there, too, at least until I can expand the apartment upstairs.

Mediator: This discussion began with my asking you to consider the ramifications of becoming neighbors. If I were either of you, I would find your situation confusing. It's hard enough to work out a separation without the complications of being neighbors.

Dennis: It sounds to me as if you don't want us to be neighbors.

Dennis was right. I was uncomfortable with their proximity. Three things bothered me:

1. I was worried that with Dennis living upstairs, Mimi could maintain an illusion that nothing had changed and that he would eventually move home.

2. But I was even more concerned that she assumed her feelings about the house *and* Dennis would never change. I could see the danger that she might lock herself into an arrangement that would make it very difficult for her to act if her feelings *did* change.

3. My third reservation was equally troubling: Did Dennis's move so close to home mean that perhaps the dependence was mutual? Maybe Mimi wasn't the only one that hadn't yet accepted the separation. Dennis seemed genuinely delighted to learn that Mimi wanted to remain in the downstairs apartment and his expression as she spoke of "that woman" betrayed more than a little pleasure in knowing that he had stirred her jealousy. Maybe her fantasy was more reality-based than I understood. Perhaps this marriage *wasn't* over. Maybe Dennis *would* come home.

As the mediator, I knew that I was coming on too strongly with my concerns about the present arrangement. They were agreed on it—they both seemed clear that they wanted this. But I wanted to be sure that in the long run Mimi wasn't in for any unnecessary continuing pain. I wanted her to have sufficient flexibility in whatever agreement they reached to make it possible for her not to be penalized if her life changed. To be free of my own concerns about overstepping my bounds, I needed to make my reservations clear to them. Otherwise, I felt, I could slip uncomfortably close to the role of Mimi's advocate. It was a thin line between supporting Mimi in thinking for herself and doing her thinking for her.

> **Mediator:** It's not that I don't want you to be neighbors. I want you to make choices that will work for all three of you. You both seem upset about not having privacy, yet you both want to be living where you are now. For the short run, it's clear that you'll do that. But it makes me nervous when I hear that you assume that you'll both feel the same in the future.

> **Dennis:** I thought that *we* would be deciding things here, not you. We're both committed to living indefinitely as we are, and you don't seem to want to let us do that.

> **Mediator:** Of course, if that's what you both want, that's what you'll do. I just want to be sure that this will make as much sense to you six months from now as it does today.

And I want you both to consider the possibility that your feelings about this may change, particularly if you go ahead with a divorce.

Dennis: Then let's figure out what would happen if either of us wanted to move.

Mediator: How do you feel about that, Mimi?

Mimi: I'm willing to listen.

Mediator: What does *that* mean?

Mimi: I haven't really thought about the long term, but I'm ready to hear what Dennis's thoughts are.

Dennis: Well, *I've* thought about it, and here's what I'd like to do. I want us both to have the right to stay where we are forever. Neither of us can force the other person to leave. But if one of us decides to leave, the other person will have the option to buy out the person leaving. If Mimi leaves, I'll pay her half of the current value of the property minus half of what we now owe on the mortgage. I'd also subtract the real estate commission that would be payable on her half if she sold it, and half of all the mortgage and real estate tax payments made by me between the date of separation and either the date of sale or the date I stop paying Mimi's share of those payments. She would also get credit for half of the rents received.

Mimi: What do you mean?

Dennis: You don't expect my paying your share of the mortgage should be considered a gift to you, do you? Your share is $750 per month after credit for the rents.

Mimi: Then I'll end up with less and less money.

Dennis: But you're never going to leave, so what difference does it make?

Mimi: I guess you're right.

Mediator: [To Mimi] Did you have a different idea about the payments?

Mimi: I thought he was going to take care of me.

Dennis: I am. I just want credit if you ever leave. And I want to be able to use the town house as security so that I can borrow some money to upgrade the top apartment. I've figured out that we can borrow another $50,000 and end up paying only $250 a month more on the mortgage.

Mimi: And you want me to be responsible for paying half of the increase in the debt, too?

Dennis: Only if you ever decide to move.

Now my earlier concern had changed to something approaching alarm. My worst fear was being realized. Mimi seemed willing to agree to terms that would either lock her into the house permanently or force her to accept a substantial reduction in her share of the equity. Such a penalty could perpetuate the inertia that was already a problem in her life. I had seen many people change their minds about staying in a house. Mimi was only forty-one years old. She had a lot of living ahead of her. But even if she did want to stay in the house forever, would she always want Dennis to be her neighbor? And how would she feel, over time, knowing that her only real asset was continually decreasing in value, while the value of the place itself was increasing? Was she still hanging on to a fantasy that they would get back together? Was she focused enough to hear my concerns?

Mediator: Let's take a closer look at this idea. Dennis, tell me what you would get out of such an arrangement.

Dennis: I don't think you like this idea, so maybe you should say more first.

Mediator: What *I* think matters far less than what the two of you think, so it makes more sense for you to tell me what you see in it.

Dennis: I *like* the arrangement. It assures us both that we'll never be forced out of the place, and it keeps the property together. Plus it allows us both to live in places that we know and love. It's a definite plus for Jeffrey to have his parents living close to each other. That way, he can go back and forth freely. And it makes it affordable for one of us to buy the other one out if one of us decides to leave without selling off any of the apartments.

Mediator: But a penalty for the person leaving . . .

Dennis: It can't be helped. Otherwise, if one of us wants to leave, the other one would have to leave, too. And I don't think that's fair.

Mediator: How could Mimi afford to buy you out if you decided to leave right away?

Dennis: I'll tell you one thing I'm sure of. I will *never* want to leave that property, so that is a strictly academic question.

Mediator: So the only real possibility is that Mimi may decide to leave someday?

Mimi: That's not too likely either. But what would I have to do if Dennis left? Could I sell one of the apartments to buy him out?

Dennis: That would probably do it.

Mimi: Then why shouldn't you do the same thing?

Dennis: Because I'm the one who's paying for them, keeping them going. And because I want to keep them together.

Mediator: And that's really your highest priority.

Dennis: Now you're getting it.

Mediator: How do you look at it, Mimi?

Mimi: My problem is that I can't imagine that a day will come when I'll want to leave.

Mediator: I know. To me, your attitude about leaving the house seems pretty similar to the way you probably thought about divorce during your marriage—highly unlikely.

Mimi: Right. And I still don't want a divorce.

Mediator: Is there a part of you that thinks you'll wake up someday and find that all this was just a bad dream and that you'll get back together?

Mimi: Yes, I guess I do think that's still a possibility.

Mediator: [To Dennis] Is it?

Dennis: Anything can happen, but to tell the truth, I don't think that we'll ever get back together.

Mediator: [To Mimi] Do you believe him?

Mimi: [With tears in her eyes] I'm beginning to. I guess I've been thinking that even if we go ahead with a divorce, we might get back together afterward.

Dennis: I doubt it.

Mediator: What's it like to hear that, Mimi?

Mimi: I don't know. It feels a little shocking. I feel sad. I keep wondering what I did wrong.

Dennis: It's not really your fault. It's me. I don't know why, but I just feel something has been missing in my life. It's true I feel angry with you a lot, but it's not because of anything you have done. It's just that I hate having your life depend so much on mine.

Mimi: [To me] What should I do, then?

Mediator: You have several choices. It's clear that you both want to live where you are right now. To have a financial agreement that could serve as the basis for a divorce, it's not necessary that you go any further now. So one choice would be to figure out how to handle the property if and when the time comes that one of you wants to leave. Another possibility is to make a longer-term agreement now so that everything is set out in advance. And a third is to figure out what you feel clear about deciding now, and put off what you don't feel ready to decide.

Dennis: It's unacceptable to me to have no long-term agreement. If we don't cover the bases now, the court could order the property sold if we disagreed about what to do with it.

Mediator: That's true. That's a risk you run now, and if there is no agreement to the contrary, you would run that risk in the future if you couldn't reach an agreement then.

Mimi: But I think we could reach an agreement then. Why not do that, Dennis?

Dennis: Because I want to protect myself against your ability to kick me off the property. It's too important to me.

Mediator: So you want an agreement primarily for your protection?

Dennis: And for the protection of the property—for our son, so he'll always be able to live there.

Mediator: So Dennis wants an agreement now. Then the next question is, what kind of agreement makes sense for you, Mimi. Dennis has figured out what will work for him and—in his view—for Jeffrey. Now you have to decide what would work for you. But to do that you have to assume that you will be getting a divorce and even that the time could come when you might decide you want to move. If the agreement for that feels fair, then you'll be covered no matter what happens. You'd have the decisions even if you never made use of them.

Mimi: But Dennis already knows what he wants.

Mediator: Right. So we'd have to come up with something that works for both of you.

Dennis: We either have an agreement or we have no agreement.

Mediator: You need an agreement that creates enough predictability to satisfy you and enough flexibility to satisfy Mimi.

Dennis: I'd like to see that.

Mediator: That's what we'd have to find. But first we need Mimi to get clear about what she thinks is right.

A TRAUMATIC CATALYST

*M*imi came to the next session very upset. She described a traumatic event that had occurred the previous weekend. A man she had recently met in a church group stopped by to see her while she and Jeffrey were out doing errands and Dennis had come down to her apartment "to get some tools." When he saw her friend he decided the man must be an intruder and insisted that he leave, threatening to call the sheriff if he wouldn't. Mimi had arrived at the end of what had almost become a fistfight and had yelled at Dennis for the first time in her life. Jeffrey had seen the whole thing and had sided with his mother.

I was almost as shocked by the story as Mimi had been by the event. Until this moment, I had had no inkling that Mimi had any male friends, much less a possible boyfriend. While she was clearly upset, there were unmistakable signs of strength now visible in her that I had not seen before. Were these new or had I misjudged her all along?

Dennis looked different, too. While he still maintained his aggressive posture, he also looked somewhat panicky, as if some deep, invisible support had suddenly deserted him. What had this event stirred up in him? In telling his version of the events, though he defended himself, from my perspective he was acknowledging the discovery of feelings of jealousy that he hadn't known existed.

Mediator: Dennis, tell me what you think is significant about what happened last weekend.

Dennis: I didn't have any idea that he was someone Mimi knew.

Mimi: You did too! I don't think you have a right to decide who can visit me.

Dennis: I was just trying to protect you.

Mediator: From what?

Dennis: I don't know. I thought he might be robbing the house.

Mediator: Really?

Dennis: [Heaving a sigh] No. I guess I just got angry that she might become involved with someone.

Mediator: How would you like it to be?

Dennis: [Looking at Mimi] I don't want you to be my wife

anymore. But it's hard thinking of you being with someone else.

Mediator: What's it like for you to hear that, Mimi?

Mimi: It feels good to finally hear the truth. I hope you can appreciate now how hard it's been for me to watch the parade of bimbos going in and out of your place.

Dennis: Who told you to watch?

Mediator: Dennis, you're missing what she's saying.

Dennis: Then tell me.

Mediator: It seems to me that you each find it hard for the other to become involved with someone new.

Dennis: I think that's only natural.

Mediator: For some people. The question it raises for me is, how will it be for you to be neighbors?

Mimi: I still think that it can work out, but I need to have an understanding with Dennis about his coming on my property. I will not allow him to come to my apartment without phoning first and getting permission.

Dennis: Except for my tools and to pick the roses in the backyard.

Mimi: What do you mean, pick the roses? They're part of *my* property.

Dennis: Who do you think did all the work to make those roses grow—the pruning, the fertilizing, the watering?

Mimi: But you're talking about my backyard. I'll have no privacy.

Dennis: I'm not about to give up all the work I've done just for your privacy.

Mimi: I can't stand your intrusiveness.

Dennis: Well, I can't stand your freeloading.

Mediator: I think we'll be able to work out this difficulty. But I want you to know that I'd be very surprised if you both stay in the town house for a long time. It would take a lot of work and cooperation to make it work for all of you, particularly when new romantic partners enter your lives.

Dennis: That's exactly why we have a buy-out agreement.

Mediator: And do you both feel settled with it?

Mimi: I guess so. But I am concerned that as the value of the property goes up, I won't get more if I move. That seems wrong.

Dennis: But I don't ever want to be in a position of not being able to buy you out.

Mediator: Is that your only concern?

Dennis: Sure, because the value of the property is going to increase faster than my earnings.

Mediator: If that's your only concern, there are other arrangements that would still allow Mimi to get her fair share.

Dennis: Like what?

Mediator: For example, if you agreed that the buy-out didn't have to be all in cash, you could work out terms for your payments that were affordable.

Dennis: But I'd still have to come up with the money someday.

Mediator: Yes.

Dennis: So that stinks.

Mimi: Why shouldn't I be able to get my money out?

Dennis: Because it'll strap me.

Mimi: But if we work it out to make it affordable for you, what's the problem?

Dennis: The problem is I never should have married you in the first place.

Mimi: [Crying] Why do you have to be so mean?

Mediator: This must be awful for both of you.

Dennis: [Eyes brimming] It *is* awful. I don't like being so difficult, but I don't know how else to deal with it. What do you suggest we do?

Mediator: I can see that you're really struggling, Dennis. Most of what you say comes out as bitter or angry, but you don't show your confusion or your pain. What is this like for you, Mimi?

Mimi: I hate it that he's so angry at me all the time.

Mediator: It seemed like *you* were angry too for a minute there, when he tried to throw your friend off the property.

Mimi: I was. It's the first time I've ever really let him know how angry I was.

Mediator: And how do you feel about having done that?

Mimi: I feel stronger. Not that I want to do it again, but if he ever tries to pull a trick like that again, I won't hesitate to let him have it.

Dennis: But not in front of Jeffrey.

Mimi: I'll try not to, but you better not try to push me around, Dennis.

Mediator: Where do you stand, Mimi, on the issue of having an agreement about either of you moving?

Mimi: I'm not ready to enter into any agreement about the long-term decisions about the property.

Dennis: What?

Mimi: Look, I'm not necessarily opposed to the terms you want, Dennis, but I'm not ready to agree to them now. First we have to work out a better relationship as neighbors.

Dennis: Sure, but I'll bet you still want to hold to the support agreement.

Mimi: Yes, I do, but when the time comes, I'll be willing to work out a long-term support agreement.

Dennis: I'm *furious.* I feel like I'm being manipulated.

Mediator: Because this is not going the way you wanted.

Dennis: And as usual, she isn't taking me into consideration.

Mimi: I think one of my problems is that I *always* took you into consideration and I didn't take care of myself. But if we're going to get a divorce, then I'm going to *have* to take care of myself.

Mediator: [To Dennis] That's good news for you.

Dennis: So what can we do?

Mediator: As I've said, you're trying to do a hard thing, changing your relationship from husband and wife to co-parents and, on top of that, neighbors. I think it's important for you to try to find some way of working together effectively. The beginning of that seems to have taken place. Dennis, you want Mimi to be more independent of you. And that's happening. She is willing to say no to you now and not just defer to what you want. I suggest that we finish off a temporary support agreement and clarify your decisions on all Jeffrey-related matters and all the details of your relationship as neighbors. Then see how that goes for a little while before trying to work out a long-term agreement on support and property.

Mimi: That's all right with me.

Mediator: How about you, Dennis?

Dennis: Do I have a choice?

Mediator: Sure. You can always go to lawyers or try to change Mimi's mind. Or you can try to be patient and let Mimi catch up with you in experiencing the separation and the reality of a divorce.

Mimi still seemed to be relatively shaky, but she had taken a big step forward. The feelings of power that had come from her anger had allowed her to differentiate herself a bit from Dennis, and she had glimpsed the possibility that she might not want to stay in the town house forever. I was pleased, even though we were clearly further from a permanent agreement than when they came in the door. Again I had to ask myself whether my focus on Mimi's independence was consistent with her desires. I still wasn't sure whether she was becoming more assertive because it made sense to her, or because she knew *I* considered it so important.

If she had decided to agree to the buy-out of the property on Dennis's terms, I would have been unwilling to accept that agreement and put it into writing—not simply because it would have been a result of Dennis's coercion, but because it would not have reflected Mimi's own independent judgment. The agreement Dennis wanted offended my basic sense of fairness, and I was relieved when Mimi refused to go along with it. That refusal *did* seem to be an independent judgment, and as such represented a very big step forward—for all three of them.

It was probable though, that I had permanently alienated

Dennis and that he would not come back to mediation. While I felt a basic empathy for his situation, particularly when I could see his pain and confusion, I didn't feel that he was ready to accord Mimi sufficient respect to enable them to reach a mutually agreeable solution. Although he remained steadfast in his desire for a divorce, the ambiguous incident with Mimi's friend had stirred feelings of emotional attachment that he had not been aware of.

Mimi wrote me a letter about a year later, saying that she was working in a yarn store, had fallen in love, and was planning to be married when her divorce came through. "You won't be surprised to learn that Bob doesn't much like the idea of being neighbors with Dennis, so Dennis and I are now in the process of negotiating a buy-out. We are doing much better, and Jeffrey seems to be very relieved at the idea of my moving. He says it will be less confusing to him. He hadn't said anything like that before. I guess he inherited some of my timidity. Dennis is doing much better, too, and doesn't pick the roses anymore. I am glad we tried to mediate, because I do feel as if I'm in control of my life now, but I am leaving the negotiations of the buy-out to Bob, who seems to be able to deal with Dennis reasonably well."

That last line concerned me, but reminded me too that my role was to facilitate an agreement that all three of us could live with. Although I wasn't sure that Mimi was serving her own interests well by handing over the negotiations to Bob, I had never expected her to become a monolith of independence and I was delighted that she was happy. I was also pleased that the decision to delay had worked well.

THE DEEP POCKET STRIKES BACK

SUMMARY

*H*ere I come face to face with my own subjective responses to my clients' attitudes and decisions which, unless checked, have the potential to destroy the necessary trust between us. My judgment of Eric not only wounds him but shows how thin is the line that separates neutrality, the mediator's proper stance, from the advocacy of one client over another, a stance that is guaranteed to sabotage the process. In this case I struggle to prevent my personal feelings from intruding on the mediation. I also analyze my own attitude toward the law, noting how my subjectivity can skew my legal predictions.

*E*ric and Becky came to me with the expectation that I would work magic for them. They had both heard about me from several sources who had recommended me highly, and they were sold on me and the mediation process before we ever met. So optimistic were they about mediation, they'd had lunch together before their appointment and arrived looking more like newlyweds than people dealing with a separation. Although Eric was in his early forties and Becky in her mid-thirties, they both looked much younger. They were a classic "California couple": blond, tan, trim, well scrubbed, and stylishly but comfortably dressed. Everything about them seemed fresh, but the atmosphere they created quickly became heavy as we began to surface their differences.

Eric immediately made it very clear that he did not want a separation. He felt that by continuing the couples counseling they had been in for the past year, they would be able to resolve their problems and strengthen the marriage. But Becky was very sure about needing a separation in order to get some distance and perspective on their situation. She was not entirely closed to the possibility that the marriage could still work, but she felt that a separation would help provide her with the clarity she needed to know how to proceed. She also wanted a financial agreement to establish her independence, since—from her perspective—what was wrong with the marriage was that she often felt lost and overwhelmed by Eric.

Becky, for years a production manager for a small toy manufacturer, had decided several years ago to change careers for something more creative. A few years after the birth of their daughter, Karen, now age seven, she had begun the process of trying to become a fashion consultant. Her ambitions were spurred by her desire to break her dependence on Eric—at least emotionally. She felt that because her work was only "a job," too much of her identity was wrapped up in her roles as mother and wife, and she envied Eric's personal investment in his work as a photographer. He was both personally and professionally committed to his own emotional and creative growth. He had been in therapy often since college. He seemed very vulnerable and throughout the first session cried easily and often. He felt sexually rejected by Becky but unabashedly said he would do whatever was necessary to make the marriage work. Given this emotional openness, I was very surprised to see him close down tightly when the discussion turned to finances and all but refuse to disclose the specifics of his situation. He spoke slowly and very carefully.

Eric: My father died eight years ago and left me a substantial amount of money. As I understand the law, that is my separate property and Becky has no legal right to any of it. If I'm right about that, then we don't need to get into the specifics.

Mediator: Yes, we do. You're right about the inheritance —if you've inherited property and you've kept it separate and in your name, Becky has no legal right to any of it. But that doesn't mean it's not relevant to your agreement. For your own protection, the agreement has to identify and describe those assets and determine what's going to happen to them. Otherwise it is possible that Becky could challenge your exclusive right to them at a later date. Second, and from my perspective more important, my willingness to mediate is conditional on your complete disclosure. I don't believe that either of you could even recognize a fair agreement without knowing the whole story. And finally, in order to work out an arrangement for the support of the family, we would need to know not only how much those assets are worth, but also how much income they produce. Even though the income legally belongs to you, a judge would consider it relevant in determining the level of support.

Eric: Well, I don't like that. The inheritance is mine. It's always been mine and it's gonna stay mine.

Becky: That's one of the reasons I want a separation.

Nothing that I know of is just *mine*. Everything seems to be either *yours* or *ours*.

Eric: The fact is, *never* have I been able to figure out how to deal with this inheritance. It's always caused problems between us, and that's why I've kept it out of our discussions. I guess the best thing to do is simply rely on the law.

Mediator: You might find the law helpful. In order for me to help you understand it, you'll have to provide us with all of the information. But if either of you felt that the law was unfair, I certainly wouldn't want our discussions to stop there.

Eric: Okay. If I have to give you the information to find out the law, so be it. As far as I'm concerned, if something is clearly the law, then it's fair.

Mediator: You have a lot more faith in the law than I do. What's your reaction to this, Becky?

Becky: I just want to do what's right. I don't have a particular feeling about the law. If it feels right, then I suppose I'll want to follow it. My biggest worry is that Eric can sometimes outtalk me and it's hard to disagree with him.

Mediator: In that case, you might find the law to be a useful check on what is going on. But both of you ought to realize that the law is not always as clear as you might think. I'll do the best I can to tell you what a court would do, but you will need to measure that information against your own sense of what's fair. If you can use the law to understand *that*, then it will be helpful.

FAIRNESS AND THE ROLE OF THE LAW

*I*t's no simple task to use the law to help a couple articulate their own sense of fairness. The ways people decide what is right vary a great deal from person to person. In this case, Eric and Becky had each staked out a different use for the law. At least for now, Eric seemed to imagine the law to be clear and impersonal and thus fair. I assumed he felt that way because he thought he knew enough about the law of community and separate property to be certain it would preserve for him all of his father's inheritance—it's easy to believe the law fair when it supports your position. But what would happen to Eric if we got into an area where the law did not cut in his favor? Would he still consider the law fair, even if it conflicted with his personal values?

With Becky, the question was quite different. She insisted she was afraid that Eric's persuasive powers could be so strong she might give up what she thought was right. Although I hadn't seen any indication that this was the case, if it were, the law might be helpful to her, but it could also boomerang. If the law supported her position, she would be bolstered by the knowledge that she could fall back on principles established by the courts. However, if the law favored Eric and ruled against her, it seemed that trying to convince him to depart from it would be practically useless.

As I saw it, my job was to try to move the focus from the law to their own internal sense of justice. The ensuing discussion might be difficult, but I saw that I had to find a way for it to take place. I also had to be careful not to use the law to become the advocate for either of them. Finally, I needed to add my own sense of fairness to the mixture. What complicated this for me was that I was finding myself irritated with Eric. In addition to seeming naively attached to the law, he seemed stingy. He professed to want Becky back, but he was unwilling to be generous with her. Not only was he creating a problem with Becky, but with me as well. The result would be a complex field of possible influences and potential resolutions.

A month later, they returned. In our second session, as we got into the issues, they reported that Becky and Karen had moved to an apartment for which Becky was paying rent of $800 per month.

But over the question of support they had come to a grinding halt. Becky wanted $2,500 per month for the next three years (if they did not reconcile within that time), and after that, child support only, at $750 per month. Eric's earnings were around $3,500 per month before taxes; his income from his inherited property was an additional $6,500 per month. Becky's before-tax income was about $1,000 per month.

> *Eric:* What would a court do?
>
> *Mediator:* A judge would probably look at how much income you each have from your work, how much you have from the inheritance, and how much time you agreed to spend with Karen, and use a formula based on that to determine a temporary support payment. I can run those figures through a computer program to give you a pretty accurate application of the formula and its results.
>
> *Eric:* Suppose I gave away my inheritance?
>
> *Mediator:* If you didn't have your inheritance and the court was convinced that it was not subterfuge to get out of paying support, then the formula would be based on your incomes and the time that Karen spends with each of you.
>
> *Eric:* Would a judge take into account the fact that Becky could get a production job right now earning at least $25,000 a year?
>
> *Mediator:* Probably not for the purposes of making a temporary order, but for the long run, yes, that could be

considered, although it's possible that it wouldn't be, since Becky has changed her occupation.

Becky: Eric, you're just trying to pay me as little as you can. You are such a cheap son of a bitch. [Bursts into tears.]

Eric: Look, I've gone over what we have spent for the past four years. Becky, if you live like that, you don't need more than $1,500 a month from me.

Becky: I need $2,500. We've gone over my budget. You can afford it and I need it.

Eric: Would she get $2,500 from a judge?

Mediator: I can give you a more precise answer if you like, but I think I can safely say that she would get more than that.

Eric: That's outrageous. Why would a court order me to do that? *She's* the one who wants out, and if she needs more money, she can go back to her old work. That doesn't seem right.

Mediator: I never said it was right. As a matter of fact, I think it was *you* who said that if it was the law, it was fair. The law has no more and no less power here than what the two of you decide it should. A judge wouldn't take into consideration who is leaving whom in deciding support. The law would simply recognize you as the deep pocket, the one who can afford to pay Becky as much as she needs. I'm quite certain you'd have to pay more than $2,500 if you left it to a judge.

The session ended shortly thereafter with Eric obviously very upset. I was concerned that perhaps I had been too heavy-handed with him in my zeal to break his dependence on the law as the repository of all fairness. Although my experience had taught me that the law is often at odds with what a good many people believe to be fair, I knew that realizing this could come as a shock. Eric had been surprised, even devastated, but his new knowledge of how the law would operate might release him from his attachment to it.

Eric had shifted in attitude toward the law, but how we would move forward was still unclear. How would Becky react to the fact that with respect to the issue of support, the law was on her side? Would she continue to operate as if the law were insignificant or would she now move into Eric's old position, invoking the law to win her point, now that it was so clear that it cut in her favor?

In my own mind, the central question was not what the law was, but rather a combination of Becky's sense of fairness, her stated need, and the practical economic reality she faced. It seemed fairly clear to me that Becky needed at least $2,500 per month to be able to live at anywhere close to the level she enjoyed when she and Eric were together. Her budget showed that after paying taxes, rent, and child care costs, she would have only $800 a month to cover discretionary expenses, including food for her and Karen.

CALLED ON THE CARPET

*T*he next session began with Eric appearing very sad and solemn.

> **Eric:** I almost decided not to come back here. I was deeply hurt by what you [looking at me] did last session. I felt that you allowed yourself to be manipulated by Becky against me because of her tears. That's what she did with our therapist and now she's done it with you. When you said that I was the "deep pocket," I couldn't believe it. I asked you for an impartial view of what a court would do.

Instead, I felt as if you were rubbing my nose in my ability to pay. I spoke with my lawyer after the session and he said you were probably right about what a court would do, but that it *was* possible you were wrong. He said I might not have to pay so much support, particularly if I could establish that for the last four years all three of us had been living on a little more than what Becky wants for support. He said a judge might also take into consideration the fact that Becky could be earning more money now. So at the very least, you overstated the situation, and when I told the lawyer you called me the "deep pocket," he was incredulous. I feel doubly hurt by you because I trusted you, and I feel betrayed.

I was very uncomfortable. I could feel my face flush. Eric clearly felt hurt, and he was accusing me of bias. My first impulse was to defend myself, to explain that I had only been describing how a judge would see Eric and that I hadn't meant anything more by the term "deep pocket."

But I also knew that he was right. He felt stung by a judgment I had made about him—that he was being stingy. This judgment put up a wall between us, and he had felt it. Usually when I make judgments about a person in mediation, I notice it first and try to take the wall down so it doesn't get in the way of our working together. It is important that I remain neutral and that the parties perceive me as so. Eric had caught me off guard. He'd sensed my disapproval and I had to do something about it. But what could I do? I thought of trying to convince him that he was wrong but knew that would be compounding the felony. I had to first understand what was happening inside me. Then I needed to see if I could repair the damage I had done to his trust in me. Stinginess on the part of others often makes me angry. The righteousness that accompanies the anger is justifiable. I think the world would be a better place if people dealt with each other generously. But there is another source of the anger, and that is my unfinished business with myself about my own struggle to be generous. Once I acknowledged that, I could try to understand Eric from a position of compassion and not condemnation.

I knew I should sit with the deep feeling I was experiencing before I started to act on it, so I remained silent for what seemed to be an interminable period of time but was probably not more than thirty seconds. Mentally, I sorted through my possible responses. There was much to say, but first I needed to respond in an honest way to Eric's feelings. This was a moment of truth for all of us, and the way we dealt with it now would probably determine all that would follow. I had to try to at once step back from what was going on and speak from my heart.

> ***Mediator:*** Eric, I'm glad that you had the courage to say what you did. I know it wasn't easy for you to do that—at least, if I were you, it wouldn't be easy for me. I also appreciate you speaking to me so directly and honestly. I hope I can return the favor. As to your feeling that I'm not sympathetic with you or feel a bias against you, I can honestly say that I don't. I feel that you (and Becky as well) have both come here sincerely intent on using this process to face the decisions ahead of you. There's a part of me that hopes that once you've reached your agreement, you'll get back together. I also appreciate your struggle about how to deal with your inheritance. I don't think that there is *a* right way to deal with it.
>
> Now for the harder part. When I said that you have a deep pocket, I was trying to give you an idea of how a judge would see you, and it's clear that I hit a nerve. I was quite convinced, and I still am, that if the two of you were to go to court, Becky would get more than $2,500 a month, but I'll come back to that. Looking at your situation from the outside, it's clear that you have enough money to be able to support yourself and to pay Becky $2,500 a month, particularly since you own a mortgage-free house.

Becky has to pay $800 a month in rent, so in that realm, I feel sympathetic to her position. When I put myself in *your* position, I feel how uncomfortable it would be to have to pay that amount of money to someone who has decided to leave me. But I think what made it so complicated for me was your strong initial statement—that it was fair if it was the law. That's a statement I disagree with, so I guess I was saying to you, "Now don't you see that the law is *not* always fair?" I have an agenda here, and that is for both of you to walk out of here with an agreement you both think is fair, regardless of what a court would do. So I needed you to see my point.

Now, it is possible, as your lawyer told you, that I'm wrong about the amount that the judge would award Becky. But you see, any uncertainty about the law only makes it more crucial that you reach an agreement that you both believe to be fair. But I *do* want you to understand that when I tell you what I think a court will do, I'm not expressing my personal opinion of what you should do or saying I think it is fair. The law is just the law, and part of my job is to interpret it.

Eric: Yes, but I think you were making a judgment that I was being tight.

Mediator: There may be something to that. You could have been picking up an emotional undercurrent that is a reflection of my own struggle with money.

Eric: It's helpful to hear you say that. Makes me think that maybe I'm not so crazy.

Becky: Well, *I* think you're crazy. I *know* I could get a lot more than $2,500 a month from a judge, but I have never wanted you to pay me because you were forced to. I hoped you would want to give us what we need to live. I know you and I have a difference of opinion about how to spend money. That was always a big bone of contention between us. But I *need* this money so I can have the breathing room to decide whether to stay separated or get back together out of choice. I'm trying to avoid being forced into something by the economic situation. I think you would be pretty miserable if I came running back only because I couldn't afford to make it on my own.

Eric: You're right. But I'm sure that if we settle on $1,500 you *will* have the breathing room, and if you need more, then your fashion consulting business will have to get bigger. I know you can do that. Or Karen could live with me. You've said you wanted more freedom. I would be happy to reverse our situation, have her stay with me and see you on weekends. That would cut your expenses.

Becky: [Her entire body stiffening, then her eyes filling with tears of anger] You have to be out of your mind. You'd do anything to try to cut support, even if it means your daughter suffers.

Eric: No. I don't think my daughter is going to suffer by spending more time with me. I wouldn't let that happen.

Mediator: I think it would be useful if we could, at least for now, separate the money discussion from the question of how much time you each spend with Karen. Which of these two makes sense to pursue right now?

Becky: We'd better talk about Karen. I want you to know that I am astounded by your cheapness, Eric. You can't have my daughter.

Eric: She's my daughter, too.

Mediator: If I'm going to be able to help you with this, I need to know what you've been doing since you separated and how that's been working for the three of you.

Eric: Karen has been staying with Becky during the week, and she has been with me every weekend.

Becky: And that's the way it's going to be. I don't give a damn what you say, Eric. I don't even want to talk about this anymore. [Starts to cry.]

I could feel my stomach tighten from the tension in the room. I had felt sympathetic to Becky when we were talking about money, but now I felt myself upset with her and sympathetic to Eric. I was angry that she seemed to be trying to shut Eric out of this decision. She seemed to think of Karen as her possession. As a father myself, I have often been disturbed by how easily some women dismiss the importance of the father-child relationship. But before I could help them, I would need to understand my anger and not push Becky away. I had to use my reaction as an invitation to understand her better, rather than use it to put up a wall between us. This is hard work for me, but vital to my maintaining my connection to both people. I turned to Becky, intentionally lowering my voice to calm us all.

Mediator: I can see how upsetting this is to you, but at some point, we need to talk about this. Are you willing to talk about this with me now, or would you prefer to wait?

Becky: This is really upsetting, but I guess we do need to talk about it. Go ahead.

Mediator: What's upsetting?

Becky: Eric knows how important Karen is to me. I feel like he's using her to get me to back off on the money.

Mediator: And, from your side, what's important in this question of your deciding about time you each spend with Karen?

Becky: Karen is the most important thing in my life. It's

true that there are times when I have resented being a mother, particularly when I have felt that there were opportunities I could have taken advantage of if I didn't have her. I think I'd be a lot further along in establishing my fashion consultancy if I wasn't taking care of her. But the flexibility of consulting is one of the reasons I chose the field—it gives me much more opportunity to spend time with her.

Mediator: So it's scary to even consider possibilities other than the schedule you have now.

Becky: Eric knows that.

Eric: How do you think it makes me feel not to have Karen more in my life now? I've not only lost my wife, but it feels like I've lost my daughter, too. This last month has been so hard. [Starts to sob.]

Mediator: So for you, being with Karen isn't really a question of money.

Eric: I'm not so happy about the way I brought it up, but it's true, I want to spend more time with Karen. That's something I need, and I think she needs it, too.

Becky: I'm open to that. What makes it hard is discussing it in terms of money.

Mediator: That's why I suggested that we separate the two issues, even though there is some relation between them.

Eric: You mean not having the amount of support depend on the time she spends with each of us?

Mediator: Yes.

Eric: I can see the advantage of that. I don't want to get into a discussion of money every time we talk about adjusting the schedule.

Becky: I'm willing to do that.

Mediator: Good. I'd also like to suggest another agreement that might help us deal with both the parenting and financial issues. I'd like us to assume that neither of you has more right to decide either issue. I have the feeling that you both assume that Becky has more right to decide the parenting issue and Eric the financial. If I'm right, then if we can start from a different assumption—that neither of you is one down in either area—we're likely to reach a better result.

Becky: But I really do know more about what's right for Karen.

Eric: And I certainly understand finances better than Becky.

Mediator: We can benefit from your expertise while still allowing you the right to disagree with each other.

Becky: That's okay. But I still want to be sure that Karen spends more time with me.

Mediator: Do you think she needs that?

Becky: Yes.

Mediator: And what about you, Eric? What do you think?

Eric: I am willing to have Karen spend more time with Becky than me. But I want to spend more time with her than I do now. I want to help her with her homework. And I would like to build up to a point when she lives with each of us half of the time. I have a lot of flexibility with my work schedule.

Becky: So do I. But I agree with you, Eric. I think it would be good for her to spend more time with you now. I think Karen would like that. She talks about you constantly.

Eric: [Beginning to cry] I've been so afraid that I would lose her.

Becky: That's not going to happen.

Mediator: And how do you feel, Becky, about her eventually spending equal time with each of you?

Becky: I don't know. That would be hard.

Mediator: It's a real challenge to be able to separate out your own needs from your kid's. If you can do that, I think it will be helpful in making decisions that work for Karen as well as you.

Becky: I've been very careful not to talk much with Karen about this. Maybe we can sit down with her and find out what she thinks. But I still want to have final say about what happens.

Mediator: How about veto power? Would that be enough?

Becky: I guess it's okay, as long as we use the same arrangement when we talk about the money.

Eric: You have a deal. Can we go back to the money discussion?

Becky: Once I make more money from my business, I'm willing to have support reduced, but that's not going to happen overnight. I need that money now.

Eric: When could I count on being able to reduce the payment?

Becky: I don't know how long it will take, but I think that in a year and a half, it should probably be time to at least talk about it again.

Eric: And when will it end?

Becky: Support for me? I told you before that three years should be long enough. But I don't want to make that definite now.

Eric: That's unacceptable. I want an outside date settled upon now.

Becky: Then I'd have to give you an outside date that's further down the road than I think I might need.

Eric: [To me] I know better than to ask you what a court would do. You'd probably say that a judge wouldn't decide how long I'd have to pay her support.

Mediator: Are you asking me to tell you about the law?

Eric: No. Let's do it differently this time. Let's work out an agreement first and then you tell us.

Mediator: [To Becky] How do you feel about that?

Becky: Fine. Eric's the one who's hung up on the law. It doesn't much interest me.

Eric: I'm actually relieved to do it this way. You're right. I think that we can do this without having to know how other people do it.

Mediator: But before you're both committed to it, I want you to know what a court would do. You'll need that to make the agreement solid and legally binding.

Eric: I thought you were the guy that said that the law's not always fair.

Mediator: I am. But I'm also the guy who feels that you need to take in what the law is to solidify your own sense of what's fair. It's paradoxical. The way to free yourself from law is to know it and know that, at least here, it's less important than what you two think.

The two went on to reach an agreement that called for Eric to pay Becky $2,500 per month after taxes as support for a year and a half, at which point they would review the amount. They also agreed that they would characterize the payments in a manner to minimize income tax consequences to each of them. They further agreed that spousal support would end in no more than four years, although they both expected it would actually end sooner. They also worked out a co-parenting agreement in which Karen would spend a couple of nights a week with Eric and the remainder with Becky, and they would alternate weekends with her. They specified that as Karen matured, she would gradually spend more time with Eric until she lived half of the time with each. They also agreed that the amount of child support would not vary with the amount of time Karen spent with each parent, but would be renegotiable based on the actual costs of raising her. Becky said the process had helped her clarify her feelings that the marriage was over. Eric also felt he had learned a great deal in the process, some of it quite painful. He sadly confessed that part of the reason he had tried to hold the line on support was he had hoped that if Becky found her life apart from him too difficult, she might be more open to reconciling. When he saw that this strategy was only alienating him from her, he recognized that he would rather have a good friendship with her than a bad marriage.

REACTIONS

*B*oth Eric and Becky expressed a sort of sad satisfaction with the agreement. My feelings about the process were quite mixed. I felt good about our recovery from Eric's perception that I had found him stingy. I was also pleased that I was able to reconnect with Becky after judging her for her maternal possessiveness. But I was still worried about something: Had I actually relied on the law myself in deciding that Becky was "right" and, in effect, that Eric's view didn't count? After all, Becky's view was *supported* by the law. Perhaps I had allowed myself to be controlled by the law while I was trying to free the parties from its control. Further, in interpreting the law I had assumed a judge would not depart from the standard formula—but at times judges do. Although, owing to court congestion judges tend to give very little time to divorce suits and deviate from using the formulas less and less, perhaps this would be a situation where a judge decided to deviate. And I had not raised that possibility. I had made the law appear to be much clearer than it was, because I had emotionally identified with Becky and was disconnected from Eric at the time I talked about the law. In short, I had allowed my subjective experiences and biases to influence my interpretation of the law—a common if rarely discussed handicap of the adversary process, in which lawyers continually make predictions based on similar influences, and judges do the same in applying the law.

Bad as it may be for a lawyer to be limited by personal emotion, in mediation this can be a cardinal sin. While there are many reasons why a mediator might interpret the law inaccurately, it would be unforgivable for the mediator to allow his prediction to be skewed because he is emotionally identified with only one of the parties. Eric's sense that I was chastising him reflected the limits on my empathy for his position. It embarrasses me to think I allowed that to happen.

While the case gave me reason to feel dissatisfied with myself, it also demonstrated the potential in mediation for correcting skewed opinions. Not many people are as sophisticated and courageous as Eric, who was willing to express his feeling that I was judging him unfairly. But if they are, the rift can be healed. Another corrective device is the use of the outside consultant. If the consulting lawyer can give a balanced and reasonably objective prediction of how a court will decide a case (as Eric's lawyer did), it can lead to a fuller understanding of the possibilities. Even if it contradicts the mediator's prediction, learning of the possibility of such a discrepancy is a significant step toward a full comprehension of the law and its fallibility.

All these "correctives" contribute to the effort to put the law into the background rather than the foreground, *informing* the parties' sense of fairness but not *determining* it. Given how confusing it can be to decide what is fair, the law can be a kind of mirror, reflecting back the collective standard of what the community thinks is fair.

But a problematic question remained open at the conclusion of this case. What should be the force of law in mediation? To what extent should one person threaten the other with court to coerce that person into agreement? The thing that makes this issue so difficult is that it feels different depending upon who is using the law. The law often exists to help a weaker party against the stronger party, which is the case for spousal support. How many spouses would voluntarily decide to pay their ex-spouses any more than they had to by law? The law in effect coerces the stronger party into adhering to the community's sense of fairness. Does such coercion cancel out the possibility of mutual agreement, the goal of mediation?

With Eric and Becky, it is still not clear to me whether their agreement resulted from their own sense of fairness or my statement of the law. Eric never objected to paying spousal support; was that because he believed it was right for him to pay or because he knew—and felt coerced by—the law? And when he finally agreed to pay Becky $2,500, was that because he thought the amount fair or because he knew she wouldn't accept less and would resort to the law to force the issue?

On the other side, how much was Becky influenced by the knowledge that the law was on her side? Even though we can say she soft-pedaled it and never expressed much interest in the law, it would certainly be hard to say that the knowledge that it supported her position did not affect her ability to stand firm in the face of Eric's resistance.

A traditional negotiator would say that Eric caved in. It was true that Eric finally accepted Becky's position, and to that extent he did cave in. At the same time, in a traditional litigation, Becky and her representative would surely have started at and probably even ended up at a much higher figure than the $2,500, particularly since the law would support such a position. The fact that she ended where she started is less of a sign that she "won" than that she felt her position to be right and fair. What made Becky's stance even more powerful was that she had not invoked the law; she had made her own personal determination of what she needed and thought was fair, not what she thought she could get. Eric finally accepted her view, and their agreement reflected that acceptance. I can't feel badly about that.

A CASE OF

ABUSE

SUMMARY

*T*he mediation of spousal abuse is a controversial issue. Dependency and power imbalances are one thing; physical threats and violence are far more problematic. As Les and Christine explain their situation, it becomes clear that they have a history of physical coercion, which has rendered verbal debate impossible. I gradually identify a dual task for myself: to help Les accept the inevitability of the separation he violently opposes and understand the seriousness of the problem. At the same time I have to support Christine in articulating her needs despite her fear and help her take steps to protect herself from Les's violent outbursts. This case also provides an opportunity to compare the degree of protection against abuse offered by the mediation and adversarial processes.

I'**d seen Les's picture** several times in our town newspaper before I met him. He was a large man, his pants and belt buckle straining to contain a belly that looked ready to burst. He owned two fast-food pizza restaurants, was a well-respected coach in the local Pop Warner football league, and had been active in town politics. He and Christine had married twenty-three years ago and owned their house outright. They had no children. Both Christine and Les had devoted themselves to volunteer work within the community.

Petite, energetic Christine had started an organization for welcoming new residents to the community and continued to be its director. She was also an ardent dog lover and over the past few years had turned their backyard shed into a de facto animal shelter. Both Les and Christine had led youth groups in their church.

So, long before these two arrived in my office, I'd felt as if I knew them. I was completely unprepared for the difficult problems about to unfold once they settled themselves in. Christine's appearance now was in sharp contrast to my past observations of her. There was a look of resignation in her eyes, and she seemed tense. She began slowly, fixing her gaze steadfastly at me as if to avoid the effect of Les's stare upon her.

> ***Christine:*** I want a trial separation, and I'd like to do it cooperatively. We need your help.
>
> ***Mediator:*** Is this something that you've talked about together?
>
> ***Christine:*** Yes, it is. I've been thinking about this for a long time. Les knows that this is what I want.
>
> ***Mediator:*** How long have you known you wanted a separation?
>
> ***Christine:*** A long time—at least a couple of years.
>
> ***Les:*** [In a booming voice] A couple of years?

Mediator: Is this news to you, Les?

Les: You bet. This woman is out of her mind. Do you mean to tell me that I've been married to you thinking we've been living together reasonably well and you've been wanting a separation for two years?

Christine: You know I haven't been happy for a long time, Les.

Les: But I didn't know you wanted out of the marriage.

Christine: We've gone over this, Les. I'm not saying I want out of the marriage. I just need to have some distance between us for a while.

Les: And then we can get back together? [Incredulous] I don't get this!

Christine: And then we'll see. I'd like to hope we can.

Les: This is completely unacceptable. Why don't you just say it? You want a divorce!

Les's voice had steadily risen to the crescendo of his last statement. He was clearly angry, bordering on losing control. Christine jumped in quickly.

Christine: No, Les. I'm not saying that. In fact, I'm pretty sure that I'm going to want to get back together.

Les: [Calmer now] Then why bother moving out in the first place? Let's go see that marriage counselor you like so much.

Christine: The one you have consistently refused to see for the past two years? I'm willing to do that—after the separation.

Mediator: Let me see if I can understand what is going

on. Christine, it seems clear to me that you have decided that a separation is necessary. And it seems equally clear that you, Les, are opposed to the idea.

Les: How can she do this to me? To us? We've been together almost twenty-five years.

Christine: Les, you know as well as I do that the last several years have been difficult.

Les: I know, but I promise that it will be different, as long as you stay.

Christine: I want to do this cooperatively, Les. That's why we're here. I want a separation. I need some time alone to make some changes. Please give me this time. And . . . I thought you understood this. I want you to move out.

Les: What? [His face reddening, his voice sounding threatening] You want *me* to move out?

Christine: I told you that when I suggested mediation.

Les: I can't believe this. What the hell am I doing here with you? You are trying to ruin my life.

Mediator: It seems as if there are two disagreements. The first is whether there is going to be a separation. The second is, if there is a separation, who is going to move out? What we need to resolve is whether this process is going to be the way you will resolve those disagreements.

Les: I want to know one thing, Christine, before we go any further. Have you already decided that you want a divorce?

Christine: [Her voice quavering] No. I want to see what happens when we separate.

Mediator: [To Les] I know that this is very painful for you, but I wondered when you asked that question if it would be easier for you, if it were true, to know that Christine is certain she wants a divorce rather than just a temporary separation?

Les: I don't know.

As we were talking, three things impressed me. First, it felt to me that Christine was talking "temporary separation" only because she couldn't bring herself to tell Les she really wanted a divorce. Second, neither of them was ready for that to be explicit, although it seemed they both knew that the separation was a step on the way to an inevitable divorce. And third, I had the ominous feeling that Les's anger could erupt in a violent manner.

ABUSE AND PROTECTION

*A*s I explained the mediation process and tried to uncover their motivations for being there, Les began to act as if he had nothing to lose. He mocked my description of the process as a way the two could work together to reach fair decisions.

Les: How can we have a fair result if I don't want a separation?

Mediator: That's the one thing you don't need to agree upon. Christine can have a separation if she wants it, even if you don't want it.

Les: So why would I want to participate in a process that leads to it?

Mediator: Good question. Maybe you don't. Still, the point of this process is for the two of you to make the remaining decisions together. If you want to do that, mediation might make sense, but if you can't accept the fact of separation, you won't be ready to make those decisions. I certainly see your point. In your shoes, if I didn't want this separation, I would find it very difficult to participate in mediation. After all, the process has to end in a result you don't want.

Les: [Beginning to cry] This woman is the only person I have ever trusted in my life. This is devastating to me. I'd do anything to keep us together.

Mediator: [To Christine] Do you feel clear that you want the separation?

Christine: [Bowing her head] I want to have some time alone. I do hope that the time will come when we can get back together. I really don't want to cause Les any more heartache than I already have.

Mediator: Then the question you have to answer for yourself, Les, is, are you willing to accept a separation and work with Christine to make the decisions to implement it? At best, it's going to be very hard, if not excruciating, for you.

Les: Tell me why I should cooperate, if I'm not going to get her back no matter what?

Mediator: I think it makes sense for you to assume she won't want to get back together. So, understanding that, do you want to make decisions together about how you will separate?

Les: I'd *like* to be able to do it, because I'm not interested in making lawyers rich and I don't want the terms of the separation to be out of my control.

Mediator: In mediation, you have to be able to make decisions together.

Les: Well, I know one thing. She can have her separation, but I'll be damned if I'm going to move out of the house.

Christine: You *know* I can't move out. I have the dogs. An apartment is out of the question. Oh, please, Les. Please. You know they can't be moved.

Les: Why should I have to get out of the house? You're the one who wants the separation.

Christine: [Hesitantly] Look, Les. I'll consider it, but you ought to know that when I talked to a lawyer, he told me I can get a judge to kick you out of the house within a few days.

An alarm went off in my head when Christine said this. In California, judges do not kick spouses out of the family residence unless they are convinced that the other spouse is in imminent physical danger, usually because of past acts of violence.

Had there been a history of violence here? Several signs suggested there had.

Christine seemed afraid of Les—at least, too afraid to be honest and admit what she wanted was a divorce. She had avoided making eye contact with him since they entered the room, and the kind of rage that I felt coming from Les was in itself abusive. Les appeared to be doing everything he could to intimidate Christine, and it seemed possible that he would be unable to restrain himself from resorting to physical violence if his frustration continued at the same level. And Christine fit a profile of an abused person: She was very cooperative, her low self-esteem was apparent, and she was clearly conspiring to keep their pattern a secret. What followed confirmed my fears.

Les: Can she really get a judge to kick me out of my own house?

Mediator: Not unless there has been some history of violence on your part and some reason to believe it could recur.

Christine: We've had more than a little of that.

Mediator: Les, I need to hear more about that to be able to help you understand the law. What has happened?

Les: Not much.

Christine: [Quietly] Not much? A couple of trips to the hospital, some cracked ribs, black eyes, and once, a broken arm.

Mediator: When was the most recent time?

Christine: Two weeks ago. And he told me last night that if I get him kicked out of the house, he'll get me.

If this were true, Christine was probably in physical danger right now. What was this couple doing in mediation? I'd had enough experience with couples in abusive relationships to understand that the abuse would undoubtedly continue if both the abuser and the abused played their parts. My sense was that if I scratched the surface, I'd find that dynamic here, with Les as the persecutor, and Christine the victim. If they played out those roles in mediation, many of Christine's needs could be overlooked, and I would be playing a central role in allowing that to happen.

On the face of it, the best option seemed to be to discourage them from pursuing mediation and make sure Christine had found a lawyer who would get her the protection she needed. Yet there are limits to the protection the adversary process can provide. If Christine obtained a court order evicting Les from the house and barring him from the premises, Les's sense of impotence and frustration, combined with the humiliation of being kicked out of his own house in a public hearing, could result in even more violence. Court orders are not sufficient to restrain irrational people who believe they have been wronged and have nothing left to lose. So a real danger to Christine could result from her decision to "protect" herself legally.

The limits of protection available through the adversary system were relevant to me as well as Christine. It was not my physical safety I was concerned with here, but rather my conscience: Casting these two out to an adversary system that could prove dangerous would not rest any easier on my conscience than reaching a bad agreement in mediation. I felt trapped and didn't like it any more than they must have. It seemed that the only way out would be to try to find a way to talk about all of this. Decisions based on understanding are always preferable to those based on power.

If the mediation proceeded, I'd have to keep a careful eye on the dynamic between Les and Christine. Les could interpret Christine's desire to mediate as a sign of weakness and then use the process to coerce her into an agreement that she would later regret. Her very stance of cooperation could play a part in tacitly allowing the abuse.

Still, Christine had initiated this process, was seeking a separation over Les's objections, and was trying to get him to leave the house, all signs she was no longer willing to be Les's victim. True, she had hedged a bit on the question of whether divorce was her goal and was perhaps even misleading Les slightly, but if her efforts kept him from exploding, who was to say she wasn't taking care of herself in the best way?

It was also a good sign that she had already consulted a lawyer. This meant she had lined up for herself both support for her choice to separate and legal advice that could affirm her position. I only hoped she had chosen a lawyer who was sensitive to the dynamics of abuse situations and would counsel her with compassion and sensitivity. I also hoped the lawyer valued his or her client's choice above all. These were especially important requirements because of the real limits on my ability to protect Christine in the process. As the mediator, I could not—or would not—act as her advocate. If I thought they were coming to an agreement that reflected their dangerous pattern, I'd have to terminate the mediation or refuse to draw up the agreement.

ANALYZING THE OPTIONS

*I*f we were to proceed, we had to settle several issues first. First and most urgent, we needed to determine how much, if any, physical danger Christine was in. Would she be safe if she stayed in the house?

Second, what made Christine's desire to stay very tricky was the fact Les knew he could scare Christine into changing her mind—he could literally chase her out of the house. If Christine stood firmly on this issue, it might be possible to break the destructive pattern between them. But Christine's stance could just as easily trigger Les's rage—a rage that might require the kind of round-the-clock police protection the local police department would not provide and Christine couldn't afford to buy.

If Christine could prove a history of violence and the existence of current threats, she could indeed have Les ejected by a judge. The question was, would she use that power in order to get him out? She had answered that question tacitly by stating her legal rights, but at the same time she had made it clear she wanted to avoid the use of legal coercion. An important influence on Christine's decision to take this position may have been her feeling that Les's current rage was a physical expression of his impotence in the face of her decision to separate. If that were indeed true, then the more willing Les was to move out voluntarily, the less likely it was that his violence would be triggered. So Christine was probably right in minimizing the use of the law that was open to her.

THE CONDITIONS FOR
PROCEEDING

*H*ow much of this could we discuss frankly in mediation? Normally, my goal is to initiate discussion of issues buried beneath the surface. Open discussion leads to the fairest results— *if* it is matched by both the participants' willingness to be strong. But in this case I wanted to restrict Les's ability to undermine Christine's strength.

Christine was now saying no—she wasn't leaving and she could call in the law if she had to. She had set her limit and I was supporting her effort to empower herself. That seemed right. But I had to be careful not to support her more than she needed or I could end up disempowering her by substituting my power for hers.

I also had to hear Les's side of it. Would he deny Christine's accusation? Had I already decided that if he did he was lying? I needed to open myself to understanding him now. I needed to be direct and sympathetic at the same time.

> ***Mediator:*** Is it true that you threatened Christine?

> ***Les:*** I didn't really mean it. And you know, the violence has not been one-way. She's fought back.

I looked at the two of them. He stood over six feet tall and must have weighed at least two hundred pounds. Christine, a slender woman about five foot two, seemed to be half Les's size.

> ***Mediator:*** You don't expect me to take that seriously, do you? Look at how much bigger you are than her.

> ***Les:*** But she provokes me.

Mediator: Are you telling me that you feel justified in hitting her?

Les: There have been times when she's deserved it.

Another potent factor affecting my ability to mediate this case was my personal reaction to violence, and its role in the mediation. Personally and politically, I have a strong commitment to nonviolence. And when the physical match is imbalanced, as it was with Les and Christine, I find violence even more abhorrent. I had to identify my own limits and limitations. For example, I knew I could not tolerate any effort on his part to intimidate Christine, and that any actual violence in a session would terminate the mediation completely.

It was easy to identify with Christine and to distance myself from Les as much as I could. It was easy to see Les as completely in the wrong, as sick. Yet for any mediation to work, the mediator must remain in the middle both in his own perceptions and from the point of view of both parties. If either party feels that the mediator has become an advocate for the other, the mediation is in trouble. If I were going to work effectively with Les and Christine, Les would need to know that I could empathize with him, too. Could I condemn his violence without condemning him? The challenge was to find the less accessible *non*violent parts of Les—his qualities as a hard worker in the community and church—and to emphathize with those, at least temporarily, viewing his violence as a distorted expression by some part of him that was frustrated or confused.

I wanted to take the same position on the law that Christine had—one that maximized Les's sense of choice and the expression of his sense of fairness, but also let him know that if necessary, Christine could invoke the law and restrict his freedom of choice. Articulating that position would not be easy; he could easily construe it as a condemnation of him as a person.

Mediator: Given your history of violence, my best guess is that a judge would order you out of the house. Of course, it would be up to Christine to be able to convince the judge that there had been violence.

Christine: There are medical and hospital records.

Mediator: That would probably be enough.

Les: But it's my house, too.

Mediator: I'm just talking about now, on a temporary basis.

Les: And then I could come back home?

Mediator: Not unless Christine decided you could. In this situation, she would have the power.

Les: That's great. *You* want a separation, and whether *I* want it or not, you get it. *You* want me kicked out of the house, and you get it whether I want it or not. You want me dead, too? Because that's what you're going to get.

Mediator: I understand that you're angry about this, but I have to tell you that I'm not going to permit you to try to intimidate Christine here.

Christine: [Beginning to cry] This is why I have to have this separation. After he broke my arm, our doctor suggested I see a counselor. I had several appointments with her, which led me into your office. Not that she encouraged me to go into mediation. She wanted me to go to the police, and then to a lawyer who would protect me. But I care for Les. I understand he has an illness, that he grew up in a horribly abusive household where both his parents hit him. He's tried so hard to lead a good life. But I'm tired. I don't want to live with this anymore. I'm continuing counseling. It's more helpful than my prayers.

Les: Whether it's prayers or counseling, it looks like you're going to get your goddamn separation. You're going to get everything.

Mediator: I can see how frustrating this must be for you. I think you're going to find this process very hard, if not impossible.

Christine: But I want to work it all out here. Please help us.

Mediator: I'm afraid you may need more protection than I can provide.

Christine: I don't think the courts can protect me. I'm afraid of what might happen if a judge kicked him out of the house, and I don't want to end up in the hospital again.

Les: Then why don't you just get out of the house? [Stands up and makes a threatening gesture.]

Mediator: [To Christine] What's it like to hear this?

Christine: I'm scared, but I really want this process to work for us.

Mediator: And what if it can't?

Christine: Then I'll have to go to court.

Mediator: It's important that you know you have that option. Ironically, mediation will have a better chance of working if you're willing to go to court if this doesn't work for you. Then your choice is freer. But if we continue this process, you'll need to separate immediately. I think it would be too stressful for you to live together while you're making these decisions.

Les: What kind of choices do *I* have?

Mediator: Fewer than Christine. Since Christine wants a separation, she'll get one. And if she's willing to go to court to get you out of the house, she can do that, too.

Your choices are to stay here and try to keep yourself under control and accept those decisions, or to hire a lawyer to fight her decisions.

Les: Some choices.

Mediator: Not very attractive, are they? But I don't honestly know what else to tell you, except that even if you were to convince Christine that she should move out, I'm not sure I would accept that, particularly if I felt that she had agreed to it out of fear.

Les: But why?

Mediator: Because I see violence as problematic for both of you, and I want you both to be free of it. It does neither of you any good if Christine capitulates to you out of fear. And I want you to get professional help. I'll give you the names of three psychologists who work with abusers. They also lead support groups.

Les: I don't want their names. And I don't want to sit around with a bunch of pathetic guys.

Mediator: Then I'm pretty sure this process won't work. Not that I'm sure it will if you do get help, but convincing you to get psychological help feels to me to be the only responsible thing for me to do.

Les: So you want to force me to see a shrink?

Mediator: Most of all, I want you to choose to do it yourself because you feel it would be helpful. What I know is that no one can help you if you aren't willing to be helped. But if I can push you to do it, and you then find reasons of your own to want to do it, it will be worth my having pushed. And I don't believe this process will work unless you get help.

Les: So what am I supposed to do?

Mediator: You can say no to me. If I were you and felt like you seem to, I might leave.

Les: I respect your directness. I know that I've been a real jerk some of the time. Maybe a separation would help. [Begins to cry.]

Mediator: What's the hardest part of this for you? What are you most afraid could happen?

Les: I'm afraid of being alone. I know that it hasn't been a great marriage, but she means everything to me. [He sobs, his huge body shaking rhythmically for what seems like several minutes] She is my life, all that's ever mattered to me. I've spent twenty-three years trying to make her happy. And I can't. [Yelling] I can't! [In a whisper] I don't want her to leave me. I don't want to leave the house. I need her. I want another chance.

Mediator: Christine has said she needs a separation. And you need help. If you're willing to get it, I'll try to see if I can help the two of you work out an agreement. So you have a lot to think over before deciding whether we'll keep going. At best, this is going to be very hard for you, and for me, too.

Les: [Meekly] I'll stay at my buddy's and get help.

CONDITIONS VERSUS PROCESS: A CONTRADICTION

The session ended on that note. I felt sad and pessimistic about our chances of working together toward a viable agreement. The conditions for continuing were so stacked against Les. There was the separation, which he didn't want; his vacating his home, which he didn't want; and my insistence that he get some counseling, which he didn't want. These would be difficult for anyone in his situation to swallow, but I suspected them to be especially hard for Les, since he seemed only dimly aware that he was in real trouble. I had tried to soften the coerciveness of the conditions, but that was probably to soothe my own conscience as much as anything else. Internally, I was struggling to reconcile the externally imposed conditions with a central goal of mediation, self-empowerment.

Yet I had no other acceptable choices. I could always terminate the mediation, but short of that, the top priority was to use the process to break the pattern of abuse. Christine wasn't the only victim of Les's abuse; Les was a victim, too. He was locked into a pattern of behavior he had learned as a child and would only be able to break it with outside help. I knew I couldn't *force* him to change; the choice was his alone. What I *could* do was try to create an atmosphere that encouraged him to change.

Had I done that? What disturbed me was the possibility that I had gone overboard—basically requiring that he seek help for something he didn't consider much of a problem. Wasn't this an example of the worst kind of professional domination? Wasn't I using whatever authority I could muster to push Les into doing what I thought he should do? Wasn't I really saying that I knew better than he? And wasn't that stance by a professional totally antithetical to what mediation was all about?

I had to answer all these questions with a yes, but a qualified one. I felt I had the right to do what I was doing because Christine was suffering. There was a possibility that she could be seriously injured or even killed if I didn't take some action. So in this instance my role as a mediator was superseded—rightly, I think—by another: the prohibitor of physical abuse. At the end of the session I was in some suspense over whether Les would accept me in this role. His openness at the end of our last session provided a ray of hope that we might succeed, that maybe this would be the beginning of a major turnaround for Les, but I also knew that at best this would be the beginning of a long, hard road for him.

A NEAR MISS

A week later, Les and Christine returned. Christine looked even more drawn and tense than in our last session. Les, casually attired in his khakis and sport shirt that didn't quite cover his paunch, reported that he had seen a therapist, didn't like him, and had an appointment with another one. Alternating between resignation and barely contained rage, he also said that he was willing to move out of the house and work out a temporary agreement spelling out the details, provided that Christine met certain conditions. Before I had the chance to find out what conditions he was talking about, Christine interrupted.

> ***Christine:*** I appreciate your willingness to do that, Les. But I want to be sure that you remove the car you're fixing up from the property, too, so I can feel we have a real separation.
>
> ***Les:*** [His face red] You wanted a separation—you got it. You want me out of the house—you got it. You wanted me in counseling—I'm doing that. Now you want my car gone. I can't believe it.
>
> ***Christine:*** I'm afraid that if you leave it on the property, you'll keep coming back to work on it. If you're willing to stay away from the car, then I guess it's okay to leave it.
>
> ***Les:*** How about this? Why don't you just burn it? Then I couldn't possibly use that as an excuse to come home.

With each word I could feel his anger rising and had the increasing sense that he was losing control of himself. At the end of his statement, he picked up a ceramic paperweight that my son had made and hurled it powerfully at Christine, striking her foot. The piece shattered and Christine screamed with pain.

Mediator: My God, Les. You can't do that!

Stunned, I moved to Christine's side. She tried to get up, managing to hobble to her feet. Then she fell into the chair in a heap. She began to sob heavily.

Mediator: Are you all right?

Christine: I don't think it's broken. I can move it. But I don't think I should continue here anymore.

Les: What are you talking about? We've just about reached an agreement.

Christine: I can't deal with you anymore.

Les: I don't get it. You're getting everything and it's still not enough.

Mediator: Did you *notice* what just happened?

Les: It was an accident.

Mediator: It was *not* an accident. It was an act of violence. It is not okay with Christine and it is not okay with me for this to happen. [To Christine] Do you want to press charges?

Christine: What do you mean?

Mediator: What I mean is that assaults like this are against the law.

Les: Look, I didn't mean to hit her. I was just upset.

Mediator: You're both lucky she wasn't hurt more seriously. I'm appalled by the violence, but I'm at least as upset by your denial of it.

Les: You're making a mountain out of a molehill.

Mediator: What do you want to do, Christine?

Christine: I want to walk out that door and let my lawyer handle this.

Les: You can't do that.

Mediator: Yes, she can. That's an option for both of you at any time. No one is forcing either of you to stay here.

Christine: But we *are* pretty close to an agreement.

Mediator: That's true, but you need to do what seems most right to you. If that means leaving, then you should leave.

Christine: [To me] What do *you* think I should do?

Mediator: What seems most right to you?

Christine: To get out.

Mediator: What's keeping you from it?

Christine: I don't know. [Starts to stand up.]

Les got up, turned toward Christine and me, started to speak, muttered to himself, "It's not worth it!" and walked out, slamming the door behind him. Christine looked at me and said, "Thank you. Do you mind if I stay in the office long enough to be sure he's gone?"

Mediator: Of course, stay. You must be really scared of him. You need to take steps to protect yourself. I'd suggest that you call your lawyer before you leave here and make sure that you don't spend the night together in the same house. You might also call the police to alert them and the women's shelter to get more help.

Christine: I think I hadn't realized until now how serious the situation is.

I was relieved that she was all right, that Les was gone, and that, for me anyway, the case was over. I was also angry and upset. I realized that my own violent feelings had been stirred. I hate those feelings because they remind me that in my self-righteousness about the wrongness of violence I act as if I don't have violent impulses of my own. But in reality, the main difference between Les and me is that I can control my actions when I feel frustrated by channeling them into safe expressions such as sports or occasional yelling. That's a big difference, but not so big that I could feel comfortable around him. Although I can usually convince myself that I am a peaceful man, Les reminded me of my own feelings of aggression.

Some mediators consider mediation inappropriate whenever violence arises. They point out that violence cancels out the mutual respect people need to have to make decisions together. Particularly dangerous is the situation in which the victim has developed a pattern of accommodation of the violence that can be confused with the spirit of cooperation necessary for a successful mediation.

Others advocate mediation for violent instances, convinced that the adversary system handles them poorly and provides no more real protection to the victim than face-to-face mediation sessions in which the problem is confronted and agreements might even emerge.

My own belief is that instances of actual or threatened violence are qualitatively different from all other kinds of situations and must be treated differently. I would not automatically rule out mediation in cases of abuse; such a determination would rest on a deep analysis of the situation at hand. Much depends upon:

- the intentions of both the abuser and the abused
- the depth of their understanding of their own interaction
- their willingness to make changes that will end the abuse permanently.

For me, the key to mediating a potentially violent conflict is the informed choice of the parties. With Les and Christine, we could go no further because there was little intention on Les's part to end the pattern of abuse, mainly because he was not even willing to acknowledge that he was an abuser. While we did not reach an agreement, Christine did have the opportunity to make her statement. By terminating the process, she made it clear that she would no longer tolerate the pattern. From where I stood, this was a necessary precondition to her refusing to be overpowered by him.

Ironically, what was missing for both of them was self-respect. If Les had developed the courage to look deep enough inside himself to understand that, and Christine had recognized her own intrinsic value as a human being and demanded that recognition from others, healing might have been possible, but probably not in mediation, and—because of my own discomfort—probably not with me.

I billed Les $15 for my son's paperweight. When he paid the bill, I gave the money to my son. I never saw either Les or Christine again. From their previous position of high visibility in the community, it seemed as if they had suddenly vanished.

IT'S YOUR FAULT

SUMMARY

*T*he central question in this case is how to move beyond blame in order to listen and negotiate. Allison has given birth to a baby that Hank absolutely, in no uncertain terms, did not want and blames for destroying their marriage. The two have fallen into a pattern of attacking each other, and real communication between them is virtually nil. I direct my efforts at helping them change their communication pattern so they can achieve at least the minimal understanding necessary to reach an agreement that will allow them to go their separate ways. For my part, I relearn a lesson that many of my cases have taught me: Empathy is the only way past blame.

A **wave of agitation** blew into the office with Hank and Allison on their first visit. Hank, a short, muscular, balding man, nervously wrung his hands and perspired profusely. Allison was tiny, but her slight build contained immense energy. She continually bounced up and down in her seat and occasionally jumped up to pace the room. They were both in their early thirties and, as I learned later, were avid mountain-bike riders. Both spoke very quickly and used hand gestures to accentuate their speech. Frankly, as soon as they entered the room, my first impulse was to jump up and leave.

Nearly in unison, they announced, "We want to finish this, *now!*" Both were anxious and impatient to undo what they agreed was a serious mistake that they had made only twenty-four months before: getting married. Complicating matters, they had had a child within a year of the marriage. The two had separated three months after the baby was born, had immediately hired lawyers, and, in six months, had spent more than $25,000 in legal fees, only to have resolved nothing. Not surprisingly, both were exceedingly anxious to put the past behind them.

I began in my usual fashion, attempting to make contact and identify their motivations for coming in. "I'd like to start by explaining mediation and see if the three of us can agree on how to proceed."

Hank was interested in none of my agenda.

> ***Hank:*** Look, here's what we want to do. Tell us what we have to decide. Then, we'll make the decisions and get out of here.
>
> ***Mediator:*** With an emphasis on the getting out of here?
>
> ***Hank:*** [Looking slightly amused] Right. You got it.
>
> ***Mediator:*** I'd like to be able to accommodate you, but I want you both to know what you're getting into here.
>
> ***Hank:*** The short version, please.

Allison: [To me] How would you like to have been married to *that?*

Mediator: You both seem in a real hurry to get it all over with.

Hank: Brilliant deduction.

Allison: I can't stand being in the same room with him.

Mediator: Then why are you here?

Allison: Because it seemed to me the lawyers were just making it way harder than they had to, and frankly, I couldn't afford to keep up the litigation.

Mediator: I need to make it very clear that, if mediation is to be effective, you two are going to need to find some way of working together.

Hank: It's *impossible* for anyone to work with Allison. She changes her mind all the time—*all* the time!

Allison: And you're really a piece of cake. All you ever do is put me down.

Mediator: I can see you both seem to meet one essential requirement for this process to work: the ability to protect yourselves. You seem pretty good at fighting with each other.

Allison: We've had lots of practice.

Hank: [Patting his forehead with his handkerchief] What else can a guy do who's being attacked literally *all* the time?

Mediator: The challenge here is to see if we can find a way for the two of you to talk, not just fight. Are you interested?

Hank: I'm willing to do whatever it takes to get this thing over with.

Allison: [Noncommittally] Mmmm.

Mediator: Then you need to agree to do two things: say what's really on your mind, and listen carefully enough to fully understand each other's views.

Allison: That would be impossible for him. He's never listened to me once in the past two years.

Hank: Allison, you interrupt me constantly. *You* never listen to *me.*

Allison: Ha! You're the expert of interruptus, Hank.

Mediator: It sounds to me as if you've got the first part down well—speaking your mind—but am I right that the listening is something neither of you has ever been able to do?

Both together: That's about right.

Mediator: Do either of you have any desire to work on listening?

Hank: I'll do whatever it takes to get the divorce done. I would really like to have as little to do with Allison as possible.

Allison: Listen, Hank, I don't want to be with you any more than you want to be with me. But I'm willing to respect your opinion if you're willing to respect mine.

Hank: Then you'll have to act respectable.

Mediator: That kind of retort isn't really helpful to the process.

Hank: I know, I'm sorry. But sometimes I just can't help it.

Mediator: So for you, Hank, the arguing is like a kind of sport.

Allison: Yeah—I'm the punching bag.

Mediator: I haven't seen too many punching bags punch back. [Both laugh]

Allison: Frankly, I wished for a long time that it could be different, but I lost hope. We seem stuck in the fighting groove. We started that way and it never changed.

OPTIMISM AND THE "HOPELESS" STALEMATE

I get a sinking feeling when I see a couple who, like Allison and Hank, are fiercely committed to doing battle but who lack any shared good times that they might fall back on as a reference point. I wonder: Why, if they've never been able to listen to each other before, would they be able to start now? What makes me think I can help them make their important decisions together when they can't even stand to be in the same room?

These questions do have answers, although they are often complex. There are several aspects of mediation that enable participants to cut through old battle patterns and begin to communicate. First, an agreement to mediate can be a signal that the participants want to let go of the old roles. In a way it is like saying to two contestants in a game, "Time-out—you don't have to play your old positions. Don't play husband. Don't play wife. You can talk to each other without the baggage that keeps you from seeing and hearing each other clearly."

Second, there is a well defined task (reaching a mutually satisfactory agreement) to be completed in mediation that serves as a kind of map. Agreed on by the participants at the start, this task provides a useful reference point to be drawn upon by the mediator or the parties when they feel sucked into an old pattern.

And finally and most mysteriously, the presence of the mediator, a third party hired by both sides, can work to facilitate communication that has, between the two alone, been hopelessly stalled. Any witness to an interaction between a couple changes the dynamic; the knowledge that there is an observer shifts both parties' perspectives. The mediator is usually described as a *neutral* or *impartial* third party, but neither of these words describes the quality that, for me, makes the crucial difference. As I have said before, that crucial quality is *caring* on the part of the person in the middle.

Of course, there is always the possibility that it won't work—that no transformation will take place. Some people are so deeply entrenched in their counterproductive patterns of dealing with each other that it is just plain impossible for them to work together. They will never move out of stalemate into resolution. It is difficult for mediators to realize and admit this and harder still to convey that insight to a couple hoping in vain for a solution.

Hank and Allison were both architects who worked in the city. Hank had set up his own firm three years before the marriage; Allison had started hers one year before the marriage. Under the law, each of them had an interest in the increase in value in the other's practice during the marriage. When their son, Morgan, was born, Allison had closed her practice; she only returned to it at the time of separation. Complicating matters, Hank had invested some of the money he had earned from his practice in a real estate limited partnership that was very difficult to value. After the separation, in order to be closer to his beloved biking terrain, Hank had rented a large houseboat for himself while Allison had remained in their rental in the city.

Before Morgan was born, Allison had been earning about $3,000 per month; when they began mediation, she was working part-time and earning about $2,000 per month. Hank had very little understanding of the economics of his business. At the time of the marriage, he had been earning about $4,000 per month; at the time of separation, he was earning $6,500 per month and at the time of mediation about $8,000 per month. Needless to say, the first issue they wanted to talk about was support.

Mediator: How do you want to go about discussing this?

Hank: As little as possible. I don't think Allison needs any support, period.

Allison: Look who's talking. I wouldn't *need* any support if I made $100,000 a year and had no responsibilities for a kid. My rent alone is $1,000 a month.

Mediator: This is a recipe for a disaster if we keep it up.

Hank: [Angrily] Look, Gary, Allison's trying to take me for all she can get. So what am I supposed to do, meekly give her whatever she wants?

Mediator: You seem to think that you have to either lie down and let her walk all over you or stand tough and give nothing. There are other options.

Hank: As soon as I give an inch, she'll take everything.

Mediator: That's your experience with her?

Hank: You're right. That's my experience with her.

Allison: [Banging her fist on the arm of her chair] Do I have to sit here and take this?

Mediator: I'm still looking for ways we might go about this. All I'm finding are ones that definitely won't work.

Allison: Look, I'm prepared to talk about this reasonably, but he's completely impossible. He acts as if we were never married and he doesn't have a child at all. I think he'd rather we'd just disappear than try to work anything out.

Hank: Not a bad idea.

Allison: Well, it's not going to happen, Hank. It's time you lived up to your responsibilities.

Hank: And it's time for you to take care of yourself.

DEFUSING FURY

I have several options in responding to an exchange like this. One is to let it go on, hoping that the very act of arguing will discharge some of the anger. For people who have rarely confronted each other, allowing them to vent can be the key to unlocking truths.

A second option is to try to cut the exchange off. Some people (like Hank and Allison) are so used to angry words that they are almost numbed to the pain being inflicted. Cutting off the exchange can make them stop simply reacting to each other and help them refocus on a more positive interaction.

But it is also possible that in pursuing their angry course the parties are making progress and that interrupting them would not be beneficial. Only the adversaries themselves can really assess whether a certain kind of exchange is truly productive. Cutting off what might be fruitful is risky for another reason as well—it sets up the mediator as the controller of the process. This can lead to a passivity by the parties and an expectation that the mediator will come up with the solution.

A third option is for the mediator to observe an angry exchange closely, both in terms of *what* is being said and *how*, and then evaluate with the parties what is going on and how to proceed. It can be very effective for the two antagonists to step back from the fray, although a moment of reflection can also yield nothing but more fuel for the fire.

A fourth alternative, and the one I chose in this instance, is a safer variation of the third: simply to comment on the process between the parties. This approach gives the parties the benefit of an outsider's view of their interaction, but does not involve actual intervention. The risk here is that the mediator's take on the situation may be wrong, but in this case I felt confident I knew what was going on.

Mediator: You both sound like you're experts on the other person. You each know what the other should do.

Hank: She's *always* operated as if I were the worst human being in the world.

Mediator: If what's going on here is any example, she doesn't have a corner on that market.

Hank: Well, of course! I have to defend myself, don't I?

Mediator: That's a natural reaction, but if you each continue to defend by attacking, we'll eventually wind up with World War III on our hands. There's at least some truth to all of your insights, but that's only part of the picture.

Allison: I'm just not willing to make myself vulnerable to that man again.

Mediator: I can understand that, and my guess is that the feeling is mutual. But where does that leave you in dealing with him?

Allison: We don't ever really talk to each other, except to attack or defend. You're right about that.

Mediator: [To Hank] Do you agree?

Hank: Yeah, but she's the one who usually starts it.

Mediator: So when you feel attacked, you defend and attack back.

Hank: Right.

Allison: No, that's what *I* do, because *he* usually starts it.

Mediator: So you each think the other one starts it.

FROM BLAME TO UNDERSTANDING

*P*eople frequently believe that a couple like Hank and Allison who blame each other for their marriage's failure are not candidates for mediation. However this is not necessarily the case. Sometimes through mediation disputants can put their blame aside and understand the other's perspective.

Blame is a defense mechanism; we use it to try to avoid some problem or pain of our own. For Hank and Allison, it was easier to see the other's failure than recognize their own responsibility for their problems. And by pushing each other away, they invited the other to retaliate in kind, rather than to consider whatever truth there might be in the accusation.

Yet blame is not all bad. In some cases, it can be useful to help people who are trying to extricate themselves from each other gain some necessary distance. And from a societal point of view, allocating responsibility for problems—in short, blaming—is central to and necessary for achieving justice.

To put this into perspective, eliminating fault is not the purpose of mediation, nor is it doing away with all notions of individual responsibility or watering down all events into shared responsibility. Rather, mediation seeks to make blame a way station on the path to empathy. It strives to create a broader view of the situation, one that encompasses *both* parties' perspectives. Unfortunately, too often blame is a place where people stop. Going past blame to compassion opens doors to a greater understanding, which in turn can lead to a just resolution.

> ***Mediator:*** From my perspective, it's not so important to get at the truth of who starts it. What's most important is for the two of you to decide whether you want to change your pattern.

Allison: If we could change, we'd probably still be together.

Mediator: Maybe there's nothing you can do, but frankly I find that hard to believe. If you could do something about it, would you think it worth the effort?

Hank: What's the alternative? Look, we're spending all our time talking about how we talk. Let's get on with it. [To Allison] How much support do you want?

Mediator: We can try to go forward without resolving the question of how you talk to each other, but my guess is that we'll end up where you started unless we do.

Hank: So tell us what to do.

Mediator: That's not my job. What I *can* tell you is what I *see* you do. Because you're both such practiced arguers, you seem reluctant to say what's really on your minds, out of fear of how the other person is going to react. You know, one function of arguing is putting the other down, but another function is protecting yourself. If that pattern continues here, we *might* make some progress, but I think it's doubtful. You *do* have other options.

Allison: Like what? Letting him walk all over me? Forget it.

Mediator: It takes a lot of courage not to react to the other person's attack with a defense or an attack, but if even one of you changes the way you react to the other, it could change your whole mode of interacting. I'm not suggesting that you just lay down and give in to each other. But you can decide not to attack.

Hank: So I'm supposed to trust her?

Mediator: Eventually, if you can find a different way of dealing with each other, you very well might find a way to be more trusting. In the atmosphere that exists now, each of you would be crazy to trust the other.

Allison: I don't know if I can change. I've been totally wiped out by this man.

Mediator: Then you may decide not to do it. Whether or not you make a change is truly up to you. If you don't trust him, you wage war to protect yourself. If you *do* trust him you risk getting taken advantage of. I guess the most positive suggestion I can make is that you take a moment before you defend or attack and see if there might be a different way to proceed.

Allison: I'd like to do that, but frankly I don't think *Hank* is capable of doing it.

Hank: Yes I *can* do it. I do it with other people all the time, but with her it's like oil and water. She gets me so angry I want to scream.

Mediator: Whatever you say, the two of you obviously have a very strong emotional connection. Some people getting divorced can be relatively calm and controlled with each other, but you two clearly fit into another category. You can't live together, but the bond between you is strong.

Hank: That's true. [Starts to become teary] I certainly don't mean you any harm, Allison. I hate thinking that we're becoming enemies.

Allison: All I want to know is that you'll help out with our finances. I'm not trying to bankrupt you. I wouldn't want a dime from you if we didn't have Morgan, but I need your help.

Hank: You're a good mother, Allison. But I know that it's better for me to be away from you. I feel saner.

ANALYZING THE SHIFT

So, a shift in the way that Allison and Hank talked to each other had occurred. It was a sweet moment, hearing them let down their guards a bit and speak more openly. What happened? It's difficult to say—the change wasn't completely open to logical analysis. Certain parts, though, were reasonably clear to me.

There were three stages: First, I called attention to their speaking patterns; second, we identified the risks and benefits of continuing the same mode; and third, we looked for alternatives. In general it appeared that the more truth they acknowledged, the more open they both became, but I still wasn't sure where this new openness would take them.

The shift away from counterproductive patterns never seems to go the same way with any two sets of people. Some people require a great deal more guidance in recognizing their patterns and their limitations. Some, even when they see the patterns, find them too strongly ingrained to change. For Hank and Allison, it was pointing out the strength of their connection that made the shift possible. Although I'm not sure why, when the power of people's connection to each other is acknowledged explicitly, they seem to find it harder to hold on to the things that separate them.

SENSING THE REALITIES BEHIND THE WORDS

When I am asked to account for a shift in dynamic like Hank and Allison's, I realize that it is difficult to describe what I am really doing in a mediation. I have reported the words that Allison and Hank exchanged, but a lot more happened in the room besides a conversation. This is always the case: Emotional reactions and reasoning are constantly guiding our actions. I don't know what the specifics of those were for Hank and Allison, but I can recall my own.

First, I was monitoring myself to make sure I wasn't attempting to manipulate them into being less defensive. My goal is to expose the truth of the situation, but I need to be willing to accept the possibility that these people are not ready, willing, or able to open up more. After all, their reluctance to change may well be protecting them from unbearable pain at what they perceive as a failure of their relationship. The trickiest part for me is to respect the parties' limits while considering the possibility that what *appear* to be limits are really just barriers to the truth waiting to be removed.

How do I distinguish between them? Experience has taught me how to use my intuition by sensing the emotional realities behind the words. The only way of doing that is to empathize with my clients as fully as I can. To do so, I have to let go of my own agendas, hopes, and expectations. Again, this does not mean I suppress my own feelings, values, opinions, or knowledge—not at all. It is impossible to sit between two married people discussing divorce and have no reaction to what they are doing.

But I do look for clues in myself—physical discomfort, feelings, or thoughts—that suggest I am alienated from one or both of the people. If unattended to, alienation can jeopardize the trust among us. Second, I look for signs that I wish to take control of the situation. I work hard to counteract my natural impulse to impose my views by reminding myself that a primary objective of the process is to empower the parties. Finally, I ask both parties to challenge me on my biases or take issue with comments that restrict them. Unfortunately, not many take me up on that—either they are too preoccupied to notice them, or they don't want to offend me—thus giving me power that I must refrain from exercising.

In the end, the point of this internal monitoring is somewhat paradoxical: To empathize fully with my clients in their difficulties, I must be highly attentive to and rigorous in identifying the content of my own internal landscape.

Hank and Allison had begun to express some compassion for each other. The blame each of them had held on to so tightly had loosened a bit—not enough so that their basic stances had been altered, but enough so that some productive dialogue could begin. This was a delicate crossroads. Each party could revert easily to the stance of blame, especially as it was providing them the distance they needed from each other. But that very distance gave them—with some help and their continued willingness—their elusive chance to meet on new ground. They had not opened their dialogue alone; I had been the catalyst. It was premature to assume that they were ready or able to continue by themselves, for they did not yet understand the process by which compassion loosens blame. And it turned out that they were not.

APPLYING THE PRINCIPLES

Mediator: Do either of you notice a shift in the way you're talking to each other?

Hank: Yes, it's different, but I'm not here for an encounter group. I want to get down to numbers.

Allison: Me, too. It's helpful to have heard Hank and to have had some straighter talk. It is a relief, in fact. But let's get down to details.

Mediator: Okay. I think it would be helpful to establish first how much time you each expect to spend with Morgan, so we can see how the expenses for him will be paid.

Allison: Of course, Hank can see Morgan whenever he wants to, but he's been with me almost all the time. Hank's hardly seen him at all.

Hank: I've been too busy. Besides, he's mostly with your mother.

Allison: You make mother sound like his nanny. She's a wonderful backup, but not Morgan's primary caregiver, and you know that!

Mediator: So we should assume that, for purposes of determining child support, 100 percent of the expenses will actually be paid by Allison.

Hank: Yes. Maybe later on that will change, but for now, that's right.

Allison: I am willing to go right to the heart of it. I know you don't want to pay spousal support, so I am willing to give up spousal support unless I get sick or hurt or some other disaster like that.

Hank: I appreciate that, Allison.

Allison: But I want $1,500 a month child support.

Hank: Are you crazy? The baby doesn't cost anywhere near that much money. You're trying to rip me off. I'm leaving. [Hank, his face flushed red with anger, gets up and walks out the door.]

Allison: [Upset and yelling after him] You want to go back to court again?

When Hank got up to leave, part of me wanted to stop him. I didn't know if he was leaving mediation forever or for a minute, but I did know that if I tried to stop him and was successful, we would all be looking more to me to run the meeting and come up with the solution. So I stood behind our original agreement—that either of them was free to leave at any time. If Hank came back, it would be on his own steam. Allison looked at me questioningly.

Allison: What do we do now?

Mediator: Let's wait to see if he comes back, unless you want to leave.

Allison: He'll come back. He always has to have the last word.

She looked almost smug as she said that. She was enjoying this moment. I was uncomfortable but determined to just wait and see what happened next. A minute or two later, Hank returned. Some of the flush on his face had dissipated, but he was still fuming.

Hank: I don't want to go back to court. You know that, but I'd rather do that than be ripped off. You know damn well that diapers, baby food, and baby-sitting don't cost more than a few hundred a month. You say you don't want spousal support, but that's what you're really asking for. Except if you call it child support, I don't get to deduct it and you don't have to report it as income.

Allison: You make $100,000 a year. The least you can do is pay $18,000 of it, less than one-fifth of what you're making, to support your son. You do nothing for him. I'm raising him all by myself. So you should be glad I'm only asking for $1,500 a month. It should really be more than that.

Hank: You're just not being honest when you say you don't want spousal support.

Allison: So now you're calling me a liar? You cheap, irresponsible son of a bitch!

Mediator: Is this productive?

Hank: No. We're getting nowhere. Allison is doing now what she did in the marriage. She's trying to manipulate me, and I won't put up with it.

Allison: And he's trying to act like our child is not his. I'm not asking for the money for me. If we didn't have a child, I wouldn't ask for a dime.

Mediator: So you each feel that you're taking a reasonable position and that the other is not? Allison, what is it that Hank doesn't understand, that would change his view if he did understand?

This intervention is useful when both parties seem unable to understand anything about the other person's point of view. It asks them to begin to consider the other person's perspective, and is thus the first step into empathy. The aim is to move beyond the question of who is right or wrong, or reasonable or unreasonable, and into a larger context.

Again, in urging the parties to broaden their perspectives, I am trying to get them to do what I try to do myself—see both points of view. This is not easy; they are bound to experience emotional dissonance at holding seemingly contradictory views. But it's easier to understand your spouse's perspective if you know that someone else—ideally your spouse but at least the mediator—understands *your* viewpoint.

I had started with Allison because I felt she was slightly less defensive than Hank and a little better able to explain her view.

Allison: He never understood or tried to understand what it's been like for me. Just as I was getting my career going, we had the baby. I'm not sorry we had him. He means the world to me. But to be suddenly thrust back into the world of competition and business so soon after Morgan was born was hard. And it's doubly hard when I have to raise him all by myself while I'm trying to get my career started up again.

Mediator: [To Hank] What do you make of that? Is that new?

Hank: Is what new?

Mediator: What did you hear Allison say?

Hank: [In an angry tone of voice] I heard her say that it's hard for her to be a mother and work at the same time. But it was her decision to have the baby. I didn't think we were ready. *I* wasn't ready, and I still think that is one of the reasons the marriage didn't work.

Mediator: Put the question of responsibility for the decision aside. Can you appreciate what it's like for Allison right now to have to get her career going again and raise your son?

Hank: Okay, I'll pay $1,500 a month, but only until you start earning more.

Mediator: Wait a second. What just happened?

Hank: I find this very uncomfortable.

Mediator: I understand that, but if you can stay with this conversation for a bit longer, I think we can get to something that could be important for both of you.

Hank: I'm very disappointed that the marriage didn't work. Having the baby made our lives so complicated that we just couldn't cope with it. And it seemed like the baby was there from the beginning.

Mediator: So it's hard for you to feel good about the baby when, if he weren't around, the two of you might still be together?

Hank: I don't think of it that way.

Mediator: How do you think of it?

Hank: I just felt overwhelmed. That's all. There just wasn't room in our lives for fun.

Mediator: For a moment, can you put yourself in Allison's position and imagine what it must be like for her now?

Hank: I don't really want to do that.

Mediator: Because?

Hank: My situation isn't so easy either.

Mediator: I know. We'll come to that. Right now, though, I think it would be useful if you could see how this all looks from her point of view. From where I'm sitting, it looks as if neither of you wants to take in what the other is going through. I think it would be helpful if you could do that.

Hank: I think I'd rather pay her the $1,500.

By saying that he would rather pay her the $1,500, Hank was making a last-ditch effort to avoid recognizing Allison's pain. He was afraid that if he opened to her, the pain of the situation would overwhelm him. He needed my support to open not only to her but, more important, to a level in himself that could change his perspective.

Mediator: I know this is hard, but I'm afraid if we just stopped it now with you agreeing to the $1,500, tomorrow morning you'd regret it.

Hank: Maybe. But I know it's not easy for her right now.

Mediator: What's hard about it for her now?

Hank: The world of architects is very competitive. It's going to take her awhile to get back into the swim of it, but she's good. She stopped at a time when she was beginning to build her business, so it's going to take a while. I know that.

Mediator: And caring for an infant won't make that easy.

Hank: I know, but damn it, that was her choice.

Mediator: That doesn't make it any easier. We can deal with the issues of who's responsible for the decision to have Morgan later. For now, I think it's important for you just to be able to appreciate what Allison's facing.

Hank: It's hard to do that when I feel so strongly that she's responsible for it.

Mediator: [To Allison] Are there more things you want Hank to know about what it's like for you right now?

Allison: I'm surprised he understands *any* of it. It makes me mad when he blames me for all of it. There was more agreement about having the baby than he says.

Mediator: We'll deal with that, but is there more about your current situation that you want him to understand?

Allison: He has financial security. He's living on this wonderful houseboat, has a big income, and he's going to make more. I'll never be able to do that, because Morgan takes so much of my time and I don't have any cash. I live from month to month.

Mediator: And what's that like for you?

Allison: In some ways I'm glad he has all that. But it's hard for me when I think about what a struggle it is for me compared to him. And then I get angry thinking that he just wants me and Morgan to disappear, as if we never existed.

Mediator: And I imagine it's a high priority for you to get on with your life, too.

Allison: Right.

Mediator: So whatever we call it, spousal or child support, for you the issue right now is getting help from Hank to get through this period. And there is a question about the long run, too.

Allison: In the long run, I'll take care of myself. I want Hank's help with Morgan, but I'll take care of myself. Believe me, I hate to be in a position where I need any help from him. And if I didn't have Morgan, or if he took care of him, which he can't or won't, then I wouldn't need any help from him at all.

Mediator: [To Hank] What are you getting from this conversation?

Hank: I'm not about to pay for her to move to a fancier house. It was just fine for her when we moved into it.

Mediator: You heard her ask for a new house?

Hank: I have a nice place to live because of the years I put into building my practice before I even met Allison.

Mediator: And you think she wants to live like you?

Hank: Yes.

Allison: You're crazy, Hank. All I said was that you are in a position that I'll probably never be in. I didn't ask you for a house. I do feel entitled to half of what was accumulated while we were together.

Hank: Okay. That's fair.

Mediator: Hank, from your side, how does all of this look? What do you think Allison doesn't understand about your side?

Hank: I think she just thinks I'm trying to run away from

the situation. It's true I want to get on with my life, and want to put the past behind me. I'm willing to support the baby, but I think that Allison should be responsible for herself.

Mediator: What does that mean?

Hank: The baby is really hers. I don't much know how to relate to him. I never really wanted to have him in the first place, at least not so early in our marriage.

Mediator: How did the decision get made to have him?

Hank: We didn't really ever decide. She wanted a child. She knew I wasn't ready yet.

Mediator: Were you using birth control?

Hank: No, but that was up to her.

Mediator: How did you conclude that birth control is strictly up to the woman?

Hank: I don't know. That's the way I was brought up. But that's beside the point. You asked me what Allison doesn't understand. What she doesn't get is that I work hard for my money. It's not as if I like putting in sixteen-hour days, and I don't want to have to pay her more than it costs to raise the kid.

Mediator: Is it because you don't feel responsible for the difficulty she may be having getting her practice going because of her parenting responsibilities?

Hank: She leaves him with her mother all the time. She can work as much as she wants.

Mediator: So let me see if I can understand you. You're saying that you want to get on with your life. You feel entirely willing to pay support for Morgan but not for Allison, mainly because you feel that the decision to have Morgan should be considered her responsibility.

Hank: Right. I don't want to be legally obligated, at least, to do more than that.

Mediator: Because?

Hank: I want to be generous with child support, but I don't want to do it out of a sense of obligation and have Allison shove it down my throat if I don't do it.

Mediator: For the mediation process, then, that shouldn't make a difference, because we're working toward an agreement that will constitute the minimum required of you. And for you, Allison, it's important that you see the ultimate agreement as the maximum, so that you don't have any expectation of more. So, Hank, do you think you've explained everything that's behind your point of view?

Hank: [Loosening his tie and unbuttoning the top button on his shirt] Yes.

Mediator: [To Allison] What do you hear Hank saying here?

Allison: That he wants to run away from his responsibilities to me and Morgan.

Mediator: You heard him say to Morgan as well as you?

Allison: He's as responsible for Morgan's being in the world as I am, and he wants to deny it. Sure, I wanted to have a kid, but I didn't sleep with the mailman to produce him. *He's* the father. I don't recall him protesting that he didn't want to sleep with me.

Mediator: Do both of you think that this point, the responsibility for having a child, is the critical difference between you?

Hank: Not really. I think that what's really going on is that Allison wants to depend upon me, and I don't want it.

Mediator: And for you there is no connection between her dependence on you and the interruption to her career to give birth to and care for Morgan?

Hank: Right. And I don't think this is getting us anywhere.

Mediator: Is that true for you, too, Allison? Are we making no progress as far as you're concerned?

Allison: I find this very difficult, but it's helpful to me to get down to the truth, and I think we're getting close to it.

Mediator: Is there anything new coming out of this for you?

Allison: I didn't realize before how much Hank blamed me for having Morgan or how much he thinks Morgan's presence interfered with our relationship. I disagree with him, but I can see that he sincerely believes it.

Hank: I believe it because it's true.

Mediator: Can you see that if you were Allison, you might see it differently?

Hank: Yes, I really do, but that doesn't change my perception.

Mediator: That's fine. It's a big step to allow someone else's point of view to be legitimate when it contradicts your own.

Hank: [Sadly nodding his head] But what do we do with that? We see it differently and say good-bye, but what do we do about support?

INTERRUPTED EMPATHY

We were now at the critical point of the mediation process. Each party now better undertood the other's view, and the fundamental conflict had been revealed—the choice to have a baby. Yet, as we talked, I sensed that although we had illuminated the central conflict, we hadn't really addressed it. Perhaps this was because I was having difficulty empathizing with Hank. I sensed that all he seemed to care about was his freedom and that Allison was right—he did want to walk away from his responsibility to her, both as a marriage partner and as a co-creator of Morgan. Yet when I examined that judgment, it didn't seem fair. It wasn't as if he were totally unwilling to support Morgan. Still, I knew that even if intellectually I could be neutral, inside I was judging him for his lack of interest in his son.

In order for the mediation to proceed fairly, I needed to overcome my biases and put myself in Hank's position. I tried to understand his ambivalence about having a child, his pain at seeing his new marriage fall apart, and his frustration at his inability to connect with an infant. I began to feel the strength of his fear of being trapped in an unhappy situation and his desire to be free, to put all of this behind him, and to start again. I suspected that for Hank, Morgan represented the anguish of a dysfunctional marriage, and that Hank was keeping his distance from his son to avoid experiencing his painful connection with Allison.

This exercise in empathy suggested that Hank didn't yet appreciate a fact that was clear to me—it would be impossible to simply erase his marriage to Allison and parenthood of Morgan. No matter what happened to him in the future, he would never again be married for the first time, and he would always be the father of this son, whether he chose to relate to him or not.

I asked myself why I could not let well enough alone and accept Hank's willingness to pay $1,500 per month, as he twice indicated he would do. The answer was, I was afraid to trust the promise because it seemed grounded in nothing but fear. Maybe that was wrong, but I was shooting for something more lasting and dependable—a solution with solid ground for him to stand on—and maybe Hank was, too.

Part of what bothered me was that while both Allison and Hank could articulate their positions and points of view quite clearly, Morgan's point of view was not represented. Even though his life would be dramatically affected by the decisions to be made here, his needs had not been clearly identified or discussed. How important was it for him to have his dad in his life? This would be a hard assessment for any of us to make. Allison's and Hank's views on the matter would likely be colored, if not muddied, by their own needs. And even if they were clear now, Morgan's needs would undoubtedly change as he grew older. Nonetheless, it was not hard to imagine that if I were Morgan, I would not only want to know that I was supported financially by my father, but would also want to form a real relationship with him, to have him be a part of my life.

I would need to find a way to make Hank and Allison aware of the difference between their perspectives and Morgan's. If I couldn't do that, we might need to bring in an expert on child development to help educate them about Morgan's needs.

EXPANDING
THE BARGAINING ARENA

*C*ommunication is only one important aspect of the mediation process; bargaining is another. For some people, bargaining means adopting classic negotiation stances to maximize their economic positions. For Hank, that would mean paying as little as he could; for Allison, getting as much as she could. At the other end of the spectrum are those people who strive for an understanding that will yield a solution satisfactory to their sense of justice.

Though achieving such an end also involves negotiation, this experience is more collaborative and less adversarial than the other.

Most mediations contain elements of both approaches, with the proportions determined by the nature of the relationship and individual predispositions. As a mediator, I often find myself urging the parties to move along a continuum toward the second approach, expanding the pie to include intangible values as well as purely economic ones.

The most difficult job a mediator faces arises when one of the parties is open to a solution based on his or her sense of fairness while the other is interested only in maximizing his or her financial position. In such a situation, the more open party is vulnerable to exploitation. It becomes the mediator's job to point out this dynamic and help them see that, along with money, less tangible bargaining chips have significance in the process.

In Hank and Allison's case, they would both benefit from expanding their perspectives and moving into a more collaborative approach. For example, with respect to support, they each stood to benefit from their being in different income-tax brackets. With some creative spousal and child support arrangements, they both could have more after-tax dollars to spend. Also, if Hank took on more of the parenting role, Allison would be free to earn more money, which would mean she would need less support. This might be a financial boon to them and, further, would give Morgan and his father more contact, which could be beneficial to all three of them.

> **Mediator:** We need to find a workable basis of agreement for you two, an idea or set of ideas that incorporates both your points of view.
>
> **Allison:** How do we do that when our views contradict each other?
>
> **Mediator:** By identifying both of your priorities and looking for solutions that address both sets as fully as possible.

Hank: That's too abstract to have any meaning to me.

Mediator: Okay, I'll try to make it more concrete. You have several decisions to make. First, you have to decide how much support Hank will pay Allison now on a monthly basis. Second, you need to decide how that support will be allocated—will it be child *and* spousal support, and if so, in what proportions. Third, you need to reach a parenting agreement on the time you will spend with Morgan and how decisions about Morgan will be made. Fourth, you need to identify and spell out the conditions that would mean a reassessment or change in the level of support and, finally, when support will end. But to make any of these decisions, you must first identify your individual priorities.

For example, so far it seems to me that for Allison a priority is getting enough support now to both mother Morgan adequately and build her business. For Hank, I imagine that knowing the limits of his obligation might give him a sense of freedom and allay his fears of being trapped into paying Allison unfairly. And for both of you, minimizing contact with each other seems to be a priority. As for Morgan, it's not clear what the priorities are for him, but we need to consider his needs, too. Are you getting what I mean?

Allison: Yes, this is very helpful. Good.

Mediator: But I'd much prefer to have this come from you than me. I'm only guessing at what your priorities are. It's really up to you to identify them, because you know much more about your lives than I.

Hank: How are we then going to make the decisions you set out, one at a time or all together?

Mediator: Either way. Until we've made them all, it will be hard to know whether you feel solid about the decisions.

> *Hank:* Okay, so Allison wants $1,500 a month. I think
> that's too high, but I would be willing to pay her that if I
> get certain things that I want.
>
> *Allison:* Like what?

Though it was important for Hank and Allison to make their
priorities clear, I was worried that my prescription for getting to
a solid solution—expanding the bargaining arena—would be cut
short by Allison and Hank. It was true that they were taking things
into their own hands, but they seemed ready to slide over the
rather difficult and delicate task of identifying their priorities explicitly and were settling into the trading or compromising mode char-
acteristic of a purely adversarial relationship. They stood to lose
the joint benefits that could expand the pie. Or they could reach
the end-point of an effective but superficial strategy to walk away
with a superficial solution that could backfire later. Still, I was inclined for the moment to check my impulse to do it my way and
see if they could find their own way. If they could not, I would fit
myself into their mode, looking for opportunities to keep things
open and pointing out potential joint gains. What they most
needed at this point was support for the obvious momentum they
were gathering on their own steam, not a shift away from it to
something more comfortable for me.

> *Hank:* [Settling back into his chair for the first time] Like
> giving me the tax advantages and reducing support at reg-
> ular intervals.
>
> *Mediator:* Explain to me what you are talking about.
>
> *Hank:* I'll give her the $1,500 a month now, but I want to
> be able to get the maximum tax advantage in doing that,
> and I want to have the amount regularly reduced every few
> months or so until we get down to regular child support.

Allison: What would that mean for me? My lawyer said that if he gets to deduct support, I have to pay taxes on it. Then I don't get $1,500 at all.

Mediator: That's right. If the goal is for you have $1,500 after taxes, it has to be all child support. If it's called part spousal or all spousal, then you'll be paying taxes on it. For you to receive $1,500 a month of after-tax money, Hank would have to pay the tax margin as well.

Hank: Why should I have to pay those taxes?

Mediator: I'm not saying you should. All I'm saying is that if she needs $1,500 after taxes, that's what would have to happen.

Hank: I don't want to pay $1,500 and her taxes.

Mediator: I think it might be clearer if we looked at the cost to Hank and the amount actually received by Allison after taxes. It seems to me you're both more concerned about that than about the amount of dollars that change hands between you.

Allison: Right.

Mediator: So, in order for Allison to receive $1,500 dollars after taxes, Hank pays Allison $2,000 dollars spousal support, because she is in the 25 percent tax bracket. Then Allison gets $1,500 after taxes, but the actual cost to Hank after his tax deduction is taken into account is $1,300 because his tax bracket is 37 percent. The difference in the tax margin is explained by the differences in your projected tax brackets for the next year.

Hank: But that would mean I'd be giving Allison a monthly check for $2,000 dollars. That's just crazy.

Mediator: Hank, you're more focused on the amount

you'd be giving her than what it would actually cost you. If you gave Allison $1,500 in child support, it would actually cost you *more* in after-tax dollars than the $2,000 in spousal support.

Hank: That doesn't make sense to me.

Mediator: It's because of the tax advantage in calling the payment spousal rather than child support. There might be other reasons you wouldn't want to do it that way, but from the standpoint of cost alone, to meet Allison's stated amount, it would be cheaper for you to call it spousal support.

Hank: What would be the reason *not* to do it that way?

Mediator: It would be harder to lock in the numbers legally, since support for Morgan can't be unchangeable and there is no differentiation between Allison and Morgan.

Hank: No, that wouldn't be good.

Mediator: So we're back to the task of identifying your priorities. You need to choose between saving money and locking in the numbers, which you can do with Allison, but not with Morgan.

Allison: I'd like the numbers to be certain, too.

Mediator: All right, fine. So we're back to the priority you both have—limiting any future economic negotiations between you.

Hank: How would I ensure that limit most?

Mediator: Calling all money you pay Allison child support and having her waive spousal support. Then the only increases could come by showing Morgan's need, not Allison's.

I had to be careful with this point. Both parties' lawyers, but most of all Allison's, would be concerned about her giving up an important bargaining chip so easily. If a judge were ruling on their case, Allison would certainly receive spousal support, probably until her business became more established. Waiving spousal support would leave her vulnerable—for example, should she get sick or hurt, she would have no recourse except to ask the court for an increase in child support. On the other hand, if the child support were high enough and were in fact a kind of disguised spousal support, then the support would only go up over time at least to meet inflation, even if Allison were to remarry. Building in that possibility would certainly alarm *Hank's* lawyer. So, from a strategic point of view, this part of the mediation was quite delicate.

The questions in my mind were how much of this Allison and Hank already understood, and how far I ought to go to ensure that they both understood the ramifications of what they were doing. Outside of our session, their consulting lawyers could help them a great deal, but at the moment it was up to me to make it all clear even if it meant there would be no agreement. But that risk was offset by the fact that the more clearly they understood the possible strategies, the more open the exchange would become and the less controlled by the strategies alone. My own first priority was still to promote openness. To do that I had to make sure I myself didn't get caught in any one solution, even if one seemed to me like the best for all three of them.

A NEW GLITCH

Hank: Okay. I'd like it to be all child support.

Mediator: Even if after taxes it costs you more than $1,500 dollars?

Hank: Mmmm. I don't know about that.

Allison: If I get $1,500 clear, then you've got a deal.

Mediator: How does that work for you?

Allison: It doesn't. I'd rather have spousal support *and* child support, but I can see he doesn't want to pay spousal support. So I'll accept child support alone, but I won't take a penny less than the $1,500.

Mediator: You don't have to do it that way, if it doesn't work for you.

Allison: Yes, but I *really* don't want to have to go to court again.

Mediator: It's true that's a possibility, but Hank doesn't want to go to court any more than you do.

What was going on here? Allison seemed to be adopting a victim's stance, a position guaranteed to push my buttons. The victim's posture is perhaps the most difficult to work with, and here I needed to assess how real it was on Allison's part. If she were genuinely feeling powerless, then suggesting she didn't have to accept Hank's position would encourage her to feel more powerful. But if, as seemed more likely, Allison was attempting to manipulate either me or Hank, then I needed her to move to a truer stance. However, if she needed to play the victim to get Hank to do what she wanted, it occurred to me that I should just stay out of the way. I decided to stick to my chosen course and make sure they understood the implications of what they were doing.

Allison: So, okay—the $1,500 child support is acceptable.

Mediator: Why does that make sense, Allison?

Allison: It's fine, because it means Hank keeps his nose out of my business and guarantees Morgan will be taken care of.

Mediator: I want you to be clear about what child support covers. Sometimes people distinguish between regular child support and such "extraordinary expenses" as health insurance, private school, uncovered medical expenses, and other categories.

Hank: Look, if I'm going to participate in any of those expenses, I'm sure as hell not about to pay $1,500 a month in child support.

Allison: You already pay the health insurance for him. You've got a good plan and it costs you practically nothing. I'll pay all the other extras except college education, which you'll pay.

Hank: No way. First of all, I haven't agreed to the $1,500, but if I did, I would want to subtract the health insurance premium cost. And by the time Morgan goes to college, you should be in as good a position as me to foot the bill, so we'll split it.

Allison: All right, but I want a cost-of-living adjustment based on inflation every year for child support. Then I'll never come to you for anything else.

Hank: It's a deal.

Mediator: Now, Hank, how do you see yourself relating to Morgan over the years?

Hank: I don't know. I don't much relate to him now. I'd like to be able to see him occasionally, but to be truthful, my first priority right now is being free.

Mediator: Do you have any interest in participating in decisions about his life?

Hank: Not really. I think that the person who is most in his life should make those decisions, and that's Allison. I trust her to do that.

Mediator: Do you think this is what is best for Morgan?

Hank: How would I know?

With a bit more conversation, we solidified the decisions and spelled out the lump sum payment to Allison for her share of their assets. After reality-testing the agreement, we were done, at least as far as Allison and Hank were concerned. They both seemed happy. I felt okay about everything but the arrangements for Morgan. Would it be the best for him, as they agreed, to hardly have his father in his life? It seemed clear that Hank wasn't much interested in being a parent now—no more than he'd ever been. And while Allison seemed open to providing Hank access to Morgan, she also seemed relieved not to have to have much contact with Hank. So the mediation process had worked for them—it had enabled them to forge an agreement they both thought they could live with. But I wondered whether either of them would regret it in the future, if not on their own behalfs then on Morgan's. As a father, I had a sense of what Hank was missing by withdrawing from his son, and I felt sad for all of them.

The mediation had turned into a traditional bargaining session, focused solely on money. They had reached a financial deal, which was something, but it was less than I had hoped for with them. In the end, despite my efforts to exercise empathy, there had been little, if any, transformation in their relationship. And they hadn't taken advantage of opportunities to structure the agreement in a way that would benefit them both. Most of all I worried what Hank's withdrawal would mean for Morgan's future. It always takes a while to disengage after a mediation, but if all of them went like this, I think I'd quit.

A
SEPARATE
GRIEF

SUMMARY

Devastated by the death of their baby and by Claudia's subsequent rage, this couple is unable to communicate with each other—in fact, they can't even be in the same room. They ask me if there's any way to mediate with them separately. In spite of my belief that seeing couples individually gives the mediator too much power, this time, because I am moved by their devastation, I do it. Shuttling from room to room, I present first one side, then the other, in an effort to reach an agreement. This one-on-one process is known as caucusing, and this case gives me the opportunity to compare and contrast it with the three-way approach I prefer.

*A*s soon as Jake and Claudia entered my office, the atmosphere changed. I could feel the muscles in my neck tense up, and I immediately anticipated an unusual mediation. The anguish on Claudia's face pinched and distorted what might have once been pretty features. In contrast, Jake's face was like a mask, revealing little of his emotional state. Neither made any effort to smile or make eye contact as I introduced myself, and only Jake managed to murmur a greeting, an audible exhalation sounding something like "Hello." The silence in the room was like a blanket of gloom. The heaviness pressed on my chest.

Both Jake and Claudia were in their early forties. She wore a neat, tailored suit; he was more casually dressed in corduroys, a plaid shirt open at the neck, and a sweater vest. He spoke in a monotone as he explained that they'd been separated for almost a year and had recently decided on mediation as the quickest means of divorce. Suddenly Claudia stood up, her face trembling, and whispered, "I can't do this."

> ***Mediator:*** What is it that you can't do?
>
> ***Claudia:*** I can't be in the same room with him. I just can't. Is there any way we could talk to you separately in different rooms?
>
> ***Mediator:*** I can see how much pain you're in, but I find that this process has greater integrity when we're all in the same room working together.
>
> ***Claudia:*** I'm not going to be able to do it. Please excuse me. I need to step outside.

She left the room.

> ***Jake:*** It's obvious how upset she is, and frankly, it isn't much easier for me to be around her. We haven't seen each other since we separated ten months ago, and we've

barely spoken. Almost a year ago, we lost our only child to Sudden Infant Death Syndrome. Both of us were at work when the baby-sitter found him. Claudia has been devastated by this and blames us both for what happened. Even though the doctors told us we're not responsible, she believes that if one of us had been there it wouldn't have happened. She's been in counseling, but I guess just seeing me is extremely painful. We would both like to mediate—we want to make the process as quick and simple as possible. We've suffered enough already. Neither of us wants to inflict more pain on the other. Won't you consider seeing us separately?

THE QUESTION OF CAUCUSING

Caucusing, or meeting separately with each party, is a controversial topic among mediators. Traditionally, labor mediators and others involved in disputes involving many parties have considered caucusing an indispensable tool. The advantages to caucusing are numerous. First, the theory is that without the presence of the "enemy," disputants are likely to be more open, disclosing information they might otherwise hide. Second, a one-on-one dialogue with a trustworthy mediator "friend" allows for a fuller and freer exploration of options. Finally, meeting separately gives the mediator a chance to better understand each party's point of view.

But the disadvantages of caucusing are also striking. By meeting individually with the parties, the mediator becomes more important to the success of the mediation—his or her point of view is likely to have a far greater impact on the disputants than if the three were working together. By extension, caucusing also gives the mediator more opportunities to manipulate the outcome, since each party depends only on what the mediator says to know what is acceptable to the other. In fact, without both parties in the room, the subjectivity of the mediator becomes the critical element, carrying much more weight than the parties' sense of fairness. If the mediator's sense of fairness happens to coincide with that of the parties, the damage is minimal. But if the mediator's sense of fairness conflicts with those of the other two, and they are not self-confident enough to register their disagreement or clear enough to know what they *do* want, the parties may find themselves with a result they later regret.

But there's a deeper level to the issue. I believe strongly that the magic of mediation comes from the direct contact between the parties in the presence of the mediator—the mediator acts as a bridge to a kind of understanding not possible otherwise. In caucusing, the vital information conveyed by body language, tone of voice, and inflection, nuances known only to the parties themselves, are all lost, and creating an understanding becomes much more difficult.

Finally, I generally oppose caucusing because of the power it invests in the mediator, particularly when he or she agrees to hold secrets between the parties. In that case the mediator must both keep the parties' secrets and respond somehow to their (often unexpressed) desire for explicit advice as to what to do.

For the mediator, the only person with a full picture of the situation, it's easy to form an opinion on what they should do. But since their agreement has to be rooted in their own sense of fairness to succeed, I have to refrain from telling them what I think.

In this case it seemed that my only options were to mediate by caucus or turn the case over to lawyers. I was moved by Jake and Claudia's obvious anguish, and their desire to minimize further suffering, so I decided to see if I could help. I suggested for speed's sake that they both come to my office but to separate rooms, and that I shuttle back and forth between them. My hope was that we might reach a point where we could come back together, even if only to make the final decisions.

COLLECTING THE BASICS— PIECEMEAL

I started with Jake. He explained that three years before, with Claudia's encouragement and financial support, he had given up his lucrative job in corporate sales and gone back to school to get a teaching certificate. When the baby died, he was in his first year of teaching history at a local high school. His salary was $20,000 per year, hardly enough for him to maintain a decent lifestyle and help support his two teenage daughters from his first marriage, who lived primarily with their mother. But Claudia, who had a well-paying job, had suggested the change knowing that he would be much happier as a teacher, even though it had meant spending their savings and depending on her salary during his schooling and student teaching.

Jake also explained that before Claudia had gotten pregnant with the baby, they had tried to conceive for years. She had undergone a rigorous fertility treatment, which, before her last pregnancy, had resulted in two miscarriages. All this had caused strain in their marriage. The successful birth of the baby had brought the joy back into the relationship, but when he died, the marriage seemed to die with him.

When I met with Claudia, it was clear that she was consumed by the loss of their child. The joy of the baby's birth had been deepened by her previous difficulties in conceiving. Now, after ten years of marriage, at forty-two, she was certain that she could not be able to bear another child. Her life felt empty. Only her job as director of marketing for a small computer company earning $80,000 per year held any interest for her, and that was marginal.

> ***Mediator:*** Do you have people you can turn to who understand your situation, any friends or family?
>
> ***Claudia:*** None. I'm all alone.

Mediator: Have you ever considered seeing a psychotherapist to help you get through this time?

Claudia: I saw someone for a while, but it didn't really help, so I stopped.

Mediator: So you feel quite stuck.

Claudia: Not really. Six months ago, I was considering suicide on a daily basis, so compared to then, it's easier now. If I can get this divorce behind me, maybe my life will begin to work.

Mediator: And what would it take to do that?

Claudia: We have our house. After we lost the baby, I couldn't stand to be in it, so I moved to an apartment. I was surprised to find that Jake moved out a month later, and since then, we've been renting it out. The rent just covers the overhead expenses. We're trying to sell it. Once that happens, and Jake reimburses me for the mortgage payments I made from the time he quit his job, then I think I'll be able to put all this behind me and move on.

When I shuttled back to the other room to meet with Jake, I was not surprised that his view was quite different from Claudia's.

Jake: Since we separated, I haven't been able to help the girls. I've been living in a small apartment complex where I do maintenance work in exchange for reduced rent. But that's cut back on my time with Allie and Natalie on weekends. I never would have considered changing my career without Claudia's financial support. The house has been on the market since I moved out and we haven't had a nibble, even though we've reduced the price twice. Until we sell it, I want Claudia to help me support the girls as we originally planned. I could go back into sales if I had to, but it feels awful to even think about that. I love teaching and I'm really good at it, and it was Claudia's idea that I teach in the first place. I don't think it's unreasonable for her to help me out.

With this significant difference in their positions, I had to consider how to best frame the situation for each party to make their views most palatable to the other. I decided to start by trying to evoke in Claudia the original spirit of her and Jake's agreement. But when I told her his side, she became enraged.

> *Claudia:* How dare he ask me for money now! If he'd stayed in his sales job where he could make a decent salary, I could have taken off at least six months from work to be with the baby. And then this never would have happened. But I had to go back after two months because *he* wanted to be a teacher. His whole life is working for him. He's doing work that he loves, which I made possible for him, and he has two healthy, loving daughters.

> *Mediator:* So you're not willing to give him any financial help.

> *Claudia:* Not a chance! He'll get his share when the house sells. I've supported him long enough.

Witnessing the distance between Claudia and Jake caused by their shared loss, I realized that blaming Jake was important in her coming to terms with the tragedy. Expressing anger could reignite Claudia's energy, and since blaming Jake would fuel that anger, it could be useful. But there would be limits to blame's usefulness. The most problematical aspect of blame is its judgmental quality. Those who condemn others strongly usually hold themselves to very high standards, reserving the strongest (though often unconscious) condemnation for themselves. So as much as

Claudia blamed Jake for the death of their child, I believed that probably she was blaming herself as well.

While the antidote to blame is compassion, the journey between the two is not easy. Blame can be a roadmark on the way to a broader understanding of a situation, but too often it is a place where people stop. Going past blame into compassion can open doors to a fuller exploration of truth which in turn can lead to a just resolution.

In mediation blame turned to anger can help a self-flagellating person assert him or herself. If Claudia could use her anger to gain the distance she needed from Jake, she would then be able to begin to rebuild her life. And if she could go a little further and find compassion, she might soften her stance toward him and ultimately herself.

It was ironic that the person who could most closely identify with the pain that she was experiencing was the one she was working hardest to push away. I didn't know what I could do about that, but I sensed that it might be the key to creating a base for common understanding. I had several ideas about how I might go about that if we were together in one room, but as the messenger I felt the distance between the rooms as symbolic of the gulf between them, and it weighed on me.

When I returned to Jake, he immediately picked up my concern.

Jake: She didn't like my idea, did she?

Mediator: No, she didn't.

Jake: What did she say?

Mediator: I know that you understand that she's in a great deal of pain. What seems to be making it harder for her is that when she looks at your life, she sees you doing work you enjoy, surrounded by loving children.

Jake: Goddamnit! She could be surrounded by loving children as well. I know she doesn't want to be around me.

But the girls! Why did she cut them off? They love her as if she were a parent, but after the baby died, she just cut them off, as if they never existed. They lost their baby brother, and then a loved stepmother, but I'm sure Claudia never thinks of that. They were—they still are—confused by her shutting them out.

Mediator: Do you think that she is aware of their feelings?

Jake: I don't know. As you know, we don't talk.

Mediator: I also imagine that the baby's death is painful for you, even though you still have the girls.

Jake: I cannot tell you how bad it still is for me. I wake up in the middle of the night sweating, wondering whether I should check the baby. And then I remember that the baby is dead, and I feel this ache that just won't go away. I've talked to our pastor and so have the girls, but the loss is immense for all of us.

Mediator: Do you think Claudia has any sense of your suffering?

Jake: She's too preoccupied with her own misery to pay any attention to anyone else's. And it doesn't make it any easier to know that she blames me for the baby's death.

Mediator: Could you imagine having any of those feelings if you were Claudia?

Jake: I can certainly imagine feeling sorry for myself, because I often do. But I can't understand how she can blame me so much. It feels like she's punishing me—and Allie and Natalie, as well.

Mediator: By pushing you all away?

Jake: Exactly. And on top of that, she's not living up to her agreement to support me. It's really for them that I need the money, not me personally. Doesn't that seem punishing to you?

Mediator: It's possible, but my guess is that she is more interested in protecting herself than in hurting anyone else.

Jake: I know that having the girls helps me a lot. I'd like Claudia to be able to have that for herself, too.

Mediator: And the financial support?

Jake: I need it. I don't want to leave teaching, and I can't help the girls without it.

Since Claudia had no legal relationship with the girls, she had no legal obligation to support them. But Jake's need for support would likely have met with success in court. At least theoretically, spousal support for men is not considered any differently than for women. However, if Claudia could convince a judge that Jake could earn more money by changing jobs, it was possible that he would receive little or no support. But since Jake had changed careers, that would be difficult.

I soon realized that all three of us were proceeding as if the full responsibility for solving this dispute were squarely on my shoulders. I was already trying to figure out "what they should do," and I knew that shifting that responsibility back to them would be very difficult.

After all, I was the only person involved who was hearing *everything,* and consequently it would be hard to avoid deciding what the settlement should be and getting them to agree to it. I was burdened by a sense of both too much responsibility and too much freedom.

Watching me move back and forth between the front and back offices, my assistant expressed some concern about the toll this was taking on me. And I admit that at times, I felt tempted to just make the whole problem go away. Since I was the one who knew what was going on, I could identify both Jake's and

Claudia's vulnerable spots, decide what the agreement should be, and then just make it happen. I could be the hero, the great problem solver. The feeling reminded me of my old trial-lawyer self who had loved the feeling of power.

But then my mediator self tapped me on the shoulder. How would I feel, I asked myself, if the agreement I produced fell apart or led one or both of my clients to regret the mediation process? I had to find a way to empower Jake and Claudia to reach their own agreement. And frankly, the only possibility seemed to be to try to get them together. I started slowly with Claudia.

> *Claudia:* Has he come around yet?
>
> *Mediator:* There's some new information that I think could be important to the solution.
>
> *Claudia:* So he hasn't come around yet.
>
> *Mediator:* I feel that there is an issue underlying your disagreement that needs to be addressed before you two are going to find your solution.
>
> *Claudia:* Like what?
>
> *Mediator:* It has to do with Allie and Natalie.
>
> *Claudia:* They don't have anything to do with this. I have no legal obligation to them.
>
> *Mediator:* That's true, but from what I understand, you have been and still are an important person in their lives.
>
> *Claudia:* They're his kids, not mine.
>
> *Mediator:* Has it always felt like that?
>
> *Claudia:* [Drawing back and looking at me, then, after a long pause, straightening her back] I don't see what this has to do with anything that we're here for.

Mediator: In that case, I'll drop it. It's up to you to decide what needs to be talked about. It just seems to me like the issues keep circling back to the girls.

Claudia: Tell me what you mean.

Mediator: Well, at least according to Jake, before the baby died, the relationship between you and the girls was important to everyone. [Long pause] I want you to know that I am feeling very uncomfortable in this role of messenger. I am afraid that I won't do justice to the importance of this communication, and I also want to respect your grieving process. The truth is, I think it's important that Jake tell you this directly.

Claudia: Tell me what directly?

Mediator: About what's been happening with the girls.

Claudia: What does this have to do with the financial issues?

Mediator: Maybe nothing. But it could be important.

Claudia: If you think that this is the only way we can reach an agreement, I'm willing to meet together once.

When I told Jake that Claudia was willing to meet together at my request, he was surprised.

Jake: She really wants to?

Mediator: I don't know if I'd go that far. She's willing to meet.

Jake: Okay, then. Let's give it a try. Any advice?

Mediator: Speak from your heart.

We set up a meeting for the following week. Claudia arrived half an hour late.

Mediator: I'm the one who called this meeting. It seemed to me that you were at a point where I was actually interfering with rather than facilitating communication. In my last meeting with Jake, I had the feeling that he should be conveying what he was telling me directly to you, Claudia. I appreciate your willingness to meet together. I know this is really hard for you.

Jake: Claudia, I appreciate your willingness, too. I know that we have a disagreement about your supporting me. I also know that you could feel manipulated by me in this conversation. So, in order for you to believe that I am not just here for money, I am willing to forgo any support and just split the proceeds from the sale of the house. As you know, money has never been very important to me. We both know that I can make a lot more than I do now, and I'll do that if that's what you want. But there are some things that I want to tell you that I've never had the chance to say.

Claudia: I'm not sure I'm ready for this.

Jake: Please. Just give me a few minutes.

Claudia: I'll try.

Jake: When the baby was born, you know how happy I was. To at last have a child together, my first son. But what touched me the most was the way that you included Natalie and Allie throughout the pregnancy, during the birth and that wonderful time afterward. When the baby died, I know how unbearable the pain was for you. I tried so hard to be with you then, but you pulled away and blamed me. I've resigned myself to the fact that you will never forgive me. But what I can't handle is that you've deserted the girls. They needed you so much. And they still do. It's true that you're not their mother, but in many ways you have been as important to them as their real mother.

Claudia: [Visibly shaken] Why didn't they ever call me after the funeral?

Jake: They didn't know what to do. They were scared. Allie wrote you several letters that she never mailed. They didn't want to intrude on your grief.

Claudia: [Softly] I can't stand hearing any more. I think this was a mistake.

She got up and left.

Jake: Maybe she's right.

I thought that it might have been a mistake, too. I had to look more closely at my own motives. Out of my desire to relieve myself of the burden of the responsibility for their communication, had I blinded myself to Claudia's clearly stated limit? Would the wall of protection she had erected so carefully now come tumbling down, exposing her to even more pain? If so, I would have a large share of the responsibility for that. Moreover, I might have jeopardized Jake's future, too. As Claudia withdrew in pain, she might well accept Jake's offer to give up the work he loved.

Two weeks later I was relieved when Claudia called to schedule another appointment. When my assistant told me that we wouldn't need both offices, I found myself eagerly anticipating the joint meeting.

This time Claudia was not late. Although she still looked sad and her face was drawn, she appeared more relaxed.

Claudia: Jake, I've thought a lot about what you said at our last meeting. I would like to spend some time talking with Allie and Natalie. I did push them out of my life without realizing it.

Jake: Oh, Claudia, I am so glad. This will mean a lot to the girls—and a lot to me.

Claudia spent some time talking about her devastation since the baby's death. She felt that during the previous session Jake had helped her unlock something inside herself that she didn't know how to get to alone. While she was now certain that she wanted to resume her relationship with the girls, she was equally clear that her relationship with Jake was over. But the blame seemed to have gone. Because she recognized the importance to Jake of continuing as a teacher, she dropped her request that he pay her back for the mortgage payments, and said she was willing to help support the girls until the sale of the house. She also expressed a desire to contribute to their college education.

Jake was visibly elated. As we closed the session, he could not stop thanking me. I was pleased that I had put aside misgivings about caucusing and agreed to mediate, especially because my biases against this method had not been borne out with Jake and Claudia. In fact, even though I did have an excessive degree of power in the role of messenger, I neither determined nor manipulated the conclusion. And while the most important work took place when Jake and Claudia were together, it was the caucus that had gradually opened the door to it. The vulnerability of each of the parties to the mediator's subjective interpretation of the other was scary, and I was glad the case worked out as well as it had.

Claudia had made a major shift in the two-week period we had been working together. She had recognized that she was not alone and was now willing to embrace the two important relationships she might otherwise have lost. It did not seem out of the question that at some point another shift might occur that would open her to a fuller relationship with Jake.

THE BALLOON THAT BURST

SUMMARY

*I*n mediation as I practice it, the parties agree at the start to have their ultimate agreement, the endpoint of mediation, reviewed by independent lawyers prior to signing it. Tom and Lainie reach an agreement in only two mediation sessions, but their accord falls apart when Tom's consulting lawyer reviews it. In this chapter I analyze the role of the outside lawyer and show what can happen when there are discrepancies between my legal predictions as a mediator and those made by a consulting lawyer. Further, I examine the relationship between the law and the parties' sense of fairness.

*T*om was a well-known physical therapist in the Bay Area, his reputation enhanced by his having had great success in the treatment of several famous athletes. As we shook hands, I was struck by his powerful grasp. His fingers were unusually long, graceful, and smooth. In the course of our time together, he seemed to be constantly pulling at his fingers as if to make them stretch. Strangely enough, Lainie, a potter, had hands that drew my attention, too. They were rough, with clay buried under the fingernails. Throughout our sessions, she seemed to be kneading her palms like a craftsperson caring for her tools.

Tom considered himself a great supporter of mediation and knew several people whom I had worked with in the past. But because she didn't trust Tom, Lainie was suspicious of mediation. Essentially she was afraid that Tom and I were planning to fleece her. However, she had interviewed a lawyer and was certain that any lawyer would have the same idea.

> *Lainie:* The lawyer will take his money and then he'll take mine.
>
> *Mediator:* So you stand a chance of being ripped off either way. It's just a question of whom you choose to allow to do that.
>
> *Lainie:* That's about the size of it.
>
> *Mediator:* If you decide to mediate, do you think there's a danger you would agree to something you consider unfair?
>
> *Lainie:* You don't know me. There's no chance of that. Over the years, living with Tom's deceits and his affairs, I've grown to distrust him so deeply that I've become a far more circumspect person than when we met.
>
> *Mediator:* Well, let me assure you that nothing happens here unless you agree to it.

THE ISSUES

*F*ree with her tears and her anger, Lainie seemed to be a good match for Tom in mediation. He presented himself as very caring, but also had more than a bit of the rogue in him.

Both of them were verbal and direct. Educated in New England at private colleges, they'd moved to California and converted their WASP, tailored, East Coast ways to an ethereal New Age attitude. They both wore clothing made from loose, handwoven, natural fibers and had long hair. Married for nine years, and now in their early thirties, Tom and Lainie had two boys, Brian, age eight and Eli, now seven. Tom had agreed to move out of the house two weeks before I met them, precipitated by Lainie's discovery of his most recent affair, but he had retained his office, which was in a wing of their house. As a result, they continued to see each other daily, which was upsetting to Lainie.

Four issues had to be resolved: the cost to Lainie of buying out Tom's interest in the house; support for Lainie and the boys; dealing with Tom's physical therapy practice as a communal asset; and a parenting agreement.

In our first session, both Tom and Lainie expressed disdain for all experts, including lawyers. Tom had talked to a lawyer whom he would see to review the agreement at the end of the mediation. Lainie wasn't sure if she would do the same, but in any event did not want to see anyone until we had reached an agreement. They also both felt that appraisers would be superfluous in order to determine the value of the house or Tom's practice. Like many clients in mediation, they were intent on getting through the mediation process quickly. For both of them, the marriage was clearly over, but it was clear that Lainie was feeling the urgency for a divorce. One too many betrayals had pushed her past the breaking point. Tom was obviously uncomfortable in Lainie's presence, but he also seemed to enjoy their barbed exchanges.

JOCKEYING FOR POSITION

Lainie came into the next session furious with Tom.

Lainie: I think that I should stop mediation. I can't trust Tom at all now. He stole a vase that one of my favorite teachers gave me several years ago.

Tom: It's true that I took it, but I did it by mistake when I was packing my things. As soon as I realized it was hers, I told her about it. I was going to give it back to her.

Lainie: When? You still haven't given it back.

Tom: As soon as we reach an agreement on everything else.

Lainie: That is unacceptable. I want it back immediately.

Mediator: [To Lainie] What do you want to do about that here?

Lainie: I want that vase back before we do anything more.

Mediator: Tom, how do you see this?

Tom: I just want to be sure that she deals fairly with me. The vase is hers. I'll give it to her.

Mediator: When?

Tom: As soon as we reach an agreement on everything else.

Mediator: Why wait until then?

Tom: So she'll be fair with me.

Mediator: So you feel as if you need to hold the vase as a hostage to be sure that she'll deal fairly with you?

Lainie: Are you kidding? Make him give me back that vase.

Mediator: I can't.

Tom: All right. I'll give it back to you later today.

Mediator: Why?

Tom: Mainly because I don't want to spend our time here talking about this.

Mediator: Okay. I just have one more question. Do you think it's right to give it back to her?

Tom: Yes. I guess I just wanted some assurance that she's not going to try to jerk me around.

Lainie: You know I'm going to be fair with you. But I don't want to play games and I don't want you to go for more than your fair share.

Mediator: Is there anything more that either of you need from each other to be able to proceed?

Lainie: I think you ought to be able to see what a weasel he is. He puts on this show of being caring and well-meaning, but deep down he's really a slippery guy. The boys adore him and it upsets me so much that they are learning this dishonest behavior from him.

Tom: But not Miss Perfect here. She has no flaws. She is always right and she always has the answer. She's the perfect parent.

Mediator: Is this how you usually talk to each other?

Tom: This is the way it has been for the last several years. You can understand why I've needed to have other relationships.

Lainie: This is getting us nowhere. Let's get on with the mediation.

What was going on during this exchange? The vase incident gave me a lot of information about their dynamic. To me they seemed more like a brother and sister squabbling over a toy than a pair of adult parents. But they both seemed to be strong enough to make and tolerate direct statements. I wondered if they were capable of listening to each other, too.

FEELING THEIR WAY

*D*uring the marriage, Tom and Lainie had lived on Tom's earnings, supplemented by money from Lainie's family. Lainie had never worked for a living, although occasionally she sold some of her ceramic pieces. Her parents had given her $100,000 for the down payment on the house and several other income-producing assets, which brought in about $1,500 per month. For the past four years, to support their lifestyle, Tom and Lainie had invaded her assets to the tune of $20,000 per year. Tom took in about $95,000 per year in client fees. His income tax return indicated that his after-tax earnings were about $45,000. We went through Tom's business expenses together to find out how much income was available to help support the family.

Mediator: How much of these expenses are real?

Tom: All of them.

Mediator: Lots of people pad their expenses for the IRS. You have to be straight with us.

Tom: Okay. About $40,000 is real.

Mediator: Let's go through them so that we all understand the situation. You indicated that you pay rent of $500 per month.

Tom: That's what it's going to cost me when I move my office.

Lainie: When is that going to happen?

Tom: In a few years.

Lainie: I don't want to wait till then.

Tom: Then you'll get less support.

Lainie: That's okay, because I don't think that it's healthy for any of us to have you around so much. You come busting into the main house all the time.

Tom: My books are there.

Lainie: Then get them out.

Tom: It's still my house, too.

Lainie: Over my dead body!

Mediator: There are two decisions you are going to need to make. First, you'll have to decide how the buy-out of the house will affect Tom's use of the office, and the second involves support—how much and what kind. They are interrelated, but I think we'll be able to get clearer focusing on them one at a time.

Tom: I want to talk about support.

Lainie: I want to talk about his moving out of the office.

Mediator: We need to talk about both. The only question is the order.

Lainie: I'll talk about support if he'll agree not to enter the rest of the house.

Tom: I only need to do that to get my books.

Lainie: I'll help you move your books to the office.

Mediator: So we're back to support?

Lainie: The first thing to figure out is how to separate his phony expenses from the real ones. He's really slippery.

Tom: [With a smile] I resent that.

Mediator: We need to do this to understand how much income is available for the family's personal expenses and because this will help us decide on the value of the practice as well.

Tom: We'll also have to talk about how much Lainie could earn when we talk about support.

Lainie: That's enough. I've had it! After all of my parents' money that you've spent, I am not about to consider how much I could be earning if I took on a job I would hate. I am not interested in playing any more of your games, Tom. Let me know when you're ready to get serious.

The bubble had burst. She walked out of the room, pausing briefly at the door to look at me, then slamming it behind her.

Tom: What do I do now?

Mediator: Talk to her and see if she wants to continue. I need you both here to be able to do it.

Lainie called several days later to schedule an appointment for the following week. After mediating for so many years, I wasn't surprised when they walked in together announcing that they had moved all Tom's books into his office and on top of that had worked out a complete agreement by themselves. The terms called for Tom to vacate the office within six months. Lainie would receive credit for the down payment from her parents and would buy out Tom's interest in the house for $60,000, one-half of the appreciation of the value in the house since they had bought it.

Tom would buy out Lainie's interest in his practice which they agreed to be worth $40,000, Lainie's half being worth $20,000. So Lainie would make Tom an equalizing payment of $40,000. Lainie agreed to waive spousal support in return for monthly child support of $2,000 based on their continued co-parenting of the boys. The boys would spend 50 percent of their time with each parent, with Tom and Lainie sharing their major expenses equally.

They both appeared elated. I spent some time helping them to be more specific in some areas, clarifying the bases for their agreements and raising some questions as to points not covered. The agreement seemed clear and workable, and met their stated needs.

> *Mediator:* Before you commit to this agreement I want to be sure that you each understand how it fits with the law.
>
> *Lainie:* What difference does that make? This is the deal. It's fair and I don't care what a judge would do. That's why we came here.
>
> *Mediator:* I understand that. You are free to make your own agreement, but to make this agreement legally binding, both of you need to understand what you have agreed upon in the context of your legal rights.
>
> *Lainie:* Okay, tell us.

I spent about forty-five minutes explaining the law. The two areas that were the least clear were spousal support and the house. Regarding the first, a court would certainly have awarded at least temporary spousal support to Lainie. As to the house, if the court decided that the down payment from Lainie's parents was a gift to them both or if it found an agreement or understanding that the house would be owned jointly, then the court might have considered it to be owned by them equally.

> *Tom:* There was always a clear understanding between us

that the down payment was hers since it came from her family.

Mediator: If you said that in court, that would decide the issue.

Neither of them felt that the law changed their feelings about the agreement.

THE QUESTION OF CONSULTING LAWYERS

Mediator: Now all that remains to be done is for each of you to have consulting lawyers review the agreement before you are legally committed to it.

Lainie: I still don't feel the need for that. What would they do that you wouldn't do?

Mediator: Maybe not much, but if you have it reviewed, it will be less subject to challenge if either of you later tries to have a court overturn it. And because we went through this so quickly, it's important that you carefully consider what you've done. It can be helpful doing that with someone who is your advocate alone.

Lainie: That's the problem. They'll just inflame us and ruin all the work we've done.

Mediator: That will only happen if they bring something out that we haven't talked about or if this agreement is so weak that it could fall apart that easily.

Lainie: You don't know Tom.

Mediator: If I did, what would I understand that I don't understand now?

Lainie: That he is inclined to just go for whatever he can get.

Mediator: He hasn't done that here, as far as I can see.

That seemed to convince Lainie. They both agreed to see consulting lawyers. But the next week I received an emergency phone call from Lainie.

Lainie: That son of a bitch went to a lawyer and now he wants half of the house. So do I have to go out and hire my own killer to deal with this?

Mediator: I don't know. Do the two of you want to come in and talk about what happened?

Lainie: I'll see, but I'm so goddamn mad at him, I can hardly see straight.

BLOWUP

*T*he session began with Lainie's accusations. She pointed fiercely at Tom.

Lainie: You make a deal and then you try to back out of it. That's why I can't trust you. This is exactly what I was afraid of.

Tom: The lawyer told me that I'm getting screwed by agreeing to anything less than half of the house.

Lainie: You and I sat down and we agreed and we both said that it was fair. We came here, and Gary explained the law to us, and you *still* thought it was fair.

Tom: That's not my recollection. He didn't say that I was entitled to half of the house—[looking at me] did you?

Mediator: No, I didn't. What I said was that a court could decide that you were entitled to half of the house if there were no agreement or understanding between you to the contrary. And you then said that it had always been clear between the two of you that the down payment was Lainie's.

Tom: But the lawyer said there would be no way Lainie could prove that.

Mediator: If there is nothing in writing, there are two ways she could prove it. First, she could testify to it. And second, you could testify to it.

Tom: Me? Why would I do that?

Mediator: What would you say in court?

Lainie: I'll tell you what he'd say in court—whatever the lawyer told him to say to win. I'm going to get out of here before I go crazy.

Mediator: You're always free to leave, but it might be worth spending a few minutes to see if we can understand what's going on.

Lainie: I know *exactly* what's going on and *I don't like it.* That's why this marriage is *over.*

Mediator: I don't get it, and I'm not sure that you do, either. I would find it helpful to hear more from Tom about what happened since the two of you were here last.

Tom: When I left here, I felt terrific. I understood what we had done and it felt like everything was resolved. But when I went to see the lawyer, she told me that I was entitled to half the house—no question about it. She wanted to know why I was giving Lainie a gift. So I started feeling like a wimp. Why should I give up $50,000? By the time I left her office, I was sure that I had been screwed.

Mediator: And now how does it look?

Tom: I don't know. I feel confused.

Mediator: Let's assume the lawyer was right, that it's an open-and-shut case that you'd get an additional $50,000 for your interest in the house. If Lainie agreed to that, would you consider it a fair deal?

Tom: I'm not sure. On the one hand, since it came from her parents, I didn't think I had a claim to it. But if the court decides I should get it, terrific. Who am I to decide what's fair?

Mediator: Good question. Let's see if we can understand what's in the law that might support that kind of thinking. The main argument you could make to a judge is that since both of you own the house, you are each entitled to half of the proceeds. Right now the law is in flux on this issue, but it states that if the house is in both of your names then it's 50–50 unless you have an understanding or agreement to the contrary. So your lawyer would be arguing that in effect Lainie gave you a gift of half of the down payment or that her parents did when the house was put in both your names.

Tom: But that's not what happened.

Mediator: Did you tell that to the lawyer?

Tom: I don't remember. I don't think so. Actually we didn't talk about it.

Mediator: If a court were to decide in your favor, it would be because a judge believed that the two of you had no agreement or understanding that the down payment was hers.

Lainie: No way. This is crazy.

Mediator: Wait a second. If you can bear with this a bit further, I think it will become clearer. The reason a court would find that there was a gift to Tom—even if there wasn't one—is that when you get married, if you buy something and put it in both your names you have joined together as a community and come into possession on an equal basis.

Lainie: But we were clear that when my parents gave the money, it was mine. Tom didn't have any part of it.

Mediator: Why did you decide to put the house in both names as joint owners?

Tom: The real estate broker said we had to do it that way.

Mediator: Did you tell that to the lawyer?

Tom: No, it didn't come up.

Mediator: Tom, the information your lawyer had to work with differed from what you gave me, I think, and that's probably why we have come up with different interpretations of how a court would decide your case. I'm quite certain that any judge who had heard our conversation of the past ten minutes would not give you half the house. I think a far more likely decision would be that Lainie is entitled to repayment of the down payment, with interest, too.

Tom: Then why would the lawyer tell me I'd get it?

Mediator: I'm not entirely sure, but I think it's a matter of missing information. If she had known that you had agreed that the money was Lainie's, I don't think she would have told you it was half yours. But there could be another reason. She might have been uncertain of what you wanted from her. If she thought you wanted her to be your advocate and take over the case, she might have looked at the situation from a vantage favorable to you because of the way in which you presented yourself. At the very least, she must have wanted you to stop and look hard at the implications of your agreement with Lainie before you committed yourself to it.

Tom: That she accomplished.

Mediator: It's also possible that she is right, that you *could* win in court. But I think that would mean you'd have to say something different than what you have said here. And if you did, we couldn't contradict you because, as you recall, we have a written agreement that says everything here is confidential and not usable in court.

There's another possibility: that the law in this area has changed again and she has read or heard of a new case I don't know about. The law concerning this specific question has changed in major ways three times in the past three years, so it could well have changed again without my knowing about it. But I consider that unlikely since I keep current with what the courts are doing. What's most likely is that the lawyer exaggerated your legal position so you wouldn't enter into an agreement you would later regret. She would have been particularly concerned about making sure you didn't hold her responsible because she hadn't made you aware of the possibility that you could win.

Tom: But couldn't I sue her for giving me the wrong opinion?

Mediator: If she's going to make an error, it's safer for her to *over*estimate, rather than *under*estimate, what you could really get. If she killed your deal with Lainie by being overly optimistic, she'd be safer than if she supported the deal and later turned out to be wrong.

Tom: It's true that I asked for her legal opinion, but that's not what I really wanted from her.

Mediator: What *did* you want?

Tom: I wanted to know whether I was getting screwed or not.

Mediator: And that's what she told you.

Tom: It wasn't quite like that. I sat down and started to talk, but she asked to see the agreement. After she read it, she asked me a few questions, and soon we were off and running. By the time I left, I was as into it as she was.

Lainie: And I was ready to kill you.

Tom: I find this all pretty upsetting. Now I don't know what I really want to do.

Mediator: You have several options. First, you have to decide whether you want to understand the law more fully. You could go back to the lawyer and discuss our conversation here. Or you could see another lawyer and get another opinion. And if you got a different opinion than mine, you could ask the lawyer to be more precise about his reasoning, and then we could discuss it. Ultimately what I want is for you to understand the law and yourself in order to make a decision.

Tom: This is so confusing.

Mediator: Try this as a frame of reference: If you won your point in court, would you consider that win fair or unfair? What about if you lost?

Tom: Actually, that is helpful. I don't think it would be fair if I won. The money is her family's. I'll get money someday from my parents.

Mediator: How does it feel to say that?

Tom: It feels okay.

Mediator: What's your reaction to this conversation, Lainie?

Lainie: I'm angry with you, Gary. If you hadn't forced us into going to lawyers, none of this would have happened.

Tom: I'm glad I went, because it feels good to know that even though I might have done better in court, this feels more fair.

Lainie: You would *not* have done better in court, and I am not going to go around thinking you are Mr. Generous. So you can forget that.

They signed the original agreement.

LAWYERS AND THE LAW

The role of the consulting lawyer is a tricky one, especially for people who are drawn to mediation because they want an alternative to litigation. Introducing the law or lawyers often triggers resistance, as with Lainie. If the purpose of the process is empowerment, then how can it cope with elements that threaten the primacy of the parties as decision makers?

This case illustrates one practical solution: The mediator can help the disputants use their personal sense of fairness as the primary reference point in deciding how much to defer to the law.

In real-world terms, did Tom's decision to agree to repay Lainie for the down payment result from his sense of fairness or from his recognition that he would probably lose in court? I suspect both factors played a role. I think that Tom's initial reaction to the question *was* based on his sense of fairness and that he had never considered the down payment his. However, I also think he was affected by the question of his chances in court. If I was right on both counts, then the law had played just the part in the mediation process that I had hoped it would—it had triggered Tom's sense of fairness while alerting him to his legal vulnerability.

Would it have been so bad if Tom had made his decision simply because he learned he would have lost in court? Two responses come to mind. First, it was not at all certain that he would have lost in court. In fact, with a skillful lawyer and some dissembling, Tom might have won, because it would have been up to Lainie to prove the existence of an understanding or agreement about her money. Or perhaps, with regard to Tom's entitlement to the house, I was wrong and Tom's lawyer was right—maybe the law had been newly interpreted in Tom's favor. If either possibility were true, I would have been very disappointed if Tom had based his decision on my interpretation of the law rather than on his own sense of fairness. To do that would have been to get the worst of both worlds: a mediation where the law—and an inaccurate interpretation, at that—was in control.

Decisions can be made on the basis of wrong information in litigation as well. Lawyers make their predictions about what a court will do, but the lawyers can be wrong. When the client's decision has gone against his or her sense of fairness *and* the lawyer's prediction proves wrong, the result can be a lot of disappointment and cynicism regarding the legal system.

But I had another reason for wanting Tom to base his decision on his sense of fairness. Over the years I have seen a kind of healing take place between separating spouses—an affirmation of both their marriage and their divorce—when their own senses of fairness determine their agreement. Ending the marriage on a note that reflects personal justice can allow each person to leave behind the unfinished business of the past. When a person makes a decision based on the fear of losing rather than fairness, the result can be frustration and a psychic continuation of the divorce. I didn't know, and still don't, whether Tom and Lainie felt as if they had achieved justice. But I do know that Tom's decision to give up any claim on his wife's family money was far more empowering for him than waiting until he and Lainie were on the courthouse steps.

TOO
EARLY TO
RUN

SUMMARY

*I*n this case, I find myself in conflict with a couple who are wildly impatient to make all the decisions regarding division of property, child and spousal support, and co-parenting before they've even separated. I try to slow down the process without usurping Sally and Jim's decision-making powers and point out the limita- tions of a binding agree- ment that is made without the actual experience of separation behind it. The result is a kind of "kill the messenger" reaction: Both become furious at me and dig into their positions more deeply. My objective with Sally and Jim is to help them see what they don't want to see in order to pro- tect their future interests.

*J***im and Sally** came to mediation with a great sense of urgency. After six years of marriage, Sally, with their three small children, was leaving Jim. She planned to return to the town in South Carolina where she had grown up. The previous June, she had attended her tenth high school reunion and had fallen in love with her high school sweetheart.

When Sally and Jim first arrived in my office, they were still living together. Their plan was to work out a divorce agreement within the next week; then Sally would leave for South Carolina to be near her boyfriend. Both were extremely distraught, but Sally was holding it together better than Jim.

As a sports enthusiast, I'd recognized Jim's name right away. He had been an All-American lineman for a southern university well known for its football. He'd played pro ball for three years, but hadn't quite measured up to sportswriters' expectations and had been wise enough to leave that arena while his body was still intact. With a few partners, he had then started three sporting goods stores.

The two made a stunning couple. Jim had maintained his great physique and resembled an oversized younger version of Harry Belafonte. Sally was tall, slender, and graceful. At our first meeting, she had on white silk pants, an aqua silk blouse, and a delicately patterned scarf pulling her thick hair back from her lovely though deadly serious face.

DECISIONS MADE IN CRISIS

*W*hen people in Jim and Sally's emotional state present themselves to me, alarm bells go off. Are they absolutely sure that they want a divorce? Could they possibly, in a week's time, make decisions about ending a six-year marriage that would make sense to them six months or six years from now? And with Jim and Sally, an additional problem would make it difficult to reach solid decisions—the fact that they were still living together.

The reality of separation offers people insights and perceptions that they hadn't yet experienced. Many people find that the experience of living separately changes their feelings about the other person. For some it reinforces the decision to separate. For others, it creates fear, doubt, or confusion. But for those who continue to live together after they have decided to separate, the pressure of the situation can blind them to their own desire to save the marriage. Although a separation does not automatically provide clarity about the state of the relationship, the information generated by a separation can be crucial to successful decision making. Without actually setting up the two households and facing the difficult problems of developing separate parenting relationships with the children, the two would be going purely on guesswork as they tried to work out the financial and parenting arrangements. But the information gathered from even a short separation can help a couple create an agreement that is flexible enough to make thoughtful, comprehensive, long-term arrangements.

What were my choices? I could flat-out refuse to mediate with them, since reaching a solid agreement in their state of emotional crisis, particularly within the week, seemed nearly impossible— and worse for them, perhaps, if they *did* manage to pull it off. Or I could decide I would help them without questioning the wisdom of what they were doing. And between those two poles lay many possible gradations: I could give them the benefit of my experience and offer all appropriate warnings while respecting their basic decisions; I could provide reality testing for the options they considered, being as honest as I could about what I saw happening in the room and the consequences of their decisions. Of course, I would be unwilling to draft any agreement that I felt was unfair, but beyond that I wanted to be sure that Jim and Sally realized what a difficult task they were undertaking.

Mediator: I have to tell you I have serious doubts about whether you can accomplish all you have set out to do by the deadline you've set for yourselves. Why do you have to get it all done now?

Sally: We both find this to be a very painful time. I want to get it over as soon as possible.

Mediator: What's the "it"?

Sally: The separation, my moving across the country with the kids, and the money decisions. I want it all over with now.

Mediator: Well, that won't be easy.

Jim: Why can't we do it quickly? [Begins to cry.]

Mediator: There's a good reason. Do you think you're in any shape to make decisions that could affect your lives for decades?

Jim: All I know is that if she moves out, I don't want to deal with her any more than I have to.

Mediator: I understand that you're in a great deal of pain now. I imagine you think that if you get the details of the separation worked out, you'll have some more control over your life.

Jim: It would give me some peace of mind.

Mediator: But in order to make solid, long-term decisions, you need to be able to project your life into the future with some clarity. But if I'm correct, right now just getting through each day is enough of a challenge.

Jim: So what can we do? You ought to at least tell us that, based on all of the people you've seen go through this.

Mediator: It's true that I've seen lots of people go through their own version of separation and decision making, but truly only the two of you can know what you are experiencing. Frankly, even from having observed you very briefly, I'd be very surprised if you could make all the necessary long-term decisions now and still be happy with them next year. But there are some decisions that you can —in fact, *must*—make now. You've already decided that Sally is going to leave and that she'll be living in South Carolina. You still need to decide whether Jim will stay in the house, how to work out long-distance coparenting, and how to manage your cash flow to support the family in two different households.

Sally: Those decisions will be easy to make. I want to do more than that, though. I want to divide our property and work out support.

Mediator: All in the next week?

Sally: All in the next week, unless we can do it faster.

Mediator: You, Sally, are probably more at risk than Jim in making those decisions now, since the kids will be with you and there are probably more uncertainties in your financial future than Jim's. My instinct is to try to slow you down.

Sally: I am afraid that if I slow down too much, I'll get so frustrated that Jim and I will end up hating each other. You don't understand—it feels to me like it's already been a long time.

Mediator: How long have you been thinking about leaving?

Sally: For more than six months.

Jim: What do you mean, six months? You told me about two weeks ago that you had just decided!

Sally: I had, but I've been thinking about it for a lot

longer. I've been unhappy since Richard [their youngest child, now two years old] was born. Meanwhile, you've put all of your time into work and left me alone with the kids for the past couple of years.

Mediator: Where do you stand on the marriage now?

Sally: What do you mean?

Mediator: In your mind, is the marriage over? How sure do you feel about what you're doing?

Sally: [After a long pause] I don't know. I know I have to get out, and I have to see this new relationship through. Right now, it feels as if the marriage is over. But I care a lot more about getting out than getting a divorce.

Mediator: Why do you need to divide the property now?

Sally: So it won't be a source of tension between us. Then we won't fight about it. It'll be a lot cleaner that way. I certainly don't want to be shuttling back and forth between here and South Carolina or trying to work this out long distance. And I think it'll be better for Jim to get it over with now.

Mediator: Will it be better for you, too?

Sally: Yeah. I'll feel less guilty. And I'll feel freer. That's my priority.

Mediator: Seeing you make your decisions out of guilt worries me, because guilt usually doesn't last too long. You might regret what you do now, particularly if the decisions are irreversible.

Sally: You mean the economic decisions?

Mediator: Right. Besides, you can't legally lock the kids into decisions that won't work for them. Because the law puts the best interests of the children first, any kid-related decisions will always be reviewable. The other decisions can be final.

Sally: I've never been much interested in money, and I'm not really concerned about it now.

Mediator: But you *are* interested in your freedom?

Sally: Yes. Still, I know that Jim will always take care of the kids, and I've always been able to manage for myself.

Mediator: Look, I don't want to try to convince you to do something you really don't want to do, but it's important that you consider future problems. The hope of this process is that the two of you will reach a fair agreement that will work for the whole family. For most people, that takes a good deal of time, not so much for mediation to take place but for adjusting to the various ups and downs that usually accompany a separation. It could be that you are the rare couple who'll be able to figure this all out before you even separate. But frankly, the more I hear, the more concerned I am that in your desire to get this over with, somebody—or both of you—might get short-changed.

Sally: I appreciate what you're saying, but I think we're both ready and determined to do it all now.

Jim: Yes. Let's get it over with.

GRAPPLING WITH THE MEDIATOR'S DOUBT

*M*y job as mediator is hardest not when the disputants disagree and fight, but when they agree on something that troubles me. The task in that case is to reconcile the parties' right to make their own decisions with my perception that something is wrong.

So how could I proceed? My reaction against rushing was so strong I felt I couldn't merely suppress it. After all, part of what I was being hired for was my assessment of the situation.

The mediator's wisdom, skill, and judgment are part of what the parties are buying. If they didn't need these contributions, they could buy a self-help book, draw up their own agreement, submit it to a court, and be done with it. Often they look to the mediator to impart his or her experience in similar matters with sympathy and objectivity.

It is the mediator's job to point out the essence and value of each person's perception, including his own, even when the perceptions seem contradictory. But this is difficult when the mediator is at odds with the parties. Such a situation illuminates the fact that the mediator has no coercive power whatsoever. The parties are free to leave and either draw up their own agreement or find someone else to do it. Nevertheless, the disputants often give the mediator power over themselves and their decisions by deferring to his or her familiarity with the journeys of others.

With Jim and Sally, I had to find a way to convey my concerns without alienating them. The more I like the people I'm working with, the harder this is, particularly when they insist they are right. It's natural for me to want my clients to like me, and when I appear to stand in the way of what they want, I don't win any popularity contests. But obviously, my purpose is to serve their needs, so I have to monitor my tendency to avoid discord between us and make sure I express myself. Equally important, I have to avoid trying to manipulate them into accepting my view of what they should do. In Jim and Sally's case, although I disputed the wisdom of their choice to make all decisions now, I decided to defer to them for the moment, but remain alert for opportunities to raise the question again.

IMAGINING THE FUTURE

*I*n the six years Jim and Sally had been married, the three sporting goods stores Jim started with his partners had been very successful, and they were in the process of opening a fourth. In addition to the stores, which had produced $200,000 for Jim in the past year, he and Sally had various investments worth about $10,000 plus $80,000 in savings, and they owned their house, in which they had approximately $150,000 in equity. Sally wanted Jim to buy out her interest in the stores, and determining a fair value for that interest would be a major issue. When we started talking about the house, I felt the difficulty that I had anticipated almost immediately.

> *Mediator:* [To Jim] What are your immediate plans for the house? Do you want to live there?
>
> *Jim:* [Starting to cry] The thought of living there without Sally and the kids kills me. I think we ought to sell it right away.
>
> *Sally:* I don't see that as necessary. Whatever you want to do with the house is okay with me.
>
> *Jim:* But if for some reason we got back together again, I'd be really sorry we sold it.
>
> *Mediator:* And we don't even know how you'll feel living in the house by yourself, because you've never done it.
>
> *Jim:* Well, I know that even when I start thinking about living someplace else, I feel as if we don't have a home anymore. But staying there alone seems even worse. I'm sure I'm going to have to get out.
>
> *Mediator:* There are other options. For example, you could

rent the house out to someone else until you're sure what will happen to the family.

Jim: I don't really care. I just know that when I think about Sally not being there and, what's worse, the kids not being there, it's so painful I can't stand it.

Mediator: What you're saying makes perfect sense to me. But it seems to me that it would be premature to make any irreversible decision about the house, because you're just not sure.

Jim: No, I want to go ahead and make a decision. We should sell the house now.

Mediator: How do you feel about that, Sally?

Sally: I don't care. It's really Jim's decision.

Mediator: Are you saying that because you feel as if you don't have any right to participate in this decision, since you're leaving?

Sally: Right.

Mediator: But the decision about the house will have an impact on you. In addition to any feelings you may have about the house, there's also the question of where the money will come from to buy you out of the stores.

Sally: I don't need the money now, so it doesn't really matter.

Mediator: Why not?

Sally: Because I assume I'll be getting enough support from Jim to live on.

Mediator: What does matter to you about this issue besides getting all of this over with?

Sally: [With a dazzling smile] Not much. I know I own half of the house, but it's really okay with me for Jim to sell it when he wants to.

Jim: Thanks, honey. If I thought there was any chance that you and the kids would come back, I'd want to hold on to it. But I guess that's a pretty unhealthy attitude. So I suppose I ought to sell it now and get it over with.

Mediator: I have to say, your intention doesn't sound very solid.

Jim: That's true, but the only thing that matters to me right now is what's happening with Sally and me. I couldn't care less about the house.

Mediator: I know that. I feel a little like a broken record when I say this, but unless the decision you make about the house now allows you to change your mind down the road, it could easily lead to regrets later.

Jim: Look, I want to be sure Sally can get her money out of the house when she wants it. Suppose we agree that I'll put the house up for sale, but if either of us decides before it sells that we don't want to sell it, then we'll hold on to it until we're both ready to sell.

With all of the ambivalence that I could feel within each of them, and the swinging back and forth about the house, their desire to make all decisions now was becoming increasingly problematic. Everything that I had worried about in the first session seemed to be borne out. Both urgently wanted to make decisions, but neither had a solid enough base of experience to make good ones. The only way I felt we could proceed safely was to build in enough flexibility for them to change their minds later on, if they needed to.

So the first thing to do was find a solution to the house problem that wouldn't be cast in stone. Otherwise, if the two ultimately disagreed on the house, one of them would end up with the upper hand. For example, if they agreed that the house should be sold now but then Jim had a change of heart, Sally could still compel him to proceed with the sale. Or, if they agreed now to postpone the sale of the house until both felt the time was right, Sally would lose control of access to money from the house and the stores, since Jim was most likely to use his half of the house proceeds to buy Sally out of the stores. But despite these very legitimate concerns, I seemed to be the only one who could focus on them.

My hunch was that Jim and Sally wouldn't be able to look directly at the house problem until they realized that their supportive feelings for one another could dissolve. Clearly, though they both felt deep anger and hurt, real separation and the feelings attending it seemed unreal. Nothing had really happened yet. My task was to help them imagine being alienated from each other.

The difficulty of conceptualizing the future is often exemplified by couples trying to reach a prenuptial agreement. What they must do is imagine a time when they no longer love each other, and then decide what will happen to their property. When two people are about to commit their lives to each other, it is difficult and at least a little crazy-making to have to think about the possibility of divorce. Though Sally and Jim were ending their marriage, not beginning it, they still couldn't conceive of a future where they wouldn't have each other's best interests at heart.

> *Mediator:* About the house. There's another option that you might consider.
>
> *Jim:* Good, what is it?
>
> *Mediator:* You could both agree to put off the decision until you are clearer than you are now.
>
> *Jim:* What would be the point of that?
>
> *Mediator:* Rather than forcing yourselves to make a deci-

sion now, you would be putting off the decision until one or both of you felt ready to make it.

Sally: But then the decision would be left up in the air.

Jim: She's right. We want to make a final decision. Let's sell the house now.

Mediator: Are you sure that's what you want to do?

Jim: Not absolutely, but if we write it up that way, if the two of us agree, we can always change.

Mediator: That's right. Where you might encounter a problem is if you disagree.

Sally: I don't understand what you are doing. You are acting as if we won't agree, and I don't think it'll turn out that way.

Mediator: Right. I am acting that way. Let me tell you why. The product of our discussions will be a written contract that will be legally binding between you. That will be submitted to court and become a court order if you go ahead with a divorce. One of the purposes of this agreement is to accurately record your intentions and agreements. Another is for you to have a reference point to solve any disagreements you might have in the future. If you never disagree, then you will be free to do whatever the two of you agree to do, no matter what the written agreement says. If you do disagree, then the written agreement will at least be the starting point for you to resolve your differences.

With respect to the house, suppose you put into the written contract that the house will be sold in the near future. Then if, say, Jim decides that he wants to live in the house for the rest of his life, the house would still be sold if Sally insisted on it. I'm not trying to produce a fight in the future, though you might feel that way. I'm just trying to elicit as much clarity from the two of you as I can, so that if you have a future disagreement you will know where you stand.

It's hard to create a neutral agreement here—something that wouldn't give one of you the upper hand in dealing with a future disagreement. Your positions are too different for that—Jim staying in the house, Sally not; Jim's money tied up in the stores, Sally's tied up in the house. As your lives unfold separately, you might well want different things to happen.

Who will have the upper hand will depend on how the agreement is worded. We can word the agreement to lock Jim into a sale of the house at a specified time; we can even write out the terms of the sale. Or we could leave it to Sally to decide when the house is to be sold. Or we could leave it somewhat vague. But if we leave any of the variables affecting the house up in the air, and if Jim decides not to sell, then he'll probably hold sway, at least in the short run.

Jim: I think you're making a mountain out of a molehill. Write it up so that I'm locked into selling it now. That seems only fair. And if I want to, maybe I can borrow the money to buy her out.

Mediator: The decision about the house might look different when we talk about a procedure for a buy-out of Sally's interest in the stores, so maybe we should leave it for now, and come back to it then.

Sally: Good, let's move on.

GOING DEEPER

*I*n the next session, I broached the subjects of the worth of the sporting goods stores and the extent of Jim's interest in them. Determining the latter was not going to be easy—the process would be both technically complex and highly subjective.

> **Mediator:** You need to decide how you're going to figure out what the stores are worth.

> **Jim:** I have the profit-and-loss statements and balance sheets for the last three years prepared by the accountant for the three established stores. But I think the only fair thing to do for the fourth store is to value it based on our investment in it, since we don't know yet how well it will do. It hasn't even opened yet.

> **Sally:** I think that's fair. We put $40,000 into it, so I would get $20,000 for it.

> **Jim:** Right.

> **Mediator:** Sally, you need to know that a court would probably decide that your interest in the fourth store would be significantly higher. As we discussed earlier, California is a community property state, which means that property acquired during the marriage through the efforts of either of you belongs equally to both of you. A court would look at the potential of the store as well as the money put in to determine its value.

> **Sally:** I don't care. Jim has worked hard getting that store ready, and I know I've made his life awful in the last few months. I feel like I am entitled to the $20,000, but nothing more. I haven't supported him doing this store. In fact, I was against it originally because I didn't want him spending more time away from the kids and me.

Mediator: Just as an exercise, say an expert appraised your share of the store's value at $200,000. Would that make a difference to you, Sally?

Jim: [Breaking in] That's crazy. I'd sell it right now if I could get a *quarter* of that.

Mediator: It might be crazy, but I'm just trying to be sure that Sally understands what she could be giving up, and for this purpose, I would rather guess high than low.

Sally: It doesn't make any difference. I tried to tell you before, money isn't that big a deal with me.

Mediator: Is that the reason you're willing to get only a return of the investment?

Sally: No. [Her voice shaking with anger] I feel like you are badgering me. I don't want more than the $20,000. I just want to move on.

It is a delicate matter to test the solidity of an agreement that differs so widely from what a court would do. While I respected Sally's right to make her own decisions, I needed to be sure that she understood what she was doing. Had she taken into account the economic effect of her decision on herself and her children? And, most difficult of all, would this decision hold up in the future? Would Sally have a change of heart once she stopped feeling guilty? This was the question that gnawed at me most and was the most difficult to explore.

Looking at Sally, cool and aristocratic, I knew she was smart and capable of understanding what she was doing, and it was also clear that at this point she had more emotional control than Jim. But I sensed that she saw herself as, if not fully responsible, then more responsible than Jim for the separation, maybe because she was doing the leaving, maybe because she had moved on to the next relationship and felt guilty about the loneliness she knew Jim would feel when she left. Whatever it was, I had to make an effort to explore it in order for us to test the stability of her agreement to take the $20,000.

At the same time, I had to accept the fact that there were limits to what I could understand about the situation. Maybe, I thought, Sally's consulting lawyer could help her understand the ramifications of her decisions better than I could. There was so much going on in her life: She was about to leave her husband to move across the country; she was already in a new relationship; she had three small children who required a lot of her attention. And she had never really handled money—she even seemed to have a distaste for it. How much of this could I get into with her? How much *should* I get into with her?

I knew that, whatever my role, Sally needed to explore the question of her share of the fourth store as freely as possible, despite her reluctance to do so. As a result of that exploration, the conclusions she was insisting on now might change or they might stand, but in either event, having thought the issue through, she would end up with a more solid footing. The problem was I didn't think she'd be willing to explore these issues in Jim's presence. Certain questions might be too sensitive for her to confront fully in front of him. It was clear that she felt guilty for inflicting as much pain on Jim as she had. I doubted she could bear to hurt him further. But how would Sally feel about the monetary agreement if her new relationship didn't work out? And, underneath her guilt, was there anger at Jim that, if tapped, would alter her thinking? How did she really feel toward Jim? Within the mediation process, sometimes the only way to do this is to caucus, or meet individually with each party.

As you know, I want my clients to stay in control of the decision making, so I usually don't caucus with them individually. But because of the deadline and the emotional intensity in this case, I wanted Jim and Sally each to have some opportunity to explore the issues of their separation privately.

Mediator: I know that you two want this over with, but

I am concerned that we're moving through these very important decisions too quickly, even though this might seem to be taking forever to you. There are certain key considerations that have to be posed for you to solidify the agreements. It's important to me, and I think to you, that they be part of this process.

Jim: What are you talking about?

Mediator: All right—for example, is Sally giving up more than her fair share of the fourth store because she feels responsible for the separation? Is Jim's agreement to sell the house now something that he will regret later? I don't want this agreement to come apart next month or next year because we skipped these questions. I also know that we can't be one hundred percent sure about any of the answers because we don't have a crystal ball. But I still think we need to do better than we have.

Jim: What do you have in mind?

Mediator: There are several ways of weighing these issues. First, we can do it here together. I know we *are* doing it, but doing it right would mean going deeper into very sensitive areas. A second option would be for me to meet separately with each of you. Some people find it easier to talk without their partners in the room. A third possibility is for you to talk with someone you really trust— your minister, a therapist, or a friend. But whichever route you choose, before you commit yourself to any agreement, I feel very strongly that you need to have this agreement reviewed by a lawyer. Perhaps that person would be a good one to talk with. Whichever of these options you choose—and of course, there's no reason in the world that you couldn't choose all of them—it's important for us to leave room here to see if any changes in the agreement are produced by those explorations.

Sally: No, now wait a minute! There's *nothing* I would say to you alone that I wouldn't say in Jim's presence. I've been talking with my friends and my minister about this for weeks, *months.* I'm through hashing all this out—I *know* what I want. Everybody I've talked with has advised me to get everything I can now because I won't be able to get anything later.

Mediator: That assumes that what you get is up to Jim.

Sally: I'll get a lawyer after we've reached an agreement—I don't have a problem with that, although I was hoping that we didn't need to see anyone but you. But frankly, right now I just want to get on with it. And the message I am getting from you is that you don't like what I am doing.

Mediator: That's not quite true. I do have two concerns, though. The first is that I feel some reluctance on both of your parts to think through the decisions you're making. That's natural when there are so many unknowns. The second, which I must continue to emphasize, is that you are making decisions that may be irreversible without having more than a fantasy of what your lives are going to look like.

At the end of this last interchange, Jim, who had moved to the edge of his chair during the early part, leaned back and breathed an audible sigh. I imagined that he was feeling that I was overdoing it. I wasn't sure he was wrong.

In any event, I didn't feel as if I could go much further with Sally. If I pressed her any further to reconsider, she might start locking herself into decisions in order to keep me at bay. I was glad she had agreed to see a consulting lawyer before she signed the agreement. But whereas Sally saw me as passing judgment on her decision, I was wondering if I wasn't being too protective of her right to more money and too tightly tied to the law as the standard of how people should decide. After all, as far as I could see, she wasn't being coerced by Jim, and she clearly wanted out. So why was I so worried?

The truth is, for me the test of a mediation is the quality of interchange between the parties and the quality of their agreement. If the agreement needs to be changed later, my hope is that the parties will have learned from our sessions how to work together, using the agreement as their reference point. But since Sally was, in my view, skimming the surface of her feelings about the conflict, I wasn't at all confident these two would have the tools to renegotiate productively. But I was also aware I had gone as far as I could in nudging Sally to go deeper. I'd have to let go and hope for the best.

> ***Sally:*** I think I understand what you're saying. I'm doing the best I can to do what I think is right.

> ***Mediator:*** I don't doubt that for a second. The point of this process is for the two of you to be in charge. If these decisions feel right to both of you, then you should do it your way.

THE OTHER STORES

We moved on to talk about evaluating the three remaining stores. I explained to them the methods of valuation and the significance of the concept of goodwill, a part of the valuation that took into consideration intangible assets of the businesses, such as the fact that it was an ongoing business with an established reputation in the community. Jim began.

> ***Jim:*** I think the fairest way to get an evaluation would be for us to use the accountant who keeps the stores' books.

> ***Mediator:*** Has he had experience doing this kind of thing?

Jim: Yes, I'm sure he would be able to do it.

Mediator: [To Sally] How do you feel about using him?

Sally: It's okay with me. I know him and I'm sure he's an honest man.

Mediator: This job requires more than just honesty, though. It requires skill in making the evaluation, and a true willingness to be impartial. Since he's the company accountant, and Jim will continue to be his client, using him would put him in a tough position.

Jim: Why?

Mediator: For two reasons. First, because of your ongoing relationship and his loyalty to the stores. And second, it is a complex and subjective judgment. If we brought in ten accountants to make this judgment, we might get three or four different opinions. Imagine what it would be like for him to decide the buy-out price between two of the partners.

Jim: We already faced that question and decided that if any of us pulls out or dies, he gets just what's on the books of the company, not anything for goodwill.

Mediator: That's one way to avoid the problem. The reason a lot of people don't use that is that they feel it is unfair to the person pulling out, because if the stores were sold, you would get much more.

Jim: Why don't we ask him to come in here, and all three of us can question him and see if we think that what he says is of value?

Sally: That's fine with me.

Mediator: Sally, do you feel as if you know enough about the stores to be able to understand what he is saying and ask enough of the right questions to be able to make it productive?

Sally: Well, it's clear you think I don't.

Mediator: You caught me. You're right, I don't, but I hope I'm wrong. I'm basing my concern on what you said before several times: that money isn't that big of a deal to you.

Sally: Look, Gary, I know what I am doing. I think I can do it this way. Besides, all the alternatives, like having an independent appraisal, would take much longer, right?

Mediator: That's true, unless you put off the decision until later.

Sally: But that wouldn't be fair to Jim, because the company would be worth more then as a result of work that he will be doing after we separate, so then I'd get more than my fair share.

Mediator: Not if the two of you agreed upon a date that would be used for valuation.

Jim: I don't want to do that. But if you do, Sally, I'll wait.

Sally: No, I'd just as soon do it now.

Mediator: That will probably mean that you'll end up getting less, unless this accountant is an extraordinary person. At the very least, there will be a tendency on his part to decide any close question in Jim's favor.

Jim: I really don't think this guy would do that. But if he did, what could we do?

Mediator: Probably the best thing would be to have another accountant here, somebody who's impartial and doesn't know either of you.

Sally: I just don't want to do that.

Mediator: How come?

Sally: Because I think this will work out okay, even if it means I end up getting less than I would have otherwise.

Mediator: Who's going to talk to the accountant?

Sally: It's fine with me if Jim does it.

The accountant came to our next meeting. Sally asked some questions that I found surprisingly perceptive, given her apparent lack of financial expertise, and using the accountant's opinion as a reference point, she and Jim agreed that Jim would buy her share for $150,000, including goodwill. Then the accountant left.

Mediator: We are in what feels to me a lot like the place we wound up over the new store. The two of you have reached an agreement that you seem happy about but that raises some concerns for me. First, I'm pretty sure that both an impartial evaluator and a judge would decide that the stores were worth more. In and of itself, that's not a real problem, at least not compared to this feeling I have again that you just want this over with, Sally. Speed here is a lot more important than fairness. I'm getting the impression that you're pretty much willing to go along with whatever Jim wants.

Sally: [Her face looking strained as she tries to contain her impatience with me] Up to a point, you're right. I want to make this workable for Jim and I don't care that much about the money. I think I've said that before. But what you don't seem to understand, Gary, is that I *do* know what I am doing, and *this* is the way I want to do it. Coming out of this with several hundred thousand dollars and support is enough for me, even if Jim ends up with a million. I hope he will, and frankly I expect him to. So it feels okay to be doing it this way.

Mediator: If it were up to you alone to decide this, how and when would you be paid your share of the stores?

Sally: Out of the sale of the house is fine.

Mediator: And if the house doesn't sell for a long time?

Sally: That's okay, as long as I get some interest on the money I am owed.

Jim: Hey, I thought you didn't care much about money.

Mediator: You think she shouldn't get any interest?

Jim: I guess it's okay, but I want us to use a friendly rate.

Mediator: [To Sally] What rate would you want to use?

Sally: If I had the money now, I'd put it in a money market savings account, so whatever that rate would be.

Jim: Fair enough. We'll get a realistic sale price from a real estate agent and I'll pay interest on that using the rate at the bank where we have our money now. I'll make quarterly payments until the house sells, but what will this mean for support?

Mediator: That would be your next decision.

Jim: I'd like to pay Sally whatever support a court would order.

Mediator: Why?

Jim: Because I wouldn't know where else to begin. Doesn't the court use some sort of guidelines?

Mediator: Yes, but those are based strictly on your income and don't take into account what your expenses will be. The guidelines are also used for temporary as opposed to long-range decisions.

Jim: Well, let's start with that.

Mediator: [To Sally] How would *you* like to determine the amount of support?

Sally: What Jim's suggesting sounds fine.

Mediator: Do you know how much it will cost you to live in South Carolina?

Sally: A lot less than here, I know that.

Mediator: How much do you spend here?

Sally: I don't know. We seem to spend just about all the money Jim makes.

Mediator: And that's just for one household.

Sally: But South Carolina's cheap compared to here, so it's not going to be a problem.

Mediator: If we are going to use court guidelines, we need to make some assumptions about your situation, such as how much income there will be and how much time the children will spend with each of you.

Jim: [His face seeming to cave in] This is the hardest part for me. I want to be with those kids a lot.

Sally: Look, I've told you I *want* you to be with them a lot, but I just don't know how we can pull that off. They're so small. Unless you come to South Carolina to see them, I can't figure out how to do it.

Jim: [Burying his head in his hands and beginning to sob] I think I can accept everything else about the separation but this. I can't stand the idea of not being with the kids.

Sally: [Her voice rising] Now, look, Jim. The truth is, you've hardly spent any time with any of them since they were born.

Jim: I know that, but that doesn't mean I don't love them. I want to be with those kids. I want them to know who their father is.

Sally: I've *always* wanted that, but you've never stopped working long enough to spend time with them.

Jim: Well, that's changing now, Sally. There are a lot of things changing, and that's one of them.

THE HEART OF THE MATTER

I turned to Jim and asked, "If you could have your way here, what would you have happen?"

I try to encourage my clients think independently on *all* issues. Sally had basically deferred to Jim in the area of finances, so in order to counteract her tendency to go along with whatever he suggested, I had asked for her opinion first when we discussed financial issues. I cannot say I was very successful, but I kept trying. Now I used the same tactic in reverse. Since the children represented Sally's area of expertise, I wanted Jim to answer first. The point was to prevent him from simply deferring to Sally and give him the chance to express his opinion in "her" area. Furthermore, focusing on Jim in the decision making regarding the children might not only legitimize his view but also force him to channel his pain and frustration into working on a solution to an unresolved problem.

Jim: I would see the kids a lot.

Mediator: How would that be arranged?

Jim: They would fly back and forth between South Carolina and California.

Sally: That's a great idea. Why don't you buy them a plane?

I was taken aback by the level of sarcasm in Sally's remark. Perhaps, I thought, she felt that her expertise about the kids was being challenged. And perhaps, too, she was trying to distance herself from Jim's pain, and maybe her own as well. At any rate, I decided to let it slide in order to keep the focus on Jim.

> ***Mediator:*** [To Jim] How could they do that? Children of two, four, and six need someone to accompany them.

> ***Jim:*** I don't know. I could go with them sometimes and maybe Sally could go with them some. After all, she isn't working.

> ***Sally:*** If you think managing Josh and Sarah and Richard at the same time isn't working, you've got a rude shock coming.

> ***Jim:*** I didn't mean it that way. I really want to be with those kids as much as possible. They're my babies.

> ***Mediator:*** Do you have an idea of what you would do with them when you were at work?

> ***Jim:*** I haven't actually thought it out, because to tell you the truth I didn't think Sally would let me have them very much.

> ***Mediator:*** You think this is just up to her?

> ***Jim:*** I have been thinking that way, but I'm starting to get the point.

> ***Sally:*** [To me] I've basically been a single parent since those kids were born, so I don't know where either of you men get off thinking that just because Jim fathered these kids, he has a right to make these decisions.

> ***Jim:*** You're right. I haven't been there for my babies because of the work, but also because you were doing such a beautiful job with them. They didn't need me. But

now they're getting to an age where there are things we can do together—play ball and go on hikes, stuff I'd like to do. Up to now they haven't been old enough. And it's true I've had my head up my ass. Well, this is shaking all of that up. I want those kids in my life, and what's more I think they need me in *their* lives.

Sally: I'll believe it when I see it.

Mediator: [To Sally] Do you think it would be valuable for the kids to have Jim participate more in their lives?

Sally: [Rising in her chair, her anger mounting] It's what I've wanted for years! If he'd thought this way before, we probably wouldn't be where we are now.

Mediator: So that makes this doubly painful for you?

Sally: [Falling back into her chair] Yes, and [in a whisper] now it's too late for us.

Mediator: How do you feel about this for the kids?

Sally: If he would really do it, it would be wonderful, but I'd really be surprised. Work's been his whole life.

Mediator: Suppose he did become more involved?

Sally: Honestly, I don't know. I'm sure it would be good for the kids. He's right; they do need a father. But it would be hard for me to see him with them suddenly because as a matter of fact I've needed a husband. Why wasn't he there for us before? Besides, the logistics of this would be a nightmare. I don't want the kids going back and forth too frequently. I think that would be disruptive to all of us. I don't want to be without them for very long either. And it's only going to get harder when the kids start going to school. [Her eyes filling with tears] It's too late. It's all just too late.

Mediator: [To Jim] What's it like to hear that?

Jim: I can understand how she feels, but I still want to be with those kids. Short of moving to South Carolina, I'm willing to do a lot to make it work for everybody.

Sally: [Looking at me helplessly] What should we do?

Mediator: My suggestion would be to take the next few months to see what arrangements make the most sense for the five of you.

Sally: And then what?

Mediator: You have several options. You can continue the pattern you established at the beginning, or review it at a set date and then see what changes if any you want to make. Or you could set up a schedule of alternate plans and try them.

Sally: No, no, no. I want to get this settled for the long term.

Mediator: You can make a plan for as long as you like, but you can't lock each other into a plan that's not working well for the kids, so this part of the agreement can't be as ironclad as the rest of it.

Sally: So you're saying we'll have to deal with each other, like it or not.

Mediator: As long as you are both going to be active in the children's lives, you can't avoid it. Did you think you could?

Sally: I want to.

Jim: You know, Sally, there's no getting around it. We have to be able to trust each other. I am, have always been, will always be vulnerable to you. I think I understand what Gary has been saying about not deciding things that could put one or both of us in a position we will regret later. We need to talk with each other, even about stuff that's hard to talk about. I'm willing to have this whole agreement be flexible, because I trust that we'll be able to work things out. We're doing it now and we'll do it then.

Sally: Okay. With the kids, we'll do it, but not with the money. I *hate* having to talk about money.

Mediator: If you're serious about participating more in the kids' lives, Jim, then you are going to need to put together a plan showing how you'll do that. It will have to be specific.

RESOLUTION

We had come through the crisis to a place where Jim and Sally could work out a specific plan. They decided that the children would stay with Jim until Sally got herself settled in South Carolina. Then they would work to create as many opportunities as they could for Jim to visit them there or for Sally or some mutually acceptable third person to accompany them back to California to spend time with Jim. Support was worked out to be reasonably flexible unless Sally moved in with her boyfriend, in which case child support would continue but spousal support would end. Jim would also give Sally a promissory note for her interest in the stores, to be paid out of his share of the proceeds from the sale of the house, which they expected would be imminent. Meanwhile, Jim would make interest payments on the note to Sally in addition to support until the house sold. They seemed comfortable with the agreement—and we had made the deadline, after all.

While I still had misgivings about the agreement, they were not so strong as to prevent me from drafting it. Part of the reason I was willing to draft it was that my concern about unfairness was not by one to the other—it was Sally's unfairness to herself that made me squirm. I drafted the agreement, Sally and Jim had it reviewed by consulting lawyers, and I then revised it to reflect the minor changes they suggested. Jim and Sally signed their agreement and Sally moved to South Carolina.

Six months later I got a call from Jim asking for advice. Since I'd seen them, he and Sally had reconciled once and separated again and now Sally objected to their original agreement. The new store had become a big success and she wanted more than the value she had settled for. She had hired a lawyer who was threatening to go to court to have the agreement overturned. I explained to Jim that he and Sally could litigate or mediate this disagreement, but they couldn't mediate unless both of them wanted to. Sally didn't seem interested in going back into mediation with me, he told me.

So the very thing I was most afraid of had come to pass: Sally had changed her mind. The law was on her side, but Jim didn't want to change the agreement, which was now legally binding. Part of me was angry at Sally for her refusal in mediation to anticipate the possibility that she'd have a change of heart, and part of me respected her for refusing to accept a situation that seemed unfair to her now. I was sorry that these two had more pain to experience, but I reminded Jim that I had no role to play unless both of them came to me to mediate.

Eight months after my conversation with Jim, I received a letter from his lawyer informing me that Jim and Sally would be going to court and that my testimony would be required. I pulled out their file and looked at my notes. I wondered how I would testify. Would I try to defend the agreement and my support of it, or would I be as forthcoming about my doubts about Sally's capacity to make sound decisions as I had felt throughout the mediation? Because Sally had a consulting lawyer review the agreement before she signed it, I thought it probable she would have an uphill battle to convince a judge to overturn it, even though she had agreed to take less than she was entitled to. My

role in the courtroom would be the same as my role in the mediation room: to say as accurately and fully as I could what I perceived and let the chips fall where they may. If I had my choice,
I would have preferred to talk with Sally, Jim, and the judge on
an equal footing for as long as it took. But dialogue is not permitted in court.

A month, then two or three, went by without further word. I
began to think the lawyers had settled the case. But one day I ran
into Jim's lawyer and she told me that Sally and Jim had gotten
back together. I was happy for them, relieved for all of us—since I
was still troubled about the strength of their original agreement—
and above all, filled with curiosity. What had happened? The
lawyer didn't really know. I thought about contacting them, but
that wasn't in keeping with our relationship, so I decided against it.

I am often asked if people who mediate are likely to reconcile.
Some people even think that the purpose of mediation is to get
back together. But usually people who have mediated don't reconcile, because one or both was intent on divorcing and because it
takes so much effort and initiative on the part of both to go
through the process. Nonetheless, occasionally people do.

Did mediation play a role in Jim and Sally's reconciliation? I
don't know. For many couples, mediation is a healing process—a
time when two people struggle to separate their lives responsibly
and honestly. While separating face to face is always painful, it is
ironically often a time of connection. Perhaps because of the presence of the witness, the parties can open up to each other, can see
each other more clearly than they had in a long time. Sometimes
this healing can bring them back together. Usually, it allows them
to separate with a measure of grace.

By mediating, Jim and Sally had tried to help each other during
their most difficult trauma. And it was clear to each of them that
the other cared even when they were most upset with each other.
And while I had had real misgivings about having mediated with
them, particularly that sense of helplessness I feel when someone
is doing something I think they might regret later, I was glad that I
might have played some small role in saving a marriage.

A CHANGE OF HEART

SUMMARY

*T*his case reveals how important it is for the parties to delve deep inside to uncover their true feelings and then be honest about them, and also with my role in helping them do that. Darla and Larry come to an agreement, but just before it is finalized, Darla admits it does not seem fair to her. When they try to renegotiate, the process not only stalls, it stops dead. My attempts to deepen their understanding of the relationship and the problems with the old agreement only reinforce the paralysis.

Darla and Larry had struggled for years with the issue that doomed their marriage and had resulted in the end of Larry's previous marriage as well, Darla explained to me in our first meeting. Larry suffered from periodic bouts of depression. Over the years he had sought treatment via therapy and antidepressants and several times had sustained long periods free of the disease, but then the darkness would return. Living with him during his depressive periods was extremely difficult for Darla.

Darla had met Larry at a bar when his first marriage was disintegrating. Strong and compassionate, she thought that she could help this handsome, sensitive older man. She was too young to realize the folly behind the phrase "All he needs is a good woman." But over the years, her patience began to wear thin. She felt herself dragged down by Larry's nihilistic outlook and by his inability to do more than just get through the day. After participating in a support group for spouses of depressives, she had decided to get a divorce. They'd been separated for almost a year.

I was surprised when Darla's lawyer referred them to me for mediation, because I knew he was highly skeptical of the process. Still, after several court skirmishes over temporary support and custody that had created more problems than they had resolved, he had called Larry's lawyer and they had both urged their clients to see me.

The tension in the room was palpable from the beginning. Larry was not depressed at the time but his pain was evident in almost every word. He wanted neither a separation nor a divorce, but he said if Darla insisted upon one, he would not oppose her. Darla was clear and consistent from the beginning: She wanted a divorce, and if Larry wanted to use mediation as a forum for reconciliation, she would resume litigation. But even with that qualification, Darla was not particularly optimistic about mediation, since she knew how intractable he could be. She had lived with Larry when he was going through his first divorce, in which he had fared very badly, and she knew he was going to be extra-self-protective to make sure that didn't happen again.

Despite her reservations, Darla very much wanted mediation to work. She was concerned that their two children, a four-year-old son, Sam, and a six-year-old daughter, Helen, be protected from further suffering. Above all, she wanted to keep the hostilities from escalating in order to minimize the damage to them. And Larry was very optimistic about mediation. "If we can each give a little," he said, "maybe we can reach a reasonable solution that we can both live with."

IDENTIFYING THE ISSUES

*D*arla and Larry both agreed they had one major difference regarding their property: what to do with two pieces of real estate they had purchased during their eight years together. But that was where the clarity ended. Neither of them was very sophisticated financially or particularly clear about the properties' financial histories, and their records were hopelessly incomplete. But with the combination of a lot of specific questions and their rummaging through files to find old receipts and invoices pertaining to home improvements and old bank records of cash they had put into the properties, we were able to piece together most of the puzzle.

When Darla and Larry began living together, Larry owned two pieces of property with a total equity of $20,000. They lived on one of the properties, and through a combination of hard work in remodeling them, borrowing from the bank, and good timing, they sold the two original properties and bought two others. One was their family residence, which was worth $150,000 with an $80,000 mortgage, and the other a rental property worth $180,000 with a mortgage of $130,000. Rent from the income property totaled $1,250 per month against monthly expenses of $1,300 for a monthly deficit of $50.

When they separated, Larry agreed to leave the house. For him, this made the separation doubly painful, because he was losing his wife, his children, and his home. Part of the reason he left voluntarily, albeit reluctantly, was to make amends to Darla for his past neglect and prove to her by committing himself to intensive psychotherapy and a new antidepressant that he could get the better of his illness. He hoped she would one day invite him back to live in the house.

Now he was suffering a great deal and was angry with Darla, but was angrier still with himself. He knew that he had destroyed the marriage. He was forty-five years old (fifteen years older than Darla) and he felt that his life was in ruins. All he wanted was to be able to come back home and be as much of a father to his children as he could.

Darla was also suffering. She had loved Larry deeply, had worked hard to make the marriage succeed, and felt great sadness at its failure. She had to work very hard to make the $700 monthly house payments she had agreed to pay in exchange for Larry's leaving. And co-parenting with Larry was no picnic. He was erratic with the kids and had very different ideas about child rearing from Darla's. But most painful of all was Sam's repeated request that he not have to see his father so much. Larry attributed this to a combination of Darla's brainwashing and the fact that he himself didn't have a decent place to live. Since he earned $30,000 a year working for a cabinet-making company and paid Darla $700 a month in support (and was willing to continue to do so, even though both knew it was at least $200 more than any court would order), he had about $1,200 per month left after taxes for himself. Darla was working full-time as a short-order cook at a coffee shop earning $18,000 per year.

In his frustration and pain, Larry had taken to calling Darla constantly about the house and arrangements for seeing the kids. Darla considered this a form of harassment and finally refused to speak to him any further on the phone. So Larry had resorted to bombarding her with letters, which Darla also found upsetting.

When I asked each of them to write out a list of their priorities regarding the decisions that had to be made, Larry was clear that he wanted to live in and own the house. Darla was willing to live elsewhere, but she also wanted to own the house she lived in. Since the difference between the equity in the house ($70,000) and the other property they owned ($50,000) was about the same as Larry's premarriage contribution ($20,000), it seemed that the only problem that needed to be solved was how Darla could convert ownership of the rental property into a house of her own. Both of them agreed that if we could figure out a way to do that, we would have a fair and workable agreement. That's what they said—but there was a tension in the room that seemed to belie their words.

WORDS VERSUS FEELINGS

*I*f I sense a discrepancy between what parties in mediation say and how they seem to feel, I have a couple of choices. I can simply treat the statements as accurate, while noting the discrepancy, and watch to see if feelings and words become more congruent or more markedly dissonant. This gives me time to determine whether my sense of discord is accurate or perhaps something else—for example, a projection on my part.

Or I can deal more immediately and directly with the discrepancy, bringing it up for discussion. The advantage of this option is that it can bring into consciousness unacknowledged feelings. The disadvantage is that it can move me into a directive role, which can sap the parties' initiative, confuse them, or lead them to distrust themselves.

With Darla and Larry, I decided that the first choice made more sense, so we closed the session agreeing to meet two weeks later, during which time they would gather the necessary information to find a way of getting Darla her own house.

Darla worked hard researching her options. She looked at a few houses to get a sense of the market, shopped for the lowest mortgage rate available, and checked with an accountant to determine how to avoid paying taxes in the transaction. She seemed relieved but slightly incredulous that it would be possible to reach her goal. By taking advantage of the decline in mortgage rates, she could afford to own a house that would cost $120,000, a relatively small step down from the family home. What's more, she had heard of some houses for sale in the area with price tags in that range. Yet while Darla described her findings, I had a nagging feeling that her stated goal differed from what she was feeling. I found myself being unusually thorough with both her and Larry to be sure that they understood everything that happened.

Their solution had obvious appeal to Larry. The family home was very important to him. He tended the garden and felt very connected to the house, having put so much effort into remodeling it. He seemed to derive a sense of security from the place that allowed him to have some hope for his future. He was pleased that the situation was working out so neatly, too. Trading the house for the rental property would reimburse him for the money and time he had put into the properties he owned before he and Darla had married. Even if Darla needed more support from Larry to buy a new house, which she thought she would, Larry seemed willing to provide it if he could stay in the family home.

After discussing how to eliminate, or at least drastically reduce, the tax consequences of the necessary transactions and minimize the amount of money needed to be borrowed from the bank, along with other details, we seemed to have hit upon a workable solution contingent only on Darla finding a house she liked:

- Darla would remain in the house until escrow on her new house closed.
- Larry would move into the rental property immediately and start remodeling and repairing it so they could sell it for the highest price.

- The money from the sale would go toward purchasing Darla's new house. Larry would apply for a loan with Darla to make sure she would qualify. He would also continue to pay her support in the increased amount of $850 per month.
- Larry would move back into their house when Darla moved into hers.
- Darla would retain custody of the kids but Larry would see them often, and they would all work toward the kids staying with him part-time.

I drafted an agreement, which they had their advisers review while Darla continued to look for a house. They each wanted to make some minor technical adjustments to the document, but the basic framework remained intact. Still, I had the nagging feeling that something wasn't right.

PROBLEMS SURFACE

*A*s we began to conclude the mediation, I asked whether they considered the agreement fair.

Larry: Yes, although I'm not particularly pleased to be paying Darla so much support. Still, I do think Sam and Helen will be better off with both of us living in homes that we own.

Mediator: How about you, Darla?

Darla: Why are you asking that question now?

Mediator: Because I want to be sure that when you look at the agreement as a whole, it will make as much sense to you as putting in each piece has seemed to.

Darla: But it's too late to make any big changes.

Mediator: No, it's not. Not that we could do it easily, but I don't want either of you to end up with a result that you'll regret later on.

Darla: Well, as a matter of fact I'm *not* very pleased with this agreement.

Larry: I'm not very happy with it, either. But, Darla, you've got to be realistic. We each gave things up.

Darla: [Crying heavily] This is all wrong. I wasn't going to say anything, but the truth is, I hate this agreement.

Larry: Maybe we should give the marriage another try.

Darla: No! I told you that that isn't what I want. The marriage is over, but I don't think it's fair that you get reimbursed so much for your premarriage contribution.

Larry: You can't have everything the way you want it. You want a divorce and you want a house. We've figured out a way for you to get both, even though it means that I'm paying you too much money.

Darla: I've been feeling guilty about breaking up the family. But damn it, it's not my fault, and I don't want to have to try to make it up to you anymore. I've given up more than I should.

Mediator: How do you know that?

Darla: When we lived together, I did a lot of the remodeling that increased the value of the house, but I'm not receiving any credit for that.

Mediator: How come you haven't brought that up before?

Darla: I don't know.

Larry: What do you mean you don't know? We've been

working on this for months. You didn't say anything about this until now. What kind of bullshit is this?

Darla: I didn't want to upset you and risk triggering another of your depressions.

Mediator: Are there other reasons, too?

Darla: Yes. I have always undervalued myself, so when Larry started talking about the money he wanted credit for, it didn't dawn on me that I should get credit for the work I put into the properties before we got married, too. But I worked hard on those places and I should get credit for that work just as much as Larry should.

Mediator: So that has only become clear to you recently?

Darla: Yes, and once I started feeling that way, I didn't want to admit it even to myself, so I tried to repress it and hoped I could live with the way the agreement was going. But when you asked me if I thought it was really fair, it began to bother me more.

Mediator: Is there more that bothers you that you haven't mentioned?

Darla: I don't want to move out of the house.

Larry: *What?*

Darla: If I move out, it'll just be another capitulation to Larry. That house is as much mine as it is his. I kept thinking that if I tried to accommodate him, he would stay healthy. But I can't dance around his depression anymore. I haven't found any houses that make sense. I just don't think I can find another house that I would want to live in that will be affordable, too.

Larry: I can't believe what I'm hearing. You want a

divorce, you want my money, and now you want to permanently eject me from the house.

Darla: You think the whole world revolves around you. Well, I'm sorry but I can't keep putting your needs first.

Mediator: I know how upset you both are right now, but I want you to stay with this conversation to see if we can understand what is going on.

Larry: I can tell you what's going on. She's trying to get everything.

Mediator: That's the way it feels to you.

Larry: No. That's what's happening.

Mediator: That's not the way it looks from here.

Larry: Then what do *you* think is going on?

Mediator: I'm not sure. The agreement we were working toward isn't holding, and it's good that that's coming out now rather than after you both committed to it. It also seems to me that Darla is getting clearer about what her priorities are and is trying to break an old pattern between you that made it hard for her to say what she really thought.

Larry: I don't know what you're saying. [To Darla] You won't sign this agreement?

Darla: No.

Larry: When did you decide that?

Darla: Just in the last several minutes.

Larry: [To me] Thanks, friend.

Mediator: You're upset with me.

Larry: Damn right I am.

Mediator: I'm sorry for that. I'm trying to stay with the agreement we made in the beginning about how we'd work together.

Larry: You pushed her right out of the agreement.

Darla: That's not what happened, Larry. You don't think I have a mind of my own. But catering to you all these years robbed me of my self-respect. I won't let that happen anymore.

Larry: If you'll recall, it wasn't me who wanted to end this marriage.

Mediator: I don't think this is going to lead you to the best solution.

Larry: Then you tell us what to do. You got us into this mess.

Mediator: I think that the first thing you need to do is to let go of the agreement. It seems dead. We need to look for a new solution.

Larry: But if we both want the house and she wants to be paid for work she didn't do, what can we do?

Mediator: That's the place we need to start from to see if we can find some solution that doesn't leave either or both of you feeling that you are giving up more than feels fair.

Larry: How can we do that if we both want the house?

Mediator: By identifying the needs that owning the house would meet for both of you and exploring other ways of meeting them.

BACK TO SQUARE ONE

*H*aving an agreement unravel is always very disorienting to everyone, myself included. I felt both disappointed that all our hard work was for naught and relieved that we hadn't ended up with a bad agreement. My first reaction was to look for whom to blame for what had happened. I concluded that we all had our part in it:

- Darla hadn't been willing to say what she thought. Still it was hard to fully blame her, since she finally did find the courage to break her pattern and say what she was thinking, even though she knew it might send Larry into a tailspin.
- Larry—owing to his self-involvement—had manipulated Darla into ignoring her sense of fairness so that he could have what he wanted.
- I had not tried to bring to light Darla's reservations earlier. I had sensed her reluctance right from the beginning and had chosen not to try to bring them out. I could understand Larry's anger with me—his charge that it was late in the game to be making such a dramatic change had merit, and I was more culpable then he even knew because I had sensed this possibility long before Darla voiced her feelings. So now the question was whether Larry had enough trust in Darla and me to continue. They had spent a good deal of time and money and it had led us to no agreement. And it was less clear to me now than ever what kind of agreement would work for them.

So why not just give up, rather than try to repair my and Darla's damaged credibility and work toward a new agreement? First, experience: I had often found that when a mediation seems most hopeless, an agreement is just around the corner. Also, the pain of their situation cried out for the beginning of a healing. And finally, there were the kids, who had no part in this process, but whose life would be very much affected by what came out of our work together.

I have never felt, as some mediators do, that it is my job to be the protector of the children in mediation, although I do keep their needs in mind. As a parent, I know, even in the best of circumstances, how hard it is to make decisions about children. And professionally speaking, while there is some expert guidance, in psychological circles there is also much disagreement about what works best for children. Most psychologists would probably agree that the particular parenting arrangement chosen by Sam and Helen's parents would be less important than their parents resolving their conflict. But to do that, these two might have to go through further conflict, at least in the short run. So from that perspective, it might be better for the kids for Darla to take her stand now than to fold her tent and agree to something that would leave her more bitter toward Larry than ever. And if they *didn't* work through this impasse, I was afraid that they'd go back to their lawyers and lock themselves into an all-out war.

It was out of this fear that I made my second mistake with Darla and Larry. At a critical juncture like this, it's particularly important for the parties to rechoose the mediation process on their own. Instead, Larry looked to me to figure out what they should do, and I played into his request and pressed for mediation, missing a great opportunity to empower them to choose to work together until they reached a mutually satisfactory solution. That choice could have taken them below the surface of property issues into their subjective experience of the conflict. But I took charge and tried to move us forward by initiating a dialogue about their separate stances.

> **Darla:** I need the house.

> **Larry:** So do I.

Mediator: Then we need to find a way to make that happen or understand what lies beneath those statements.

Larry: Like what?

Mediator: When you say you need the house, are you each making statements about *living* in the house, or owning it, or both? What time frame are you talking about? Is there a way you could both own the house until one or both don't want to do that?

Darla: Look, I want a separation. I don't want to own the house with Larry.

Mediator: I'm just giving examples of possibilities that might emerge when we look deeper into your positions.

Larry: But you asked us to do that at the beginning. We went through this already.

Mediator: Yes, but things have changed since then.

Larry: Maybe they'll change again.

Mediator: They could.

Larry: Then we will have wasted *more* time.

Mediator: I'm not sure that the time we've spent so far has been wasted, but it's possible.

Darla: What do we do once we both get underneath the surface?

Mediator: Then the three of us look at possible solutions to meet those fully explored needs.

Larry: Why should I want to think of what's going to help her? Look what happened last time.

Mediator: You might not want to, but you need to weigh that decision in the context of your alternatives.

Larry: Okay, I'll give this one more try and that's it.

Darla: I'm not sure I understand how to do this.

Mediator: After you leave tonight, think about not only what is most important to you in this, and *why* it's important, but see if you can articulate those feelings.

ONE LAST TRY

At the next meeting, I began:

Mediator: Were you each able to do what we talked about?

Larry: All I know is that I want that house and I want the money back that I brought into the marriage. And Darla, you have to face the fact that you are being compensated for all you did by owning half the house and all except $20,000 of the rental property without having put in a dime of your own money.

Darla: I want the house because I'm afraid I won't have enough money to handle a new situation, even if I get support from Larry. Anyway, I don't like having to be dependent on him. All I want is child support, the house, and some cash to give me something to fall back on.

Larry: I'd be glad to have that myself. That's a really good deal. You know, every time you talk like that, you forget all the work I've done to get you where you are.

Darla: That's the way *you* think about it. You've never seen how much *I've* done. You think you've done it all. I put up with so much and you don't see it.

Mediator: Larry, what's behind your desire to have the house?

Larry: I planted every flower that's growing there. I put so much of myself into that place. I miss it a lot. She's not watering the plants or weeding or doing anything to maintain it. It's falling apart.

Mediator: Forget what she's doing or not doing for now. What would it mean for you to give up the house?

Larry: I find that question too painful to think about.

Mediator: I'm trying to get at what's behind your desire to have the house. You've given us some of that, but I'm trying to find out if there's more.

Larry: I know what you're trying to do, but it's just too hard for me.

Mediator: What's too hard?

Larry: Thinking about not having the house.

Darla: That's pretty much the way I feel. I want to work this out with him, but I think he's just too stubborn. That was why I tried to work around it before, but then I ended up agreeing to something that wouldn't work for me or for the kids.

Mediator: Of course, another alternative is that *neither* of you get the house. That's likely to be what a judge would do—order it sold.

Larry: Is that what you want, Darla? Would you be happy then?

Darla: No, I'd be happy if *I* got the house. The point is not to prevent you from getting it—it's to keep it myself.

Larry: And you want to keep me from being compensated for the time and money I put into the previous houses?

Darla: No, I just think I should be compensated for my effort, too.

Larry: But you didn't pay anything toward the mortgage payments when we were living together. This is useless to keep going. We're not getting anywhere.

Mediator: I agree that we are not moving right now. But this is showing where we're stuck, I think—both of you feel unappreciated, I believe, for your contribution to the marriage, and you both see each other's desire for appreciation as a denial of your own contribution. Does that sound right?

Larry: She wants everything. She wants me to just drop out of sight, disappear.

Mediator: That's the way it feels to you, I know. I imagine that it would be very difficult for you, Larry, to consider losing the house.

Larry: I just wouldn't do it. And I'm not going to give it up. I think that I'm willing to be reasonable and compromise, but Darla isn't.

Mediator: I'd like to ask each of you a question. Do you think you each understand each other's point of view and what's behind it?

Darla: Yes, I do. He wants to live in the house and doesn't want to recognize my contribution or the importance of the kids spending most of their time in the house.

Mediator: And does it make sense to you why he would feel that way?

Darla: Sure. That's the way he is.

Mediator: And if you were Larry, could you imagine feeling the same way?

Darla: Yes, except I don't think I would be insensitive to my wife's contribution.

Mediator: Larry, do you think you could put yourself in Darla's shoes and understand how she sees this?

Larry: [Beginning to cry] I just don't think it's fair that she should get a divorce *and* the house.

Mediator: I understand how you feel. But do you also see how it is for her right now?

Larry: [Sobbing] How can she do this to me?

Mediator: I can see how hard this is for you. Right now I think we're stuck, and I'm trying to help each of you see a slightly bigger picture than you're seeing now. Doing that could help options surface that will take us past the impasse.

Larry: I find this too painful.

Mediator: By "this" do you mean trying to take care of yourself and see what it's like for her at the same time?

Larry: That's right.

Mediator: I can understand that. But if we're going to be able to get to something that will work for the whole family, you each need to be willing to look at the whole picture, and that includes the other's point of view.

Larry: I don't think I can go on.

Within about five more minutes, it was over. They both decided that it didn't make sense to continue mediating now. We spent a little time talking about how they might pursue the case with their lawyers, and then they left.

THINKING IT OVER

I felt a little relieved, but as with most cases that don't reach resolution, I also felt frustrated. The mediation had broken down. Why? The truth was, I didn't know. It was possible, I suppose, that these two should never have tried mediation in the first place, and that the process had simply revealed that to be true.

But I wondered, too, whether I could have done something to break the stalemate. Perhaps I had betrayed Larry's interest by becoming Darla's advocate. Perhaps I should have emphasized the legal dimension, as their lawyers undoubtedly did. I could have pushed Darla to see that she probably wouldn't have done better in court, at least from the point of view of economics. She would have gotten less support, might not have gotten the house, and would never have gotten a judge to order Larry to help her buy a new house if she had to do that.

Perhaps Darla would consider the mediation worthwhile in raising her up from reticence to self-assertiveness. Larry, though, seemed unlikely to consider the process beneficial—his pain was too intense. In fact, I was reasonably certain he would continue to blame me for killing an agreement that was "fair." Above all, I was concerned that the mediation breakdown might escalate their differences and weaken Larry's somewhat tenuous relationship with his son. But that was out of my control. Perhaps, eventually, Larry would see the connection, now obscured by pain, between old perceptions and ongoing problems.

RESOLUTION

I was surprised to receive a note from Larry a few weeks later along with a payment of my bill. He wrote that he did not regret having mediated, that he thought that both he and Darla had learned more about themselves and their relationship in the process than they had in dealing with their lawyers, and that that experience had been valuable even though it had not resulted in agreement. As a result of the mediation, he said, they were dealing with their lawyers in a different way, and he felt they were on the way to a "mediative" settlement of their case. He also told me he had found a new psychiatrist and was happy with his course of therapy. I was relieved that he was taking active steps to break his cycle of depression.

In the end, this case set before me the mediation lesson I find most difficult to learn: I need to trust the parties' deepest instincts in deciding not only whether to mediate, but whether to quit as well. And I need to follow up on all my perceptions, without holding back or brushing aside my hunches. Finally, this case reminded me that it takes a lot of guts for people to mediate, and that even without the objective success of a solid agreement, the effort can yield other important rewards.

CAUSE
FOR HOPE

*I*n these cases, I have tried to give you an accurate picture of what actually happens in mediation. As you now understand, it is impossible to know in advance how any mediation will go and I often find myself surprised by the turns that sessions take. It would be as much a mistake to assume that because you and your soon-to-be ex-spouse get along well your mediation will go smoothly as it would be to assume that because you have a hostile relationship there is no possibility of success.

But there are certain indicators that can help determine the prospects for a successful mediation. These include both parties genuinely wanting to mediate and being able to stand up for their own points of view. But more than anything else the success of a mediation rests on the willingness and ability of both people to end the marriage with a minimum of bitterness. With the mediator— someone you both believe understands you—you have the opportunity to make decisions that will preserve the best of your relationship and allow you to go your separate ways without enmity.

Given the fact that I work a great deal with people who are in the throes of divorce, many people are surprised I am so optimistic about life. There are so many signs that the world is in danger of becoming unraveled that it is hard to hold onto the belief that the suffering around us will be alleviated in any significant way. What gives me cause for hope are my almost daily observations of the little miracles that occur when people who are deeply estranged come together to forge an agreement that will make both of their lives more workable. As an observer and participant in those moments, I feel deeply privileged and satisfied to be part of a process which heals rather than exacerbates old and deep wounds.

A GUIDE TO FINDING A MEDIATOR NEAR YOU

O nce you and your spouse have decided to mediate, the next step is locating mediator. Depending on where you live, this may involve some work. I have found there are three approaches to this process; you may want to try a little of each.

LOOKING LOCALLY

I t makes sense to start your search right in your community. Begin by asking your friends, neighbors, and co-workers for referrals; word-of-mouth suggestions are often your best bet. Also look in the Yellow Pages, checking various listings, such as: Mediation Services, Attorneys Guide—Mediation, or Dispute Resolution. Call your local bar association and inquire if it has an attorney/mediator referral service. Also call your local psychological association, community dispute resolution center, and any marriage and family therapists organization for names of mediators in your area.

Contact your Chamber of Commerce and ask if its membership includes any mediators or if it has information on any professional groups for mediators in the area. When reading the newspaper keep an eye out for feature stories on mediation and note any advertisements that appear for mediators. If there is a community college or law school nearby, check to see if either offers any classes on conflict resolution, and if so, ask the instructor for names of any qualified professionals. Ask your local public librarian for assistance. He or she may keep membership lists of professional mediation organizations on reserve or know of publications written by or that contain names of mediators in your area.

THE NATIONAL APPROACH

*T*his approach involves tapping into national resources. The Academy of Family Mediators, headquartered in Minneapolis, Minnesota, can provide you with leads on qualified mediators in your area. The American Bar Association's Dispute Resolution Section, located in Washington, D.C., will also furnish information about attorney/mediators in your area. Either the San Francisco or New York office of the American Arbitration Association will also provide names of mediators near you. In addition, you can call the Society of Professionals in Dispute Resolution (SPIDR), headquartered in Washington, D.C., for information on the SPIDR chapter nearest you (however, SPIDR policy does not allow the organization to provide names of their members to the public).

- Academy of Family Mediators: (612) 525-8670
- American Bar Association Dispute Resolution Section: (202) 331-2258
- American Arbitration Association, New York: (212) 484-4000
- American Arbitration Association, San Francisco: (415) 981-3901
- Society of Professionals in Dispute Resolution: (202) 783-7277

REGIONAL RESOURCES

*T*he middle ground of your search for mediators should include state and/or regional organizations. Start with your state's Association of Marriage and Family Therapists (call the national headquarters in Washington, D.C. for information on the chapter nearest you: 202-452-0109). If you're looking specifically for an attorney/mediator, call the family law section of your state court system (frequently state courts will assemble lists of potential mediators for family law cases). In addition there may be a regional organization or association of mediators, as well as one specifically for lawyer/mediators. State universities can also be useful resources: Call the law school, the psychology department, and any dispute resolution department and ask if they maintain lists of mediators in the state. In addition, your state's Department of Consumer Affairs could inform you of any individuals or organizations involved in mediation near where you live.

Finally, the Center for Mediation and Law, of which I am a founder and a director, trains attorney/mediators, and will be able to tell you if any of its trainees work in your area. This is also a good organization to contact if you are an attorney interested in learning to become a mediator. Write the Center at 34 Forrest Street, Mill Valley, CA 94941, or call 415-383-1300.

Finding the right mediator may take time, patience, and perseverance. Before you start interviewing potential mediators, it would be worthwhile for you and your spouse to determine some basic criteria, such as, How far are you willing to travel? What hours are you available to mediate? How much have you budgeted for it? Once you have determined these parameters, you can make decisions about which mediators to interview. Look over the chapter "Choosing a Mediator" in Part One, to refresh your memory about interviewing potential mediators.

INDEX

A

Abuse, spousal, 221–42
  appropriateness of mediation
    in instances of, 241–42
  conditions for proceeding
    with mediation in
    instances of, 231–37,
    241–42
  legal protection and, 228–29,
    230, 233, 234, 240
  during mediation session,
    238–41
  signs of, 227
Academy of Family Mediators,
  368
Accountants, 22, 55–56, 111,
  332–35
Adversary culture, 36, 46
Agree, willingness to, 25
Agreements:
  prior, 52, 324
  see also Separation agree-
    ments
American Bar Association, 368
Arbitration, mediation vs.,
  147–52
Arbitrators, 15, 17
Arguing, 244–57
  changing pattern of, 252–57
  mediation's affects on,
    247–48
  mediator's options in
    responding to, 250–51

Assets, 40
  businesses, 297, 303, 321,
    322, 326–36, 342, 343–44
  expanding, 54–55
  real estate, 347, 349, 350–51
  see also House

B

Bargaining, 269–70, 272, 278
Blame, 243–57
  changing pattern of, 252–57
  constant arguing and, 244–57
  judgmental quality of, 285–86
  mechanisms of, 252
"Bringing reality into the room,"
  31
Businesses, as communal assets,
  297, 303, 321, 322, 326–36,
  342, 343–44
  valuation of, 332–35

C

Cash flow, 40, 139–40
Caucusing, 36–37, 62
  advantages of, 281
  case history of, 279–93
  in dealing with coercion, 121
  disadvantages of, 281–82
  in emotionally-charged cases,
    329–32